The Trauma-Informed Borderline Personality Disorder Group Curriculum

30 Group Session Plans for BPD Programs Serving Clients with Complex Trauma

The Trauma-Informed Clinical Curricula Series, Book 3 of 4

Jeevan Holden Rutto

This curriculum is intended for use by licensed clinical professionals in structured treatment settings and is provided for educational and informational purposes. Nothing in this publication constitutes clinical supervision, individualized clinical advice, medical diagnosis, or the practice of medicine. The author and publisher make no representations or warranties regarding the accuracy, completeness, or suitability of this material for any particular clinical population or program context. No guarantee of clinical outcomes is expressed or implied.

The evidence-based therapeutic frameworks referenced throughout this curriculum are established clinical methodologies with their own bodies of published literature. These include Dialectical Behavior Therapy, the Biosocial Theory of Borderline Personality Disorder, Schema Therapy and Schema Mode Theory, the ACE Research Framework, Mentalization-Based Treatment, the Window of Tolerance Model, Acceptance and Commitment Therapy, and Post-Traumatic Growth research. This curriculum applies and adapts these frameworks specifically for trauma-informed BPD group treatment in IOP, PHP, and residential settings. It does not claim ownership of the underlying theoretical models.

The reproducible client handouts in Appendix C (Handouts 1A through 30A, including Handout 12B) may be photocopied or digitally distributed for clinical use with individual clients within a licensed treatment setting only. **A download link is provided in Part Three: Appendices.**

Readers bear full responsibility for applying this curriculum in accordance with applicable professional standards, ethical guidelines, licensing requirements, mandatory reporting obligations, and the specific clinical needs of the populations they serve. The author and publisher shall not be liable for any harm, loss, or damage arising from or related to the use or misuse of this material.

All case studies, clinical vignettes, and character names in this publication are fictional composites drawn from clinical observation across many years of practice. They do not represent any specific individual, and any resemblance to actual persons, living or deceased, is coincidental and unintended.

Table of Contents

Preface

Borderline personality disorder is one of the most researched diagnoses in contemporary clinical mental health, and one of the most consistently undertreated. The evidence base for Dialectical Behavior Therapy is genuine and robust: DBT reduces self-harm, hospitalization rates, and treatment dropout in BPD populations with outcomes that no other single-modality intervention currently matches. That evidence is not disputed here. What this curriculum addresses is a parallel body of research that has accumulated alongside the DBT literature and has been slower to reach clinical practice.

A 2020 meta-analysis of ninety-seven studies found that individuals with BPD are nearly fourteen times more likely to report childhood adversity than non-clinical controls. Emotional abuse shows the strongest independent association with BPD symptoms, followed by emotional neglect. These findings are not background statistics. They describe the developmental origins of the regulatory, identity, and relational deficits that DBT treatment is specifically designed to address, and they establish that the majority of clients presenting in BPD programs carry a developmental history that the standard DBT protocol was not designed to explicitly account for.

The gap this curriculum fills is specific and documented. Standard DBT skills training assumes that clients can acquire and apply regulatory and interpersonal skills within their Window of Tolerance and gradually extend that application to more activated states. What it does not systematically provide is the somatic regulatory foundation that makes skills accessible under stress, the ACE-informed developmental explanation that repositions the client's self-understanding from shame-based to explanatory, or the schema mode framework that maps the internal states the skills are designed to regulate. For the majority of BPD clients, whose nervous systems were shaped by emotional adversity during critical developmental periods, skills acquisition without this preparatory architecture produces a predictable and preventable outcome: clients who can accurately define the skills and cannot reach them in the moments they are most needed.

This curriculum responds to that gap across thirty sessions in four sequential modules. Module A builds the regulatory and dialectical foundation before any pattern recognition work begins. Module B maps seven BPD-specific patterns with the clinical precision that makes skills training genuinely targeted rather than generic. Module C delivers all four DBT skill modules with each skill connected to its Pattern Map location and its mode-state access barriers named. Module D builds the identity, relational, and values-based forward direction that DBT's goal of a life worth living requires.

This is the third volume of the Trauma-Informed Clinical Curricula Series. It follows volumes on addiction recovery and eating disorder treatment. Each volume applies the same ACE-informed, regulation-first, somatic-aware architecture to a specific clinical population. This volume adds what BPD treatment specifically requires: the biosocial theory extended by the adversity research, the schema mode framework for the internal states DBT skills address, and the clinical protocols that BPD presentations demand, including the self-harm and suicidal behavior distinction that governs clinical response throughout the program.

This curriculum is written for licensed clinical professionals with foundational familiarity with DBT concepts and is not appropriate as a self-help resource. Program directors and clinical supervisors will find the implementation guides and three-domain supervision framework directly applicable to staff development. This curriculum is not a replacement for individual DBT therapy, does not address presentations requiring stabilization before group work is appropriate, and makes no promise of specific clinical outcomes.

What it provides is the structured clinical architecture within which the evidence-based work of DBT becomes more consistently accessible for the clients whose developmental histories the ACE research has documented, and whose treatment has too often proceeded without that documentation's clinical implications.

Series Introduction: The Trauma-Informed Clinical Curricula Series

There is a particular kind of clinical exhaustion that does not announce itself. It builds slowly, in the space between what you were trained to do and what the clients in front of you actually need. You have the evidence-based tools. You have the clinical training. You have the supervision. And yet something in the most complex presentations, the presentations that consume the most of your clinical attention and produce the most uncertain outcomes, does not respond to what you have been given.

This series was built to close that space.

The Trauma-Informed Clinical Curricula Series is a four-volume collection of structured group therapy programs for intensive clinical settings. Each volume addresses a specific population whose clinical complexity sits at the intersection of developmental adversity and a primary presenting condition. Volume one addresses addiction recovery. Volume two addresses eating disorder treatment. This volume addresses borderline personality disorder. Volume four addresses dual diagnosis populations. Each volume can be read and used independently. Each is more clinically powerful when read alongside the others, because the clinical principles connecting them, the role of adverse childhood experiences in producing the specific regulatory deficits that each population manages, are the same principles expressed in different clinical forms.

What every volume in this series shares is a central theoretical commitment: the presenting condition is not the primary clinical target. The nervous system that learned to produce it is. That distinction sounds subtle. In practice it changes the entire design of treatment.

Borderline personality disorder is characterized by nine diagnostic criteria organized around instability of emotion, identity, and relationship. Each of those criteria has been the target of clinical intervention for decades. Dialectical Behavior Therapy, the gold standard treatment for BPD, addresses them with considerable effectiveness. The research on DBT is genuine and the outcomes are meaningful. This curriculum does not dispute that.

What this curriculum adds is the question that DBT's original design did not require it to ask: where did the instability come from, and does understanding that origin change what treatment can offer?

The answer, as this volume documents in Part One, is yes. Individuals with BPD are nearly fourteen times more likely than non-clinical controls to report childhood adversity. The specific adversity that most consistently predicts BPD is emotional abuse and emotional neglect, the forms of adversity that disrupt attachment, impair the development of identity, and produce the specific quality of relational terror that abandonment fear represents. Understanding that origin does not invalidate DBT skills. It makes them more accessible, because clients who understand why their nervous systems produce the patterns they do are more able to use the skills that address those patterns.

That is the clinical claim this series has always made and this volume makes specifically in the BPD context: adversity is not background. It is the causal mechanism. Addressing it changes the clinical work.

How the Series Is Organized

Book 1 is the series anchor. It establishes the ACE-informed, regulation-first, somatic-aware architecture that all subsequent volumes build on. Every facilitator who delivers Book 3 should have read Part One of Book 1. The foundational clinical chapters there, on ACE research, nervous system regulation, somatic awareness, and group facilitation, provide context that this volume assumes rather than repeats.

Book 2 extends the architecture into eating disorder treatment. It addresses the specific regulatory functions that eating disorder behaviors serve and the clinical challenges of body-based work in populations where the body is already a primary source of distress.

This volume, Book 3, takes the architecture into BPD treatment. It adds what BPD specifically requires: an understanding of the developmental origins of emotion dysregulation, a clinical vocabulary for the schema modes that organize BPD behavior, and a structured integration of the four DBT skill modules with the trauma-informed regulatory framework that makes those skills genuinely accessible for clients whose histories make them difficult.

Book 4, forthcoming, takes the widest clinical lens: dual diagnosis populations where mental illness and substance use disorder interact in configurations too complex for any single-modality approach to contain.

What Standard DBT Does Not Address

The case that changed how I understood DBT came in the third year of my clinical career. The client, a thirty-one-year-old woman I will call Reese, had completed a full-year DBT program at a well-regarded outpatient center. She had a skills binder three inches thick, organized by module with color-coded tabs. She could identify her emotions accurately, name their functions, use TIPP when her nervous system was above the window, and articulate a DEAR MAN conversation with more clinical precision than some of the counselors I had trained alongside. She knew DBT.

She also called the crisis line fourteen times in the six months following discharge and was in my office eight weeks after leaving the program asking whether she was untreatable.

I did not know what to tell her. I knew she was not untreatable. I did not yet know what had been missed.

What had been missed was not a skill. It was the understanding of why her nervous system produced the states that the skills were designed to address, and where that nervous system had come from. Reese had an ACE score of nine. She had grown up in a household with a physically violent father, a mother with untreated depression, a history of sexual abuse by a family member between ages seven and eleven, and the specific quality of relational unpredictability that comes from a childhood in which safety was never reliably available. She had never been asked about any of it in a systematic way. It had appeared in her intake as a notation: complex trauma history. Then the DBT skills training had begun.

The skills binder was real. The skills were real. But the nervous system that needed them had been built in a household that Reese had never had language for, and the skills were being applied to states whose origins she had never been given a framework to understand. She was using accurate tools to address a problem she could not name.

What the Research Establishes

Dialectical Behavior Therapy is the most extensively researched treatment for borderline personality disorder in existence. The outcomes literature is not ambiguous: DBT reduces self-harm, decreases hospitalization, improves emotional regulation, and produces better treatment retention than most alternatives. None of this is under dispute in this curriculum.

What is under dispute is whether DBT's skills-training architecture, applied without an explicit developmental and trauma-informed framework, is adequate for the majority of clients presenting with BPD in clinical settings. The research suggests it is not for a specific and well-documented reason.

A 2020 meta-analysis of ninety-seven studies found that individuals with BPD are nearly fourteen times more likely to report childhood adversity than non-clinical controls, with emotional abuse showing the strongest specific association to BPD symptoms (Porter et al., 2020). A study using the National Epidemiologic Survey on Alcohol and Related Conditions found that each of the ten ACE categories independently predicted BPD diagnosis, with emotional abuse demonstrating one of the strongest independent associations (Fall, 2020). The neurobiological research on the ACE-BPD relationship is not indirect: childhood emotional abuse and neglect disrupt the development of the hypothalamic-pituitary-adrenal axis, impair prefrontal regulatory capacity, and produce the specific relational hypervigilance that abandonment fear represents at the neurobiological level.

Yet the standard DBT treatment manual does not include a protocol for addressing co-occurring PTSD or developmental trauma, a gap the original research team has acknowledged directly (Harned et al., 2014). The skills training proceeds. The developmental origins of the states the skills are designed to regulate are not addressed. The result, in the author's clinical observation and in the emerging literature on Trauma-Focused DBT adaptations, is skills acquisition without the contextual understanding that makes skills genuinely available in the states when they are most needed.

What This Curriculum Does

This curriculum is built on a specific and modest clinical claim: DBT skills work better when clients understand the developmental origins of the nervous system states they are being asked to regulate. That understanding does not replace DBT skills. It provides the explanatory context that makes skills acquisition feel meaningful rather than mechanical, and it provides the de-shaming reframe that the ACE research demands for this population specifically.

The curriculum delivers the four DBT skill modules, in their standard form, across Module C of Part Two. It does not modify the DBT skills themselves or claim to improve on Marsha Linehan's foundational work. What it does is build, in Modules A and B, the ACE-informed regulatory foundation and the clinical pattern map that make Module C's skills training genuinely accessible for clients whose histories have given them every reason not to trust their own ability to change.

The result is a thirty-session program organized across four modules. Module A establishes safety and the dialectical foundation, including the biosocial theory of BPD in ACE-informed language. Module B maps the specific BPD patterns, including abandonment fear, splitting, identity disturbance, schema modes, the impulsivity chain, and chronic emptiness, with explicit connections to the developmental adversity that produced them. Module C delivers the four DBT skill modules with trauma-informed framing and somatic awareness integrated throughout. Module D addresses identity, relational repair, and the forward direction of a life organized around values rather than around managing the disorder.

Who This Curriculum Is For

This curriculum is written for licensed clinical professionals in IOP, PHP, and residential BPD treatment settings. It assumes familiarity with the foundational DBT concepts and presumes that facilitators have access to DBT skills training or basic familiarity with Linehan's work. It does not assume specialized trauma training, though the Facilitator Competencies section and Appendix F provide specific guidance for facilitators whose training does not include it.

This curriculum is not appropriate as a self-help resource and is not designed as a replacement for individual DBT therapy. It is a group skills curriculum with a trauma-informed architecture, and it requires a licensed facilitator with access to clinical supervision.

The client in a standard DBT program who is acquiring skills without the context that makes them meaningful deserves more than a thicker binder. This curriculum offers the context. The skills remain.

How to Use This Curriculum

This section governs how the curriculum is delivered. Decisions made before Session 1 determine whether the clinical architecture holds or collapses under the specific pressures that BPD presentations produce in group settings. Read this section before facilitating any session.

Program Structure Options

This curriculum contains thirty group sessions organized across four modules. The session count differs from Books 1 and 2 in this series because Module C's DBT skills content requires two sessions per skill module rather than one, and because the BPD population typically requires more thorough Module A work before the pattern recognition in Module B can proceed safely.

12-Week IOP Structure (Three Sessions Per Week)

The 12-week, three-sessions-per-week format delivers thirty-six sessions, allowing delivery of all thirty sessions with six review or make-up sessions across the cycle. Module A is delivered in weeks one and two. Module B in weeks three through five. Module C in weeks six through nine. Module D in weeks ten through twelve.

At three sessions per week, pacing within Module B requires clinical attention. Sessions 9, 10, and 11, which address abandonment fear, splitting, and identity disturbance respectively, should not be delivered on consecutive days. The activation potential of these sessions compounds across the week. Allow at least one session between major pattern recognition sessions for somatic consolidation. If the group's collective zero-to-ten number suggests elevated baseline activation entering any Module B session, begin with an extended Module A regulatory practice before proceeding with new content.

The complete 12-week IOP sequencing guide, including specific recommendations for managing the higher activation density of Module B and the skills practice requirements of Module C, is in Appendix E.

8-Week PHP Structure (Five Sessions Per Week)

The 8-week, five-sessions-per-week format delivers forty sessions, allowing full delivery of all thirty sessions with ten available for review, skills practice reinforcement, and the diary card work that DBT protocols typically include. This format is the most clinically appropriate for the BPD population because it provides the consistent, high-frequency contact that the attachment-disrupted nervous systems in this population respond to most effectively.

Module A is delivered in week one. Module B in weeks two and three. Module C in weeks four through seven, with each DBT skill module receiving two dedicated sessions. Module D across week eight. The specific pacing recommendations for the PHP format, including guidance on the diary card integration that residential and PHP programs often use alongside group skills training, are in Appendix E.

Rolling Admissions Adaptation

The rolling admissions adaptation for BPD programs requires more clinical care than the adaptation for addiction programs described in Book 1. The reason is specific: Module B's pattern recognition work, particularly Sessions 10 through 15, depends on the group's collective relational safety in ways that Module B in Book 1 does not. A new group member entering a cohort in the middle of Module B's work on splitting and identity disturbance carries relational disruption risk that is not merely logistical.

The recommended adaptation is the same structural model as Book 1: Module A as a continuous open group, Modules B through D as a closed cohort. The Module A group accepts new members on a rolling basis. The Module B cohort opens when a sufficient group of Module A completers is available, at intervals no shorter than eight weeks, and operates as a fully closed group through Session 30. Under no circumstances should new members join an existing Module B or Module C cohort mid-cycle.

The clinical rationale for the closed cohort is more urgent in BPD treatment than in addiction treatment. The relational patterns that Module B maps, including splitting and idealization-devaluation, are activated by changes in group membership in ways that predictably disrupt the clinical work for the entire cohort. A new member joining an existing Module B group does not merely need to catch up on content. Their arrival reorganizes the relational field of the group in ways that can require multiple sessions to restabilize.

Session Plan Format Guide

Every session in this curriculum follows the same fourteen-component structure established in Books 1 and 2. See Chapter 6.0 for the complete format guide. Several components have BPD-specific modifications that are worth noting here.

The opening ritual is structurally identical to Books 1 and 2: feet on floor, weight in chair, orienting scan, zero-to-ten check-in. The clinical function of this ritual is amplified in BPD treatment. For clients whose relational template has been organized by the experience of environments that were unpredictable and unsafe, the repetitive, absolutely consistent opening ritual is not merely a regulatory tool. It is an attachment signal: I am regulated, this space is predictable, we begin together, and it is the same as last time. Any facilitator who varies this ritual, even occasionally, produces a measurable disruption in the group's relational climate.

The closing grounding practice carries an additional function in BPD treatment: it explicitly returns the group to the present before anyone leaves the room. The ending of each session is, for many clients in this population, a small enactment of abandonment. The closing ritual is the clinical management of that enactment: it acknowledges the ending, provides a regulatory anchor for the transition, and explicitly frames what continues even after the session closes.

The diary card, used in standard DBT programs as a between-session tracking tool, is not a formal component of this curriculum's session plans but is referenced in Appendix E's implementation guides. Programs that use diary cards alongside group skills training should review the integration guidance before Session 1.

Adapting Sessions for Individual Therapy

All thirty sessions can be adapted for individual therapy use with the same general modifications described in Book 1: eliminating group processing questions in favor of dyadic processing, adapting group exercises for individual delivery, and adjusting time to standard session formats.

Several sessions in this curriculum have higher group-specificity than comparable sessions in Books 1 and 2. Sessions 2, 10, 12, 26, and 30 use the group relational field as a live clinical instrument. Session 10 on splitting, in particular, is designed to allow the facilitator to observe and gently name idealization-devaluation dynamics as they emerge in real time within the group. In individual therapy, the equivalent clinical material must be generated through the individual therapeutic relationship, which is appropriate but requires a different clinical approach than the session plan provides.

Dosage and Sequencing Recommendations

The single most important sequencing principle in this curriculum is identical to Books 1 and 2: Module A must be completed in full before Module B begins. In the BPD population, this principle carries additional clinical weight because the pattern recognition work of Module B includes content, particularly Session 14 on self-harm and Session 15 on chronic emptiness, that requires the regulatory foundation of Module A not as a preference but as a clinical safeguard.

Facilitators who observe that a cohort has not adequately established Module A's regulatory foundation before the Module A completion date should extend Module A rather than proceeding on schedule. An additional Module A review session, using any combination of Sessions 1 through 8's content, is always preferable to beginning Module B with a group that cannot yet reliably access the grounding practices that Module B's higher activation content will require.

Within Module C, the DBT skill modules should be delivered in the sequence presented: Mindfulness (Sessions 17 to 18), Distress Tolerance (Sessions 19 to 20), Emotion Regulation (Sessions 21 to 22), and Interpersonal Effectiveness (Sessions 23 to 24). Mindfulness is foundational to all other DBT skills and its deliberate placement first is not arbitrary. The Wise Mind concept introduced in Session 4 and extended in Sessions 17 and 18 is referenced explicitly in every subsequent Module C session. A cohort that has not adequately established Wise Mind as a working concept will find that the distress tolerance and emotion regulation skills feel mechanical in ways that the Mindfulness sessions are specifically designed to prevent.

Facilitator Competencies and Training Recommendations

Minimum Competency Requirements

This curriculum is designed for licensed clinical professionals. The minimum competency requirements for solo facilitation are: licensure in a mental health discipline, at least two years of post-licensure clinical experience including work with personality disorder presentations, familiarity with the foundational DBT skills through personal reading of the DBT Skills Training Manual (Linehan, 2015) or equivalent training, and access to clinical supervision from a supervisor with experience in personality disorder treatment.

These are minimum requirements, not ideal ones. Facilitators who meet only the minimum requirements should begin with Module A sessions under supervision and should complete at least one co-facilitated Module B cycle before facilitating independently. The pattern recognition content of Module B, particularly Sessions 10 through 14, carries the highest activation potential of the curriculum and requires the most experienced facilitation.

Competencies That Strengthen Facilitation

Several competencies beyond minimum licensure meaningfully improve the quality of this curriculum's delivery.

DBT skills fluency. Facilitators who have personally practiced the DBT skills they are teaching deliver Module C's sessions from a different position than facilitators who know the skills only from training. This does not require formal DBT certification, though that is valuable when available. It requires genuine familiarity with the four skill modules at a level that allows facilitation without reference to notes.

Biosocial theory literacy. The biosocial theory of BPD, Linehan's foundational account of how emotional sensitivity combined with an invalidating environment produces the BPD presentation, is the theoretical spine of Sessions 2 and 5. Facilitators who cannot explain the biosocial theory in accessible language without clinical jargon cannot deliver these sessions with the clinical authority they require. The relevant reading is Linehan's 1993 original text and her 2015 skills training manual.

Schema mode awareness. Session 12 introduces the five schema modes most relevant to BPD: the Vulnerable Child, the Angry/Impulsive Child, the Detached Protector, the Punitive Parent, and the Healthy Adult. Facilitators unfamiliar with Young, Klosko, and Weishaar's schema therapy framework should read the relevant chapters in the practitioner's guide before facilitating Session 12 and the Module D sessions that reference schema mode concepts.

Somatic awareness in group settings. The somatic regulation framework from Books 1 and 2 applies throughout this curriculum. Facilitators who are delivering this curriculum without prior experience of Books 1 or 2 should read Part One's Chapters 2 and 3 of Book 1 before beginning, as those chapters establish the neurobiological rationale for the regulatory practices that this curriculum assumes rather than re-explains.

Self-harm clinical competency. Session 14 addresses self-harm directly as both communication and regulation. Facilitators must be clinically current on the distinction between non-suicidal self-injury and suicidal behavior, must have reviewed their program's self-harm protocol before facilitating Session 14, and must have clear individual referral pathways in place before delivering Module B's higher-activation sessions.

Training Recommendations

The ideal training pathway for facilitators new to this curriculum includes: completion of at least a foundational DBT skills training before beginning; supervised delivery of at least one Module A cycle before facilitating independently; reading of Young, Klosko, and Weishaar's Schema Therapy practitioner's guide (2003) before facilitating Module B; and participation in a consultation team or peer consultation group that includes clinical discussion of the facilitator's own responses to BPD presentations.

That final element is not incidental. The countertransference that BPD presentations produce in clinicians, including idealization, devaluation, rescue pulls, boundary erosions, and the specific quality of clinical fatigue that sustained high-activation work produces, is among the most documented and most under-addressed phenomena in personality disorder treatment. Facilitators who do not have regular space to process their own responses to BPD presentations are not adequately supported for this work, regardless of their clinical skill level.

Co-Facilitation Recommendations

Co-facilitation is recommended, though not required, for Modules B and C. It is most strongly recommended for Sessions 10, 12, 13, 14, and all of Module C. The clinical rationale is specific: Module B's pattern recognition sessions and Module C's skills training sessions require the facilitator to hold the group's relational field, track individual regulatory states, manage disclosure boundaries, and deliver complex clinical content simultaneously. In a cohort with active BPD presentations, the relational demands alone can occupy the full clinical attention of one facilitator. A co-facilitator attending specifically to individual regulatory states while the primary facilitator holds the content reduces the risk of the specific clinical failure that Chapter 5 addresses: content delivery with underdeveloped regulatory monitoring.

When co-facilitating, assign the primary narrative role and the regulatory monitoring role before each session. Rotate assignments across sessions rather than establishing permanent role divisions.

A Note on Group Safety, Self-Harm, and Clinical Supervision

The Safety Container in BPD Treatment

The safety container in BPD treatment differs from the safety container in addiction treatment in one clinically essential way: it must hold not only the risk of trauma contagion from disclosure but also the specific relational dynamics that BPD presentations produce within the group itself. Splitting, idealization-devaluation, testing behaviors, and the activation of abandonment fears in response to routine clinical events, a facilitator running late, a session ending, a co-facilitator absent from one session, are not merely management challenges. They are live clinical material, and how the facilitator responds to them in real time is itself a clinical intervention.

This does not make the BPD group container more fragile than the addiction group container. In the author's clinical observation, a BPD group that has been well held through the inevitable relational storms of Modules A and B develops a quality of cohesion that few other group therapy contexts produce. The clinical discipline required to build it is specific and learnable.

Self-Harm: The Clinical Priority Above All Others

Every facilitator delivering this curriculum must have a current, program-specific self-harm and suicide risk protocol reviewed with their clinical supervisor before facilitating Session 1.

The BPD population carries elevated self-harm and suicidal behavior rates that are not analogous to any other population this series addresses. Up to 10 percent of individuals with BPD die by suicide. Between 69 and 80 percent engage in non-suicidal self-injury at some point in the course of the disorder. In the group setting, the disclosure of self-harm or suicidal ideation by one member activates both mandatory clinical responses and the group's collective relational field in ways that must be managed simultaneously.

The clinical distinction that governs this curriculum's approach to self-harm is the one that DBT established and that Session 14 applies specifically: non-suicidal self-injury and suicidal behavior are clinically distinct and require different responses. Non-suicidal self-injury is most commonly a regulatory strategy, a form of communication, or both. Suicidal behavior, including suicidal ideation with intent, plan, or means, requires individual crisis assessment that cannot occur within the group setting. When a group member discloses suicidal ideation with intent in session, the facilitator pauses the group, expresses direct regulated concern, and activates the individual crisis protocol. A co-facilitator or additional staff member manages the group while the disclosure is addressed. The group is not abandoned. The individual is not assessed in front of the group.

The complete self-harm and suicide safety planning protocol for this curriculum is in Appendix D. Every facilitator must read it in its entirety before Session 1 and must have reviewed it with their clinical supervisor. This is not optional.

Disclosure Boundaries in BPD Groups

The disclosure framework from Books 1 and 2, that group members share the impact of their history rather than the specific content of traumatic events, applies in full here. It carries an additional layer in BPD treatment: the specific disclosure risk of graphic self-harm descriptions in group settings.

When a group member begins to describe specific self-harm behaviors in graphic detail, the clinical response is identical in structure to the trauma disclosure management protocol from Chapter 5 of Book 1, adapted for the specific content. The facilitator intervenes: "I want to slow us down here. What you are starting to describe is important, and it belongs in your individual therapy where there is more time and privacy. What I hear from you is that you have been in significant pain. Can we stay with that?" The graphic content is redirected. The emotional truth is received. The group's regulatory state is managed.

This intervention is not a suppression of the client's experience. It is the clinical recognition that graphic self-harm descriptions in group settings produce contagion effects with predictable consistency in a population that already includes elevated rates of self-harm behavior. Protecting the group container is protecting every member of it, including the member who was redirected.

Splitting in the Group Room

Splitting, the alternation between idealization and devaluation, is not merely a within-client dynamic. It appears in groups as a between-member and member-to-facilitator dynamic, and it is one of the most clinically demanding challenges in BPD group facilitation. A group member who is currently idealizing the facilitator will defend the facilitator against any challenge. A group member who is currently devaluing the facilitator will find every clinical intervention inadequate. Both states are live material. Neither is an emergency.

The clinical response to splitting in group settings is the dialectical response: acknowledge what is true in the member's experience while holding a wider view. If a member says the curriculum is not helping them, the response is not defensive justification and it is not wholesale agreement. It is: "Something about the curriculum feels wrong or missing for you. That's real and I want to understand it. Can you tell me specifically what isn't landing?"

Facilitators who take splitting personally, who either capitulate to the devaluation or are destabilized by the idealization, lose the regulated presence that is the primary clinical tool of this curriculum. The pre-session regulatory check described in Session 1's facilitator notes is the primary protection against this loss.

Clinical Supervision Requirements

Every facilitator delivering this curriculum must have access to clinical supervision at minimum weekly frequency. Supervision for BPD treatment must address three domains, not two.

The first domain is clinical decision-making: what is happening with specific clients, how are the clinical judgments being made, is the pacing appropriate for the current cohort.

The second domain is facilitator state: what the clinical content is producing in the facilitator's own nervous system, what the facilitator is carrying from prior sessions, where the facilitator's own attachment history intersects with the material.

The third domain, specific to BPD treatment and not formally required in Books 1 and 2, is countertransference to the specific presentation: the idealization, the devaluation, the testing behavior, the rescue pull, the specific quality of fatigue that comes from sustained work with high-activation presentations. Facilitators who are not given regular clinical space to name and process their countertransference to BPD presentations are the facilitators most likely to enact it, either by over-identifying with clients at the expense of clinical clarity or by distancing from clients in ways that reproduce the invalidating relational environments the curriculum is designed to address.

Facilitators who do not currently have access to supervision that addresses all three domains should raise this explicitly with their clinical supervisor before beginning the curriculum. The request is a clinical requirement, not a personal one.

Part One: Clinical Foundations

Chapter 1.0: The Diagnosis That Missed Its Own Origin

Fourteen. That is how many times more likely an individual with borderline personality disorder is to report childhood adversity than a person with no BPD diagnosis, according to a meta-analysis of ninety-seven studies covering more than eleven thousand people with BPD and more than thirteen thousand clinical controls (Porter et al., 2020). Fourteen times. The relationship is not correlational in the loose sense of two things that tend to appear together. It is among the strongest associations in all of personality disorder research.

So here is the question that that statistic demands: why does the primary evidence-based treatment for BPD include no protocol for addressing the childhood adversity that characterizes the majority of people who receive the diagnosis?

That question is not a criticism of DBT. It is an invitation to understand what DBT was designed to do and what it was not designed to do, and to ask what becomes possible when the adversity history that produced the BPD presentation is treated as the clinical mechanism rather than the biographical background.

Most clinicians who work with BPD believe the adversity is relevant. Most do not have a systematic clinical architecture for making it therapeutically active. That is the gap this chapter addresses. By the end of it, you will approach the ACE-BPD relationship differently than most clinicians in your field: not as a risk factor to note at intake, but as the developmental mechanism that determines what treatment must provide.

This chapter covers: the ACE research specific to BPD and what it establishes about the adversity-BPD connection; the specific adversity types most strongly associated with BPD and why they matter clinically; the neurobiological pathway from adversity to BPD symptom expression; the de-shaming reframe that the ACE data demands for this population; and the clinical application of ACE-informed thinking in group BPD treatment. The question this chapter raises but does not answer is how the neuroscience of that adversity pathway explains the specific symptom picture of BPD, including emotion dysregulation, identity disturbance, and abandonment fear. That is Chapter 2.

Common Belief:

BPD is primarily a biological condition, likely with a significant genetic component, and while adverse childhood experiences may increase severity, many people with BPD had unremarkable childhoods and many people with high adversity burdens do not develop BPD.

What the Evidence Shows:

The genetic contribution to BPD is real but modest, with heritability estimates ranging from 37 to 69 percent depending on the study population and methodology (Torgersen et al., 2012). The adversity association is substantially stronger. Porter and colleagues' 2020 meta-analysis documented the 13.91 odds ratio for childhood adversity in BPD across 97 studies including over 11,000 individuals with BPD. Of the specific ACE types, emotional abuse shows the strongest independent association with BPD symptom expression, with emotional neglect closely following (Fall, 2020). The apparent exceptions, individuals with high adversity burdens who do not develop BPD and individuals with BPD who do not report significant adversity, are explained by temperamental vulnerability, protective relational factors, and the documented underreporting of emotional abuse and neglect by populations who experienced those adversity types as simply normal. The adversity is frequently present whether or not it was named.

1.1 The ACE-BPD Relationship: What the Research Establishes

The ACE-BPD relationship is not a recently discovered clinical observation. It has been documented across decades of research. What is relatively new is the systematic meta-analytic evidence that establishes its magnitude.

Porter and colleagues' 2020 analysis is the largest and most methodologically rigorous examination of the relationship to date. The 13.91 odds ratio holds across case-control, epidemiological, and prospective cohort study designs, meaning it is not an artifact of any single methodological approach. The relationship is consistent whether adversity is measured prospectively in childhood or retrospectively in adulthood, which addresses the common objection that retrospective self-reports are inflated by current clinical state.

The NESARC-III analysis by Fall (2020) provides the most granular picture of which ACE types most strongly predict BPD, using a nationally representative sample of 4,301 adults with BPD diagnoses. Every one of the ten standard ACE categories independently predicted BPD after controlling for other variables. The adjusted odds ratio for emotional abuse was 3.00, meaning that adults who experienced emotional abuse in childhood were three times more likely to meet criteria for BPD than those who had not, after accounting for all other ACE types. Emotional neglect showed an adjusted odds ratio of 2.30. Physical abuse was 1.89. Sexual abuse, which is often assumed to be the primary adversity type in BPD, showed an adjusted odds ratio of 2.10 for BPD alone, but a substantially higher 4.45 for BPD with comorbid substance use disorder.

The clinical significance of the emotional abuse finding cannot be overstated. Emotional abuse is the adversity type that most directly disrupts attachment, the primary mechanism through which children develop the capacity to regulate emotion, tolerate distress, and maintain a coherent sense of self. A child who is repeatedly told that their emotions are wrong, excessive, or shameful, who is ridiculed for emotional expression, or who experiences the specific form of relational cruelty that adult contempt for a child's inner life produces, does not develop the regulatory capacities that BPD treatment will later ask them to use. The therapy is attempting to build what the adversity prevented from developing.

1.2 Emotional Abuse and Neglect: The Adversity Types That Matter Most

The primacy of emotional abuse and neglect in the ACE-BPD relationship is not clinically surprising to anyone who works regularly with BPD presentations. The clinical surprise is how rarely these adversity types are systematically assessed, named, and addressed in treatment.

Emotional abuse in childhood takes several specific forms relevant to the BPD presentation. Chronic ridicule of emotional states, particularly the child's distress and fear, teaches the child that their internal experience is unreliable, excessive, or shameful. This does not produce a child who stops having emotions. It produces a child who experiences emotions with full intensity and simultaneously experiences shame about having them, a configuration that maps directly onto the BPD symptom of intense emotional experience combined with self-loathing about that experience.

Emotional invalidation, Linehan's (1993) foundational concept in the biosocial theory of BPD, is the specific adversity mechanism she identified as producing the BPD presentation in combination with emotional sensitivity. An invalidating environment is one in which the child's emotional responses are consistently met with messages that those responses are inaccurate, inappropriate, or evidence of a personal deficiency. The child learns to distrust their own internal states, which produces the identity instability characteristic of BPD: if I cannot trust my own emotional experience to accurately reflect my internal state, I cannot know who I am.

Emotional neglect, the absence of attunement and care rather than the presence of abuse, produces a different but equally consequential developmental injury. The child whose emotional states are consistently ignored, who has no reliable experience of having their distress met by a regulated other, does not develop the neural infrastructure for co-regulation that Session 7 of this curriculum addresses. They arrive in adulthood with a nervous system that has never reliably experienced the specific quality of being regulated by another, which is precisely what the BPD presentation's relational intensity, abandonment fear, and desperate searches for connection represent: the attempt to get, from adult relationships, what early relationships never provided.

1.3 The Adversity-to-BPD Pathway: A Developmental Account

Understanding the pathway from adversity to BPD is not merely academically interesting. It changes what the facilitator looks for in clinical history, how they understand the behavior in the room, and what the clinical intervention needs to provide.

The developmental account begins with the interaction between emotional sensitivity and environmental response. Linehan's (1993) biosocial theory proposes that BPD develops when a child with above-average emotional sensitivity grows up in an environment that consistently invalidates their emotional experience. The sensitivity is not a deficit. In a validating environment, high emotional sensitivity is associated with empathy, creativity, and relational attunement. In an invalidating environment, it becomes the mechanism through which emotional neglect and abuse produce the most damage.

The adversity does not simply produce unpleasant experiences. It disrupts the developmental processes that emotional attunement, predictability, and safety are designed to produce. Specifically, it impairs the development of emotional regulation capacity, the learned ability to tolerate, modulate, and express emotional states in flexible rather than rigid ways. It impairs the development of a coherent sense of self, which requires consistent attunement from caregivers to develop. And it produces the specific relational template, described in Chapter 2 of Book 1, that treats closeness as simultaneously necessary and dangerous, which is the precise relational configuration that splitting, abandonment fear, and the idealization-devaluation cycle represent.

The ACE research does not explain why emotional abuse and neglect produce these specific developmental impairments rather than others. The neuroscience of the next chapter does. What the ACE research establishes, and what the clinical application of this chapter depends on, is that the BPD presentation is the predictable developmental outcome of specific adversity types in emotionally sensitive individuals, not a genetic defect or a moral failure. That distinction, held consistently by the facilitator and gradually received by the client, is the foundational clinical intervention of Module A.

1.4 The De-Shaming Reframe in BPD Treatment

The ACE research demands a de-shaming reframe in BPD treatment that is, in the author's clinical observation, more clinically charged and more clinically essential than the equivalent reframe in addiction treatment.

Addiction carries significant cultural stigma. BPD carries something different and in some ways more isolating: the specific stigma of being a disorder that many clinicians are reluctant to treat, that is frequently blamed on the person who has it, and that is described in the clinical literature in language that has historically positioned the person with BPD as the source of clinical difficulty rather than as a person with a clinical presentation that has developmental origins and clinical treatment.

The de-shaming reframe in this curriculum is not a reassurance or a positive reframe in the therapeutic sense. It is an evidence-based explanation: your emotional intensity, your fear of being left, your difficulty knowing who you are, your history of relationships that swing between closeness and collapse, these are not character defects. They are the predictable outcomes of a nervous system that experienced emotional abuse and neglect during the developmental period when the regulatory, identity, and relational capacities that BPD treatment addresses would otherwise have been built.

This reframe does not eliminate personal responsibility for current behavior. A client who understands the developmental origins of their BPD presentation is still responsible for how they act in their current relationships and in treatment. What the reframe changes is the shame that has prevented genuine engagement with that responsibility. A client who believes they are simply defective has no reason to expect that learning skills will change them, because defectiveness is not a skill deficit. A client who understands that their presentation is a developmental outcome has a reason to expect that building the developmental infrastructure that was not built has clinical value.

The Adversity-Origin Principle

The recognition that a client's BPD symptom presentation is the developmental outcome of specific adversity experiences, not a character defect, and the clinical use of that recognition to replace shame-based self-understanding with an explanatory framework that makes skill-building clinically meaningful.

Apply it by delivering the ACE framework in Session 5 with enough specificity and warmth that the client's first response, whether relief or anger or grief, becomes the first emotionally present moment of treatment.

Key Insight Box

BPD's emotional, relational, and identity instabilities are the developmental consequences of specific adversity, not evidence of personal deficiency.

1.5 Apply This in Practice

Quick Win First

Before your next clinical intake for a BPD presentation, add one specific question that the standard intake almost certainly does not ask: "When you were upset as a child, what typically happened?" Not "did you experience abuse or neglect?" The specific question: what happened when you expressed emotional distress. The answer will tell you more about the developmental adversity most relevant to the BPD presentation than most of the standard intake form combined.

When to Use This

The ACE-informed framework applies to every clinical contact with a BPD presentation. It is most immediately actionable in three specific moments: when a client describes their BPD diagnosis as evidence that something is fundamentally wrong with them; when a client's treatment history includes multiple programs that addressed skills without improving them; and when a client's shame about their clinical presentation is preventing engagement with the skills work that the curriculum offers.

Steps for Use

Step 1: Administer the ACE questionnaire at intake or in Session 5 using the group protocol in Appendix A. Present it as an explanatory tool, not a risk instrument. The framing matters as much as the instrument.

Step 2: Connect the client's specific ACE profile to their BPD presentation in language that is specific rather than general. "Your ACE history includes sustained emotional invalidation, which is the exact adversity type most strongly associated with the identity instability and emotion dysregulation that BPD describes. What you are experiencing is not a surprise, given that history."

Step 3: Use the Adversity-Origin Principle consistently across sessions. When a client describes a clinical pattern with shame, the clinical response returns to the developmental frame: "That pattern makes developmental sense. Let's look at where it came from and what built it."

Step 4: Distinguish the reframe from excuse. "Understanding why your nervous system produces this pattern does not mean you have no responsibility for how you act in recovery. What it means is that the work ahead of you is harder than most people realize, and that the difficulty is not evidence of your personal deficiency."

When It Does Not Work

The adversity-origin reframe does not produce immediate clinical change in clients whose shame has been thoroughly internalized. Initial resistance, particularly anger at the suggestion that their history explains their diagnosis, is common and clinically appropriate. The anger is the beginning of the grief work that Module C addresses. Do not mistake early resistance for clinical failure.

The framework also does not address the full complexity of BPD presentations in clients with significant genetic vulnerability, neurological conditions, or developmental differences that are not primarily adversity-produced. The ACE framework is clinically essential but not clinically sufficient on its own.

1.6 Case Study: Riley

Background

Riley was forty-two years old, a former middle school teacher who had lost her teaching position following a boundary violation with a parent that ended in a formal complaint. She had been in and out of outpatient mental health treatment since age nineteen and had received the BPD diagnosis in three separate clinical contexts. Each time, she described her response to the diagnosis as the same: a specific combination of relief at having a name for her experience and deep, sustained shame at what the name seemed to mean about her.

She had been in standard DBT skills training for fourteen weeks at a prior program before being referred for IOP treatment following a self-harm episode. Her skills binder was complete and organized. Her diary card compliance had been, in her description, excellent. The self-harm had occurred two days after receiving a text from her mother that she described only as "the usual."

Riley's ACE score, completed at intake, was eight. Her history included sustained emotional abuse from a mother with untreated narcissistic features, emotional neglect from a father who was physically present and emotionally absent, and a period of peer victimization in middle school that she had never connected to her ACE history because the standard ACE questionnaire does not include it.

Presentation

Riley presented as articulate about DBT, genuinely skilled in the regulatory practices she had learned, and entirely unable to explain why she had harmed herself two days after receiving a text message from her mother. She described the self-harm as arriving without warning: "I wasn't even particularly upset. I was fine. And then I wasn't, and then I had done it before I registered that I was making a decision."

The dissociation-like quality of the episode, the sense of having arrived somewhere without having chosen to travel, is clinically recognizable as an emotional expression of her state at the time: she had, in fact, been activated by the text message at a level her interoceptive awareness could not detect because the emotional abuse had been so chronic and so thoroughly externalized as normal that its activation produced physiological responses below her conscious threshold.

Analysis

Riley's fourteen weeks of DBT skills training had addressed the regulatory deficit without addressing the developmental history that produced it. She had skills. She did not have the understanding of why her nervous system produced the specific states the skills were designed to regulate, which meant she could not detect the chain's initiation at the sensory and somatic links. The text from her mother was not a situational trigger in the cognitive behavioral sense. It was a somatic cue: a sensory input associated with fourteen hundred consecutive instances of emotional invalidation, activating the regulatory collapse that the childhood environment had reliably produced.

When Riley's ACE history was reviewed in the context of the developmental pathway described in Section 1.3, she was quiet for a long time. Then she said something that has become a clinical touchstone in the curriculum's field testing: "I never thought of it as something that happened to me. I thought it was just how I am."

Response and Intervention

The clinical work began with the Adversity-Origin Principle delivered specifically, not generally. "Your emotional sensitivity is real. The environment you grew up in treated that sensitivity as evidence of a problem. Your nervous system spent fourteen years learning that your internal states were untrustworthy. DBT asks you to trust your internal states enough to regulate them. We need to address that specific gap before the skills can fully work."

The ACE questionnaire was reviewed in detail in Session 5. Riley's response to the emotional abuse item was the first time in her treatment history that she had seen her mother's behavior named as an ACE category. The naming was, in her words, "disorienting and also a relief." The disorientation was the beginning of the identity work. The relief was the beginning of the de-shaming process.

Outcome

Riley completed the full thirty-session curriculum. She did not self-harm again during the program. At the six-month follow-up, she reported one high-risk episode that had not resulted in self-harm, which she attributed to having used the somatic early warning sign map developed in Session 6. She also described an ongoing and difficult process of reconsidering her relationship with her mother, which she was addressing in individual therapy. She remained distressed. She was not in crisis.

Teaching Points

Riley's case illustrates the specific clinical gap between skills acquisition and skills accessibility in BPD treatment: she had the skills and could not access them in the state the trigger produced because the trigger activated a developmental response rather than a cognitive one.

The mother's text as a somatic cue, rather than a situational trigger, illustrates why the trigger chain model from Book 1 applies in BPD treatment: the chain initiates below conscious awareness, at a sensory and somatic level that standard DBT trigger analysis does not systematically address.

The naming of emotional abuse as an ACE category producing a response of "this is just how I am" illustrates the clinical effect of thorough internalization: when adversity is chronic and relational, it stops being experienced as external and starts being experienced as self. The ACE framework is the first clinical intervention that makes the externalization possible.

The outcome is realistic: Riley did not resolve her relationship with her mother, did not eliminate her BPD symptoms, and remained in active therapeutic work. What changed was her self-understanding and her capacity to interrupt one specific high-risk chain.

Reader Mirror Moment

If Riley's "I never thought of it as something that happened to me" resonates with your clinical experience, it is because it is among the most common clinical presentations in BPD treatment. Clients who have internalized chronic emotional abuse as normal, as simply the environment they grew up in, cannot access the developmental reframe without someone providing it explicitly. This is not a therapeutic observation the client can reach alone. It requires a clinician who knows the ACE-BPD research and who delivers the developmental explanation with enough specificity to make it about this client's specific history rather than about BPD in general. The specificity is the clinical intervention.

Comparison Table: The Clinical Difference Between Treating BPD Without and With the ACE Framework

Clinical Element	Without ACE Framework	With ACE Framework
Diagnosis meaning	Label for a behavioral and emotional pattern	Developmental outcome of specific adversity types
Explanation for symptoms	Dysregulation and skills deficits	Developmental impairments produced by adversity
Shame position	Implicit: the BPD person has a disordered personality	Explicit: the BPD presentation is an understandable response
Treatment target	Skills acquisition	Skills acquisition plus developmental understanding
Client engagement	Compliance with skills training	Engagement with skills plus the developmental narrative
Response to relapse	Evidence of insufficient effort	Evidence of the gap between skills and their developmental prerequisites
Facilitator stance	Skills trainer	Developmental witness and skills trainer

There is one question the Adversity-Origin Principle does not answer on its own: why does childhood adversity, and emotional adversity specifically, produce the particular symptom picture of BPD rather than some other clinical presentation? Why emotion dysregulation rather than flat affect? Why identity instability rather than rigid identity? Why abandonment fear rather than social withdrawal?

Chapter 2 addresses those questions through the neuroscience of emotion dysregulation. The answer is specific, it connects directly to the ACE research this chapter has established, and it changes what the facilitator understands about what is actually happening in the room during a BPD crisis.

"Your emotional intensity is not a flaw. It is a nervous system that was taught the wrong lesson about its own experience."

Chapter 2.0: The Nervous System That Never Got to Rest

Avery was in the middle of Module B when she said the thing that stopped the group. They had been discussing the abandonment fear, working through the behavioral chain that the fear produced, and Avery, who had been quiet throughout the psychoeducation, said: "My nervous system has never stopped working since I was seven years old."

Nobody in the room spoke for a moment. The facilitator noted, later in supervision, that what Avery had described was not a metaphor. It was a neurobiological fact.

Emotion dysregulation, the regulatory core of borderline personality disorder, is not a learned habit or a cognitive error. It is the specific product of a nervous system that developed under adversity conditions and never got the developmental opportunity to build the regulatory architecture that safety would have produced. Understanding how that happens, in biological detail that is now well established in the research literature, is the prerequisite for understanding why the four DBT skill modules work when they work and why they sometimes do not.

This chapter is stranger than most chapters in clinical curricula, in the best sense. The neuroscience of BPD is not dry. It is the story of a specific thing that happened to a developing nervous system, in a specific sequence, that produced exactly the symptoms that will sit across from you in group sessions and resist exactly the interventions that would work if the developmental history were different.

This chapter covers: the neurobiological mechanisms through which early adversity produces emotion dysregulation; the specific brain structures implicated in BPD's symptom profile; the Window of Tolerance in BPD and why it is narrower, less stable, and more reactive than in other presentations; and how substance use, self-harm, and impulsive behavior function as regulatory tools in this specific neurobiological context. The question this chapter raises but does not fully resolve is why DBT skills, which directly target the regulatory deficits described here, sometimes fail to generalize from the therapy room to the high-activation moments that matter most. That is Chapter 3.

Common Belief:

The emotional dysregulation of BPD is primarily a problem of emotional sensitivity: people with BPD feel things more intensely than other people, and the treatment task is to help them tolerate that intensity and respond more flexibly to it.

What the Evidence Shows:

Emotional sensitivity, elevated emotional reactivity, is one component of the BPD emotional profile, but it is not the primary clinical problem. The more clinically significant issue, documented across neuroimaging and psychophysiological research, is impaired return to baseline after emotional activation: the regulatory capacity to down-regulate the intensity that has been activated. Linehan (1993) described this as the three-part BPD emotional profile: high baseline sensitivity, high reactivity, and slow return to baseline. The neurobiological research supports all three, with the slow return to baseline showing the strongest association with clinical severity and the most direct relationship to impulsive and self-harming behavior (Carpenter and Trull, 2013).

2.1 The Amygdala in BPD: A Threat Detector on Permanent Alert

The amygdala's role in BPD is well documented across neuroimaging studies and directly relevant to clinical facilitation. Individuals with BPD show elevated amygdala activation in response to emotional stimuli, including stimuli that non-BPD individuals do not register as emotionally significant, and show reduced amygdala-prefrontal connectivity, which impairs the capacity for cortical down-regulation of the amygdala's responses.

What makes the BPD amygdala picture clinically specific, and distinct from the general pattern described in Chapter 2 of Book 1, is the particular sensitivity to social and relational threat cues. Research using facial expression paradigms has found that individuals with BPD show heightened amygdala activation to emotionally neutral faces, which they consistently rate as hostile or threatening at rates significantly higher than non-BPD control participants (Domes et al., 2009). This is not a cognitive error in the standard CBT sense. It is a calibration: a threat detection system that was trained in an environment where neutral faces could precede harm and that has maintained that training into adulthood.

The clinical implication is specific. When a group member with BPD interprets a facilitator's neutral expression as displeasure, or a co-group member's silence as contempt, they are not being irrational. They are reporting the output of a threat detection system that was accurately calibrated to the specific emotional environment in which it developed. The clinical task is not to correct the interpretation as a cognitive distortion. It is to provide enough consistent, reliable, and explicitly warm relational experience that the threat detection system's calibration gradually updates.

Case Study embedded illustration: Avery's description, "my nervous system has never stopped working since I was seven years old," is a precise somatic account of a permanently alert amygdala. Her history included a father with severe untreated bipolar disorder whose affect was unpredictable and whose explosions bore no reliable relationship to what preceded them. Her amygdala learned what any well-functioning amygdala in that environment would learn: that neutral moments could not be trusted, that calm preceded storm without warning, and that the only adaptive response was continuous monitoring. That learning was not disordered. It was correct. It became clinically significant when it persisted into an adulthood in which the father's unpredictability was no longer present but the nervous system had no reliable mechanism for knowing that.

2.2 The Prefrontal Cortex and the Regulatory Collapse

The prefrontal cortex is the primary regulatory structure for emotional states, and its relationship to the amygdala in BPD is the neurobiological core of the disorder's primary clinical challenge.

Under ordinary activation conditions, the prefrontal cortex maintains inhibitory connections to the amygdala that allow emotional responses to be modulated, contextualized, and extinguished when the threat that produced them has resolved. This prefrontal-amygdala regulatory circuit requires two conditions to function adequately: it must have been built through sufficiently consistent co-regulatory experiences during development, and it must be operating within the arousal range in which prefrontal function is not suppressed by cortisol.

BPD presentations are characterized by both failures simultaneously. The adversity history that Chapter 1 documented produces exactly the developmental conditions under which the prefrontal-amygdala regulatory circuit is built incompletely: insufficient co-regulation, insufficient experience of having emotional states met by a regulated other, and the specific developmental injury of having emotional expression consistently met with invalidation. The circuit is structurally impaired.

And because the emotional responses that result from the impaired circuit are more intense and more frequent than in non-BPD presentations, the prefrontal cortex is more often operating in the high-cortisol range in which its function is additionally suppressed. The result is the regulatory collapse that clinicians observe as escalating distress, impulsive behavior, and the inability to access skills that the client demonstrably has and uses in lower-activation contexts.

This is why the DBT skill "opposite action" sometimes works in session and fails in crisis. In session, the client is within their window and the prefrontal cortex is available. In crisis, the window has been exceeded and the prefrontal cortex is partly offline. The skill is not accessible not because the client has failed to learn it but because the regulatory architecture required to access it has been temporarily overwhelmed.

2.3 The Window of Tolerance in BPD: Narrow, Unstable, and Reactive

The Window of Tolerance concept introduced in Book 1 applies in BPD treatment with three BPD-specific modifications that significantly affect how the curriculum uses it.

First, the window in BPD presentations is typically narrower than in other clinical populations, and the narrowing is more reactive to relational cues specifically. A client with BPD whose zero-to-ten number is five, within the window, can be moved above the window within seconds by a specific type of interpersonal event: a perceived slight, a moment of disconnection, a change in the facilitator's tone. This reactivity is the amygdala's relational threat sensitivity manifesting in real time. Facilitators who understand this do not take it personally. Facilitators who do not understand it often either become overly careful in a way that produces its own disruption, or become frustrated in a way that confirms the client's threat detection.

Second, the BPD window is less predictable in its position across sessions and across times of day than the window in addiction populations. A client who arrived within the window in the previous session may arrive above it in the current session for reasons that appear unrelated to session content. The zero-to-ten check-in that opens every session in this curriculum is not merely a regulatory tool in BPD treatment. It is a real-time clinical assessment that determines how the session must be paced.

Third, the return to baseline after window exceedance is significantly slower in BPD presentations than in most other clinical populations. This is the slow return to baseline that Linehan (1993) identified and that Carpenter and Trull (2013) associated most directly with clinical severity. A group member who is above the window during Module B's Session 14 may not return to window by the end of the session even with extended grounding practices. Facilitators must plan for extended closings in the sessions with the highest activation potential, and must have individual follow-up contacts available for group members who leave sessions in dysregulated states.

2.4 Regulatory Functions: Self-Harm, Impulsivity, and the Substitution Problem

Every behavior that standard treatment positions as a symptom of BPD to be eliminated has a regulatory function that the elimination of the behavior does not address. Understanding those functions is the prerequisite for understanding why behavior change in BPD treatment without the regulatory infrastructure to replace the function of the behavior is not merely ineffective. It can be destabilizing.

Non-suicidal self-injury is the most clinically charged example. Its regulatory function has been well documented across multiple research frameworks: it produces a rapid shift in autonomic state through the parasympathetic activation of pain response, provides a concrete somatic experience in clients who are dissociating, converts an unbearable emotional state into a physical state that feels more manageable, and, for some clients, functions as communication directed at others who have not responded to verbal expression of distress. Removing the behavior without replacing its regulatory function leaves the nervous system without a tool it was using to manage a state it cannot otherwise manage.

This is not an argument for tolerating self-harm. It is an argument for understanding the function before designing the clinical response. When a client self-harms following a session, the clinical question is not only what triggered the behavior. It is what the behavior provided that the trigger had taken away, and what the treatment plan offers that will provide the same regulatory outcome without the harm.

Impulsive behavior, splitting, substance use, and binge-purge behavior in BPD presentations with eating disorder comorbidity are all amenable to the same functional analysis. Each represents the nervous system reaching for its most reliable regulatory tool in the absence of something better. Chapter 3 examines why standard DBT's skills-training approach sometimes fails to provide that something better for the specific population this curriculum addresses.

The Regulatory Collapse Sequence

The predictable neurobiological sequence in which relational threat activation exceeds the BPD nervous system's prefrontal regulatory capacity, producing behavior that serves a regulatory function but that DBT skills were designed to replace.

Apply it by treating every high-activation behavioral episode as clinical data about the regulatory gap rather than as evidence of treatment failure or insufficient motivation.

Key Insight Box

BPD's impulsive and self-harming behaviors are regulatory tools for a nervous system whose regulatory architecture was impaired by adversity.

2.5 Apply This in Practice

Quick Win First

After your next group session with a BPD population, identify one behavioral episode that occurred in the session and ask yourself the regulatory function question: what did that behavior provide for the nervous system that produced it? Not what triggered the behavior. What the behavior gave the person who did it. The answer, which should take under three minutes to generate, will change how you understand the episode and how you respond to it clinically.

When to Use This

The neurobiological framework applies most directly in four clinical moments: when a client engages in self-harm despite having completed extensive skills training; when a client's in-session behavior escalates in ways that appear disproportionate to the session content; when skills fail to generalize from session to high-risk real-world contexts; and when a client describes their behavioral patterns as incomprehensible even to themselves.

Steps for Use

Step 1: Teach the three-part BPD emotional profile, high sensitivity, high reactivity, and slow return to baseline, in Session 2's biosocial theory psychoeducation. Use the zero-to-ten scale as the practical monitoring tool for all three components.

Step 2: In every session, use the pre-session zero-to-ten check-in to assess window position before any content delivery. If the group's collective number is above seven, begin with somatic regulation rather than content.

Step 3: When a behavioral episode occurs in session or is reported from outside session, conduct the regulatory function analysis before the behavioral intervention: what state was the nervous system in before the behavior, and what did the behavior do to that state?

Step 4: Connect the regulatory function analysis explicitly to the skills curriculum in Module C. Each skill in the four DBT modules is introduced in this curriculum with an explicit statement of which regulatory function it is designed to replace.

When It Does Not Work

The neurobiological framework does not produce behavioral change independently. Understanding why the nervous system produces regulatory collapse does not give the client the regulatory alternative. That is what Module C provides. The framework is the prerequisite for skills acquisition, not a substitute for it.

The framework also does not adequately address BPD presentations with significant dissociative symptoms, where the regulatory collapse is complicated by disconnection from internal states that the Window of Tolerance model assumes the client can access.

2.6 Visual Element: The Regulatory Collapse Sequence

The following process sequence describes the neurobiological events that connect a relational threat cue to a self-harming or impulsive behavioral response in BPD presentations.

Stage 1: Relational Threat Cue

A sensory or contextual input that the amygdala's relational threat detection system, calibrated by adversity history, registers as potentially dangerous: a change in tone, a perceived slight, a moment of disconnection, an ambiguous facial expression, or the specific sensory qualities of a situation associated with prior relational harm.

Stage 2: Amygdala Activation

Rapid, pre-cortical threat response. The amygdala fires before the prefrontal cortex has processed the cue. In BPD presentations, the activation is higher in magnitude and the threshold for activation is lower than in non-BPD presentations.

Stage 3: Window Exceedance

The activation exceeds the Window of Tolerance. The prefrontal cortex's capacity to modulate the response begins to degrade. The regulatory collapse is underway. Skills that are available within the window become progressively less accessible.

Stage 4: Regulatory Deficit State

The nervous system is in a state for which it has no adequate internal regulatory tool. The slow return to baseline means this state will persist. The intensity of the emotional experience is high. The prefrontal cortex is partly offline.

Stage 5: Behavioral Regulation

The nervous system reaches for its most reliable external regulatory tool: self-harm, substance use, impulsive behavior, or the relational escalation that at least produces a response from the environment. The behavior serves a genuine regulatory function for the nervous system that produced it.

Stage 6: Post-Behavioral State

The regulatory behavior has addressed the acute regulatory deficit. The shame that follows is frequently the trigger for the next regulatory cycle. The Shame-Use Cycle from Book 1 operates here as the Shame-Behavior Cycle: behavioral shame deepens the state that the behavior was recruited to address.

Chapter 2 has described the neurobiological mechanism that Chapter 1's adversity data produces. The regulatory collapse sequence, the specific pathway from adversity-calibrated amygdala to prefrontal offline to behavioral regulation, is the mechanism that DBT skills training was designed to interrupt. The question it does not yet answer is why that interruption is sometimes incomplete: why do clients who have genuinely acquired the skills sometimes fail to access them in exactly the states they were designed for?

That question points toward the gap that Chapter 3 addresses: the specific ways in which standard DBT, as designed, does not account for the developmental origins of the regulatory deficit it is treating, and what a trauma-informed architecture adds to make the skills genuinely accessible in the states when they are most needed.

"The behavior was not a choice. It was the nervous system finding the most efficient route out of a state it could not otherwise survive."

Chapter 3.0: Why the Binder Is Not Enough

I have made the mistake this chapter describes, and I made it more than once before I understood what I was doing.

The first time, I was three years into clinical work and running my first DBT skills group. The client, a twenty-six-year-old man I will call Marlowe, had been in DBT for six months in a previous program and had left after a crisis admission. He arrived at my group with a skills binder from the prior program, a confident DBT vocabulary, and a quality of engagement in the group that his previous facilitator had described as excellent. I assumed the prior program had built the foundation. I assumed my task was to extend it.

The second time was Marlowe's crisis call at eleven-thirty on a Tuesday night, seven weeks into our group, the third in a two-month period. He had done everything right, he told me. He had used his TIPP skills. He had called someone. And then the state had continued anyway and he had done the thing the skills were supposed to prevent.

I spent a long time thinking about what I had assumed that I should not have assumed. The binder was complete. The skills were real. What Marlowe had not been given in either program, and what I had not thought to provide, was an understanding of why his nervous system produced the states the skills were designed to address. The skills were tools for managing a regulatory deficit whose origins had never been examined, whose developmental logic had never been explained, and whose persistence in the face of genuine skill use had therefore never been understandable.

This chapter covers: the specific gaps in standard DBT's architecture that the adversity data from Chapter 1 and the neuroscience from Chapter 2 reveal; what a trauma-informed architecture adds to the DBT skills training without modifying the skills themselves; the case for integrating ACE-informed psychoeducation and somatic regulatory work before skills training begins; and the question every DBT facilitator eventually faces, which is not whether DBT works but when it does not work and why. The question this chapter raises but does not resolve is how to identify and address the specific internal states that inhibit skills access in real time, which is the domain of schema mode theory in Chapter 4.

Common Belief:

DBT is the gold standard treatment for BPD, and when it does not produce adequate outcomes, the primary explanation is treatment engagement: the client was not sufficiently compliant, did not practice skills between sessions, or was not yet ready for treatment.

What the Evidence Shows:

DBT has strong evidence for reducing self-harm and hospitalization in BPD populations, but its effect sizes on the core features of the disorder, emotional dysregulation, identity instability, and chronic emptiness, are modest (Linehan et al., 2015). The explanation for non-response is not primarily engagement: research on Trauma-Focused DBT adaptations, specifically DBT-PTSD (Bohus et al., 2020) and the broader DBT-for-PTSD literature (Prillinger et al., 2024), suggests that explicitly addressing trauma history and its developmental effects alongside skills training produces better outcomes than standard DBT alone. The standard DBT manual does not include a protocol for addressing co-occurring PTSD or developmental trauma, a limitation the field has documented and is actively working to address.

3.1 What Standard DBT Was Designed to Do

Marsha Linehan developed DBT in the late 1980s and early 1990s as a treatment for chronically suicidal women who met criteria for BPD and whose presentations had been resistant to existing treatments. The specific problem she designed it to solve was not BPD in general. It was the specific clinical challenge of maintaining therapeutic alliance with clients who were chronically in crisis, who were frequently dropped by therapists who found the work unmanageable, and who needed a treatment that could hold a suicidal client in outpatient treatment without abandoning her at the point of crisis.

The solution was elegant and effective: DBT combined the acceptance-oriented principles of mindfulness and radical acceptance with the change-oriented principles of cognitive behavioral therapy, organized around a biosocial understanding of BPD that positioned the disorder as the outcome of emotional sensitivity in an invalidating environment rather than as a character defect. The four skill modules provided concrete regulatory and interpersonal tools. The treatment hierarchy, which prioritizes life-threatening behavior above therapy-interfering behavior and above quality-of-life behavior, gave clinicians a structured approach to the clinical complexity that BPD presentations produce.

Standard DBT works. That is not under dispute here. What is worth examining clinically is what it was designed to address and what it addressed less explicitly.

3.2 The Three Gaps a Trauma-Informed Architecture Addresses

The trauma-informed architecture of this curriculum addresses three specific gaps in standard DBT's design, none of which invalidates the skills training that DBT provides.

The first gap is developmental context. Standard DBT's biosocial theory acknowledges that BPD develops from the interaction of emotional sensitivity with an invalidating environment, but it does not systematically integrate the ACE research that establishes the magnitude and the specific adversity types of that environment. A client who understands the biosocial theory abstractly knows that environment matters. A client who has reviewed their ACE profile, who understands that emotional abuse has an adjusted odds ratio of 3.00 for BPD, and who has made specific connections between their history and their presentation has a different relationship to both their diagnosis and to the skills designed to address it.

The second gap is regulatory preparation. Standard DBT skills training assumes that clients can practice skills when they are within the Window of Tolerance and gradually extend that practice to higher-activation states. It does not systematically build the somatic regulatory foundation, the grounding toolkit, the interoceptive awareness, and the zero-to-ten monitoring practice, before skills training begins. This curriculum builds that foundation in Module A before any DBT skill is introduced. The skills in Module C are not more effective because they have been modified. They are more accessible because the regulatory infrastructure required to use them has been built first.

The third gap is schema-level understanding. Standard DBT addresses automatic thoughts and behavioral patterns but does not systematically address the schema modes, the deep internal states organized around early relational experiences, that produce the specific emotional states the skills are designed to regulate. A client who knows that she has a TIPP skill but does not know that she is in the Vulnerable Child mode when she most needs it is applying a cognitive-level tool to a pre-cognitive-level state. The schema mode framework in Chapter 4 provides the internal map that makes the skills clinically targeted rather than generically applied.

3.3 What a Trauma-Informed Architecture Does Not Change

Naming the gaps in standard DBT requires equal clarity about what this curriculum does not change.

The four DBT skill modules, Core Mindfulness, Distress Tolerance, Emotion Regulation, and Interpersonal Effectiveness, are delivered in this curriculum exactly as Linehan's skills training manual describes them. The skills have not been modified, supplemented, or replaced. The research base supporting them is valid and this curriculum depends on it.

The dialectical philosophy at the heart of DBT, the principle that acceptance and change are both necessary and that neither alone is sufficient, is the organizing philosophical framework of this curriculum as much as it is of standard DBT. Module A's radical acceptance session (Session 6) is not a supplement to DBT's acceptance framework. It is a deliberate extension of it, delivered in the context of the ACE research that makes its clinical necessity clear.

The biosocial theory is not replaced but extended. This curriculum takes Linehan's biosocial account of BPD and places it within the larger ACE research framework, making the developmental adversity that the theory describes specific rather than general and measurable rather than assumed.

The Preparation Gap

The clinical failure mode in which DBT skills are taught to a nervous system that does not yet have the regulatory infrastructure to access them under the activation conditions in which they are most needed.

Apply it by assessing, before beginning Module C's skills training, whether the client's Window of Tolerance is adequately established, their somatic early warning signs are identified, and their understanding of the regulatory collapse sequence is in place.

Key Insight Box

DBT skills fail to generalize when the regulatory foundation required to access them under stress has not been built before skills training begins.

3.4 Apply This in Practice

Quick Win First

Before your next Module C session delivering a DBT skill, review the client's Window of Tolerance map from Session 3 and their zero-to-ten log from Module A's take-home practices. If the client does not have a working zero-to-ten monitoring habit established, extend the Module A somatic work before proceeding to skills training. This review takes five minutes and prevents the most common skills training failure mode.

When to Use This

The Preparation Gap framework applies when: a client has extensive prior DBT exposure but continues to experience regulatory crises; when skills practice in session does not generalize to high-activation real-world contexts; when a client describes themselves as "bad at DBT" despite compliance with skills training; and when self-harm or impulsive behavior occurs in clients who can articulate the skills they were supposed to use.

Steps for Use

Step 1: Before beginning Module C, review each group member's Module A outputs: the Window of Tolerance map, the somatic early warning sign map, and the grounding toolkit. The toolkit should include at least one technique rated three out of three for regulatory effect on that specific nervous system.

Step 2: Open every Module C session with an explicit connection between the skill being introduced and the regulatory collapse sequence from Chapter 2. "We are learning opposite action today. Opposite action is a prefrontal cortex intervention. It works when the prefrontal cortex is adequately online, which means it works when you are within your window."

Step 3: At every Module C session, conduct the zero-to-ten check-in before skill instruction. If the collective window is above seven, begin with grounding before proceeding.

Step 4: After Module C, evaluate each skill's real-world accessibility: has the client had an opportunity to use it under moderate activation conditions? Practice under low activation is necessary but not sufficient. Graduated real-world practice under increasing activation is the generalization pathway.

When It Does Not Work

The Preparation Gap framework addresses the regulatory accessibility problem but not the schema mode problem. A client who has adequate regulatory preparation and still cannot access skills during a high-activation episode may be encountering the Punitive Parent or Detached Protector modes that Chapter 4 addresses. The preparation gap and the schema mode barrier are distinct clinical problems requiring different interventions.

3.5 Case Studies: Marlowe and Ellis

Case Study 1: Marlowe

Marlowe was twenty-six, a graphic designer who had been in DBT twice before the IOP admission. Both prior programs had described him as highly engaged and intellectually capable. Both had ended in crisis admissions within three months of discharge.

When he arrived at the IOP, his skills binder was genuinely impressive. He could articulate the four skill modules with clinical precision. His conceptual grasp of dialectical thinking was more sophisticated than that of some clinicians in training. And his zero-to-ten regulatory awareness was, in his own description, essentially absent: he had never developed the monitoring practice because it had been presented in prior programs as preparatory material before the "real" work of skills training began.

The clinical architecture of the IOP reversed this order: Module A's somatic and regulatory foundation work preceded all skills training. Marlowe's initial response was frustration: "I've done DBT twice. I know this material." The clinical response was direct: "You know the skills. You can't access them in crisis. The work we are doing now is building the infrastructure that makes access possible."

The shift in Marlowe's engagement occurred in Session 6's zero-to-ten monitoring exercise, when he identified, for the first time, that his baseline resting number had never registered below five. His regulatory ceiling for skill use had been systematically lower than the activation level at which he most needed skills, which explained the consistent pattern of skills failure at precisely the moments of highest need.

Outcome: Marlowe completed the full curriculum. At the nine-month follow-up, he had had two crisis calls, neither resulting in hospitalization. He described the Module A foundation work as "the part I didn't know I needed because I thought I already had it."

Case Study 2: Ellis

Ellis was thirty-two, a retail manager who had never been in DBT, had received the BPD diagnosis six months before IOP admission following a serious self-harm episode, and had no prior experience of any structured clinical program. They arrived at Module A's first session expecting to receive information about their disorder and were visibly surprised when Session 1 began with the group agreement and the zero-to-ten scale.

"When do we talk about the actual BPD stuff?" they asked after Session 2.

The clinical response was: "We are talking about the actual BPD stuff. Your nervous system needs a regulatory foundation before skills training can work. We are building it now."

Ellis's trajectory through the curriculum was the opposite of Marlowe's: where Marlowe already had the skills without the foundation, Ellis had neither. The sequential architecture of Modules A and B was for Ellis exactly the sequence it was designed to be. By Session 12, Ellis had a schema mode map that gave them language, for the first time, for the internal shifts they had been experiencing for decades. By Session 21, the emotion regulation skill of opposite action had, in Ellis's description, "actually done something when I needed it, for the first time."

Reader Mirror Moment

Marlowe and Ellis represent the two most common presentations in clinical BPD settings: the client who has the skills without the foundation, and the client who has neither. The curriculum's sequential architecture addresses both, but the clinical error to avoid is the one the author made with Marlowe: assuming that prior DBT engagement means the foundation is in place. It frequently does not. The only way to know is to assess it directly, using the Module A tools, before proceeding to skills training.

Decision Framework: When to Extend Module A Before Proceeding to Module B or C

Assessment	Standard Progression	Extend Module A
Zero-to-ten baseline	Client has established daily monitoring habit	Client has not established daily monitoring habit
Window of Tolerance	Client can describe their personal window signs	Client cannot identify hyper- or hypoarousal signs
Grounding toolkit	Client has at least one three-rated technique	Client has no reliable grounding technique
Somatic early warning signs	Client has at least two identified	Client cannot identify body-level warning signs
ACE framework reception	Client has made at least one personal connection	Client remains in intellectual distance from the framework
Regulatory baseline	Client's resting zero-to-ten is typically below six	Client's resting number consistently above six

Chapter 3 has named the gaps that a trauma-informed architecture addresses and specified what it does not change. The preparation gap it describes is real and the framework for addressing it is clear. But there is a layer beneath the regulatory problem that the Preparation Gap does not reach: the specific internal states that produce the regulatory collapse in the first place. A client whose regulatory foundation is solid and whose skills are genuinely accessible sometimes still cannot use them, because the internal state they are in is organized by a schema mode that operates before the prefrontal cortex can engage. Chapter 4 addresses that layer and introduces the clinical vocabulary that gives both facilitators and clients access to it.

"Skills training without the developmental context is giving someone a map without telling them what country they are in."

Chapter 4.0: The Inner Cast Nobody Named

Have you ever sat with a BPD client in a high-activation moment and had the thought that you are talking to someone different from the person you spoke with twenty minutes ago? Not a different mood. A different person. A different relationship to the self, a different voice, a different quality of engagement, a different set of implicit rules about what is happening in the room and what you, the clinician, are about to do?

If you have, you have observed schema mode activation. And if you have not had language for what you observed, you have been in the same position as the majority of clients in BPD treatment: in the presence of something real and organizationally significant that has never been named.

Schema mode theory, developed by Jeffrey Young and colleagues from the schema therapy framework, provides the clinical vocabulary for the specific internal states that produce the behavioral and relational presentations characteristic of BPD. It does not replace DBT. It provides the map of what is happening inside the nervous system that DBT's skills are designed to regulate, and it gives clients a language for their own internal shifts that is, in the author's clinical experience, among the most relieving clinical gifts that BPD treatment can provide.

This chapter covers: what schema modes are and how they develop from adversity experience; the five modes most clinically relevant to BPD; how mode activation relates to the regulatory collapse sequence from Chapter 2; how schema mode awareness changes both the facilitator's clinical understanding and the client's self-understanding; and the specific clinical uses of mode awareness in group settings. The question this chapter raises but does not resolve is how the facilitator maintains their own regulated presence in the face of mode activation that is directed at them, which is the domain of Chapter 5.

Common Belief:

The internal states that characterize BPD, the switches between vulnerability and rage, the sudden devaluation that follows idealization, the experience of the self as bad or unworthy, are manifestations of emotional dysregulation that DBT skills training addresses at the correct level.

What the Evidence Shows:

Schema therapy research demonstrates that the schema modes most characteristic of BPD, Vulnerable Child, Angry/Impulsive Child, Detached Protector, and Punitive Parent, are stable internal states with distinct physiological, cognitive, and behavioral signatures that are not fully addressed by emotional regulation skills training alone. Schema therapy has shown clinically meaningful outcomes for BPD in randomized controlled trials (Nadort et al., 2009), and schema mode awareness specifically has been associated with reduced BPD symptom severity independently of skills acquisition.

4.1 What Schema Modes Are and How They Form

A schema mode is an internal state, a specific configuration of emotion, cognition, bodily sensation, and relational orientation, that is activated by triggers relevant to the deep beliefs that organized it. Schema modes are not personalities in the dissociative sense. They are the emotional and behavioral expressions of early maladaptive schemas, the core beliefs about the self, others, and the world that formed through early adverse experience.

The mechanism of mode formation is the same mechanism Chapter 1 described in the developmental pathway from emotional abuse to BPD: a child who experiences chronic emotional invalidation does not simply learn that their emotions are wrong. They develop an internal structure that contains the specific emotional states the abuse produced (terror, grief, shame, rage) alongside the internal voices that narrated the abuse (you are too much, you deserve this, no one will help you), alongside the protective strategies the adversity required (becoming small, becoming unreachable, becoming compliant). These states do not disappear when the adversity ends. They become the modes that the adult nervous system activates when sufficiently triggered.

Young, Klosko, and Weishaar (2003) identified and described these mode states across extensive clinical research and organized them into a taxonomy that is particularly well-fitted to the BPD presentation. The five modes most clinically relevant to BPD are described in the following sections. Each has a distinct presentation in the group room, a developmental origin in the adversity history, and a clinical implication for how the facilitator responds.

4.2 The Five Modes in the Group Room

The Vulnerable Child is the mode that carries the original emotional injuries: the terror, the grief, the longing for care, the sense of being fundamentally alone. When the Vulnerable Child mode is active, the client presents as fragile, distressed, and genuinely reaching for care and connection. The clinical challenge is that many BPD presentations' previous relational experiences have taught this mode that reaching for care produces either rejection or harm, so the vulnerability is simultaneously present and defended against.

In the group room, the Vulnerable Child appears as genuine emotional openness, but also as the specific quality of helplessness that can pull facilitators toward rescue responses that exceed appropriate clinical limits. The clinical response to the Vulnerable Child is consistent regulated warmth, acknowledgment of the vulnerability without merger with it, and explicit connection between the current state and the developmental experience that produced it: "That part of you that is in so much pain right now learned that pain had no reliable answer. In this group, the answer is consistent: you are heard, you are not alone in this, and the work we are doing is specifically for this."

The Angry/Impulsive Child is the mode that holds the rage at what was done, the entitlement to have needs met, and the impulsivity that acts before the prefrontal cortex can engage. When this mode is active, the client presents as explosive, entitled, or behaviorally dysregulated in ways that feel personal to the people in the room.

In the group room, the Angry/Impulsive Child frequently appears as the testing behavior, the interpersonal escalation, and the direct confrontation of the facilitator that new BPD group facilitators experience as the most clinically destabilizing element of the work. The clinical response is firm, non-defensive, and empathically connected to the underlying need: "I hear that you are angry. The anger makes sense given what it is pointing toward. I am not going anywhere, and I am not going to react to this the way earlier experiences may have taught you to expect."

The Detached Protector is the mode that learned to survive by becoming emotionally unreachable. When this mode is active, the client appears flat, compliant, intellectually engaged, and emotionally absent. This is the mode that produces the most clinical confusion because it looks like engagement while being precisely its opposite.

In the group room, the Detached Protector is the client who completes every assignment correctly and reports no improvement. It is the mode that generates excellent skills binders without skills access. It is, in the author's observation, the mode that most often leads to the clinical error of assuming the client is progressing because they are not visibly struggling.

The Punitive Parent is the mode that internalized the abusive or invalidating voice of the adversity environment and turned it on the self. When this mode is active, the client experiences intense self-contempt, self-blame for distress, and the specific conviction that their suffering is deserved.

In the group room, the Punitive Parent appears as self-attacking statements, minimization of genuine pain ("I shouldn't be complaining about this"), and the rapid movement from vulnerability to self-contempt that represents the mode transition from Vulnerable Child to Punitive Parent. The clinical response requires the facilitator to name the transition: "I noticed that you just moved from sharing something painful to telling yourself that you have no right to feel it. That voice has a history. Let's look at it."

The Healthy Adult is the mode that is the treatment goal: the regulated, self-compassionate, values-connected internal state that can hold the other modes without being controlled by them. The Healthy Adult does not eliminate the other modes. It becomes the organizing internal presence that can recognize them, respond to them, and choose behavior from values rather than from the mode's historical emotional logic.

4.3 Mode Awareness as a Clinical Intervention

The most immediate clinical use of schema mode theory in group settings is giving clients language for their own internal shifts. Many BPD clients have spent years experiencing mode transitions without having any framework to understand what is happening. The shift from calm to enraged, from open to unreachable, from vulnerable to self-attacking, has felt random, uncontrollable, and evidence of their fundamental instability. Mode language gives the internal experience a structure that the client can observe and eventually work with.

The clinical introduction of mode language in Session 12 of this curriculum is not a lecture about schema therapy. It is a simple recognition practice: what mode is active right now, what does it feel like in the body, and what did it just do to the way you are relating to the people in this room? That practice, repeated across Modules B, C, and D, builds the internal observer capacity that the Healthy Adult mode represents and that the entire curriculum is organized around developing.

Mode Mapping

The clinical practice of identifying the active schema mode in real time, connecting it to its developmental origin, and using that identification to create the observational distance from which skills use becomes possible.

Apply it by introducing the five modes in Session 12, naming mode activation when it occurs in subsequent sessions, and teaching clients to identify their active mode as a prerequisite to using any DBT skill.

Key Insight Box

Naming the mode that is active in a moment of distress creates the observational distance from which skills become accessible.

4.4 Apply This in Practice

Quick Win First

At the end of your next clinical contact with a BPD client, spend three minutes identifying which schema mode was most active during the session. Not which emotion was most visible, which mode. Was the client in Vulnerable Child, reaching for connection? Angry/Impulsive Child, escalating or testing? Detached Protector, present but unreachable? Punitive Parent, self-attacking? Or Healthy Adult, regulated and genuinely engaged? The mode identification, done privately before your next session, will change how you respond to the same client in the next contact.

When to Use This

Mode awareness applies to every session in this curriculum but is most immediately actionable in three specific clinical moments: when a client's behavior shifts dramatically within a session and the shift cannot be explained by session content; when skills training is not generalizing despite solid acquisition; and when the facilitator notices a strong countertransferential pull, either to rescue, to distance, or to react, which frequently reflects accurate attunement to the mode the client is expressing.

Steps for Use

Step 1: Introduce the five modes in Session 12 using the accessible language in the session plan. Do not use technical schema therapy vocabulary in the group room. Use the mode descriptions: the part of you that is in pain, the part that is angry, the part that shuts down, the part that judges you harshly, and the part that holds all of this with some perspective.

Step 2: Practice mode identification in each session from Session 12 onward. The zero-to-ten check-in is extended in Module B to include a mode check: "Where are you on the scale, and which mode feels most present right now?"

Step 3: Connect mode identification to skills use. Before any DBT skill, in Module C, ask: "Which mode is active right now? What does that mode need from the skill we are about to practice?"

Step 4: Model Healthy Adult responses to mode expression. When the Punitive Parent speaks in group, the facilitator's regulated, compassionate, non-colluding response is itself a Healthy Adult demonstration.

When It Does Not Work

Mode awareness requires a degree of internal observational capacity that is not available to clients in acute mode states, particularly the Angry/Impulsive Child and the Punitive Parent modes. When a client is flooded by either of these modes, naming the mode may escalate rather than settle the state. The clinical sequence is always: regulate first, then name. Grounding before mode identification.

The Detached Protector mode presents a specific challenge: it may appear to engage with mode language as intellectual content without producing any genuine internal shift. Facilitators should monitor for intellectualized mode identification that does not produce behavioral or emotional change, which is itself a Detached Protector expression.

4.5 Case Study: Quinn

Background

Quinn was twenty-nine years old, a social worker whose professional training had given her extensive knowledge of BPD, DBT, and schema therapy, all of which she applied with considerable clinical sophistication to her own presentation with the specific effect of keeping herself at a safe analytical distance from the clinical work. She had been referred to the IOP following a hospitalization after a suicide attempt that she described, in the intake interview, as a "cognitive error" she was confident she had now resolved.

Her ACE score was seven, including sexual abuse by a relative between ages nine and thirteen, emotional neglect from both parents throughout childhood, and household mental illness. She had been in individual therapy for four years, had read extensively about schema therapy, and could describe her own schema modes with more clinical precision than most clinicians in training.

Presentation

Quinn's group participation in Module A was exemplary, in the sense that Detached Protector mode participation is exemplary: accurate, compliant, articulate, and emotionally absent. Her zero-to-ten numbers across Module A averaged between four and five, which is within the window and presented as appropriate. Her somatic early warning sign mapping produced detailed, technically precise observations that were disconnected from any apparent somatic experience.

The clinical shift came in Session 12, not when the mode content was delivered, but when the facilitator asked the group: "Which mode feels most present to you right now, in this room, in this moment?"

Quinn answered after a long pause: "The one that knows all about the other ones and doesn't feel any of them."

The room was quiet. The facilitator said: "That is the Detached Protector, and you just named it from the inside. That's different from knowing about it analytically."

Analysis

Quinn's presentation illustrates the specific clinical challenge of the Detached Protector mode in clinically sophisticated clients: intellectual mastery of the schema therapy framework can function as an extension of the Detached Protector mode rather than as an exit from it. The knowledge is real. The emotional distance it maintains is also real, and it is organized by the same adversity experience that produced the vulnerability the Detached Protector is protecting.

The clinical contribution of Session 12's specific framing, asking which mode is present right now in this room, rather than asking which mode the client tends to use, was to make the mode visible from the inside rather than from outside. The Detached Protector can narrate itself abstractly indefinitely. It cannot remain invisible when it is asked to report on its own presence in the present moment.

Response and Intervention

The facilitation of Quinn's subsequent sessions adjusted to explicitly acknowledge the Detached Protector's presence rather than attempting to bypass it. "The part of you that keeps you safe by keeping you far away has been running this session. That part kept you alive. We're not trying to get rid of it. We're trying to help it feel safe enough to let some of the other parts be present."

The Vulnerable Child first appeared visibly in Session 18's Core Mindfulness session, during a brief guided practice. Quinn began to cry and then immediately, in the room, moved to self-contempt: "I don't know why I'm crying. This is embarrassing." The facilitator named the mode transition in real time: "The Punitive Parent just arrived. Notice that."

Outcome

Quinn completed the full curriculum. At the twelve-month follow-up, she described the mode awareness as "the first thing I've encountered in treatment that I couldn't intellectualize my way out of." She remained in individual therapy and had not been hospitalized in the follow-up period. Her self-contempt responses, the Punitive Parent mode, were more frequently observed and more frequently interrupted by her own Healthy Adult responses.

Reader Mirror Moment

If you have worked with clients who know their own psychology with considerable accuracy and still cannot change the patterns that knowledge describes, Quinn's presentation is representative. Intellectual knowledge of the schema modes is not the same as mode awareness from the inside. The clinical contribution of Session 12's group exercise is precisely the shift from outside knowledge to inside observation, and it is a shift that many clients, particularly the most intellectually sophisticated ones, have never made before the group work creates the conditions for it.

Concept Map: The Five Schema Modes in BPD and Their Clinical Relationships

Schema Mode	Emotional Signature	Behavioral Expression	Developmental Origin	Clinical Response
Vulnerable Child	Terror, grief, longing, helplessness	Reaching for care, distress, fragility	Emotional abuse, neglect, abandonment	Consistent warm acknowledgment; no rescue
Angry/Impulsive Child	Rage, entitlement, urgency	Escalation, testing, impulsivity	Unmet needs, insufficient response to distress	Firm, non-defensive, empathic; stay present
Detached Protector	Flatness, compliance, absence	Intellectual engagement, emotional unavailability	Chronic invalidation; closeness was unsafe	Name the absence; invite rather than confront
Punitive Parent	Self-contempt, self-blame, worthlessness	Self-attacking statements, shame escalation	Internalized abusive or invalidating voice	Name the mode; challenge the voice's authority
Healthy Adult	Regulation, compassion, perspective	Flexible response, values-based behavior	What treatment is building	Model it; recognize and name it when it appears

There is one condition under which the clinical knowledge in this chapter becomes temporarily unavailable to the facilitator, and it is the condition that Chapter 5 addresses directly. When schema mode activation is directed at the facilitator, either through idealization, devaluation, aggressive testing, or the specific pull of the Vulnerable Child mode toward rescue responses that the clinical relationship cannot sustain, the facilitator's own regulatory system and attachment patterns are activated in ways that the clinical training alone does not prepare for.

Chapter 5 addresses those dynamics specifically: how to maintain regulated clinical presence when the group room becomes the therapeutic relationship, and why the facilitator's response to splitting and mode activation is itself the most powerful clinical intervention available.

"The mode that shuts everything down is not the absence of feeling. It is the last thing standing between the client and a pain they learned they could not survive."

Chapter 5.0: When the Group Room Becomes the Treatment

"Are you angry with me?"

The question came from Skyler, a thirty-four-year-old who had been in the group for six weeks, directed at the co-facilitator who had not spoken in the previous twelve minutes while the primary facilitator led a Module B discussion on splitting. The co-facilitator, Morgan Vale, had not been aware of any change in her affect or expression.

"No," Morgan said. "I'm listening."

"You look like you are."

What came next was the moment that the group's clinical value either holds or collapses.

Morgan said: "I appreciate you telling me that. My face isn't angry with you. I wonder what made you read it that way."

Skyler was quiet. Then: "It's what I always expect."

That exchange, six words from a client who had been in and out of treatment for twelve years, is the entire clinical logic of Chapter 5. The BPD group room is not primarily the place where skills are delivered. It is the place where the relational patterns that the adversity history produced are activated in real time, in the presence of a clinician who has the opportunity to respond differently than every prior relational experience has taught the client to expect. That opportunity is either taken or missed, and the outcome has more clinical significance than any individual skill session.

This chapter covers: why the group room becomes the therapeutic relationship in BPD treatment; the facilitation competencies required to use that dynamic clinically rather than being overwhelmed by it; the specific management of splitting, idealization, and devaluation in the group context; how the facilitator's regulated presence is itself the primary intervention; and the supervision structures that make sustainable delivery of this work possible. The clinical urgency of this chapter is specific: the mistakes that BPD group treatment produces, the abandonment of the clinical frame, the retaliatory response to testing behavior, the rescue response to vulnerability, occur quickly, with lasting consequences for the client, and can be prevented by the specific preparation this chapter provides.

Common Belief:

The primary clinical challenge in facilitating BPD groups is managing client behavior, including escalation, self-harm disclosure, and interpersonal conflict, and the primary skill required is de-escalation and limit-setting.

What the Evidence Shows:

The primary clinical challenge in BPD group facilitation is not behavior management but relational attunement: the capacity to maintain a regulated, consistent, warm, non-retaliatory clinical presence across a full range of client emotional expressions, including expressions specifically designed, at the schema mode level, to test whether this relationship will behave differently than the developmental relationships that produced the BPD presentation (Bateman & Fonagy, 2004). De-escalation and limit-setting are clinical tools within a relational framework; they are not the framework itself. Research on the therapeutic alliance in BPD treatment consistently finds alliance quality, not skills training compliance, to be the strongest predictor of treatment outcomes (Barnicot et al., 2012).

5.1 The Testing Behavior Is the Treatment

The testing behavior that every BPD group produces, the challenges to the facilitator's authority, the boundary explorations, the provocations that seem designed to confirm a specific feared outcome, are not obstacles to the clinical work. They are the clinical work.

A client whose developmental history taught them that authority figures were unpredictable, that care came with conditions, that closeness preceded harm, and that their emotional needs were excessive has a specific and legitimate question that they are asking with their behavior rather than their words: will you respond the way every prior relational experience has taught me to expect? The testing is the asking.

The clinical opportunity is in the answering. Not in the words the facilitator uses, though the words matter. In the regulated presence, the consistent warmth, the non-retaliatory response to provocation, and the willingness to remain present and engaged across the full range of the client's emotional expression. Each consistent response to a test is a piece of data that gradually, over many sessions, updates the relational template that adversity produced.

This is not a passive process. The facilitator who maintains regulated presence in the face of direct devaluation is not merely being tolerant. They are providing a relational experience that the client's nervous system has never had access to, and they are doing so consistently enough that the nervous system's predictive model of relationships begins to update. That updating is slow, incomplete, and non-linear. It is also the mechanism by which the most durable clinical change in BPD treatment occurs.

5.2 Managing Splitting in the Group Room

Splitting is the most disruptive dynamic in BPD group settings and the most clinically significant. When splitting operates in the group room, it typically produces one or more of the following configurations: one facilitator is idealized and the other is devalued; one group member is elevated to a position of specialness while others are positioned as less worthy; or the group itself is split into the valued members and the dismissed ones, with the configuration changing unpredictably across sessions.

The clinical management of splitting begins with the facilitator's non-defensive response to both poles. The facilitator who is currently being idealized does not lean into the idealization or work to maintain it. They receive it with warmth and with gentle curiosity about what the idealization is responding to: "I notice you are feeling close to the work we are doing today. What is it about today that feels different?" The facilitator who is currently being devalued does not become defensive, withdraw, or attempt to re-earn approval. They receive the devaluation with the same consistent regulated presence they bring to the idealization: "I hear that this isn't feeling useful to you right now. That's worth understanding. Can you tell me more?"

The co-facilitation model is particularly valuable for splitting management because it prevents the facilitation pair from being split along the same lines as the group. When co-facilitators discuss splitting dynamics in pre-session consultation, align their responses before session, and debrief together after sessions in which significant splitting occurred, they model the dialectical principle of the treatment in their own relationship: two people who hold different positions can remain in genuine relationship without one being right and the other wrong.

5.3 The Facilitator's Regulatory State as the Relational Treatment

Chapter 5 of Book 1 established the facilitator's regulatory state as the primary clinical tool in trauma-informed group work. In BPD treatment, this principle operates at a higher level of clinical urgency because the mode activations the BPD presentation produces, particularly the Angry/Impulsive Child and the Punitive Parent modes, are specifically calibrated to dysregulate the people in the relational field.

A facilitator who becomes anxious in the presence of the Angry/Impulsive Child confirms the mode's expectation: this person will be overwhelmed. A facilitator who becomes cold or clinical in the presence of the Vulnerable Child confirms the mode's expectation: this person will withdraw when I need them. A facilitator who becomes irritated or contemptuous in response to testing behavior confirms the adversity history's core lesson: the people in authority over me are unpredictable and unsafe.

The pre-session regulatory practice described in Chapter 5 of Book 1 is, in BPD treatment, extended to include a specific mode-awareness check. Before entering the room, the facilitator not only assesses their zero-to-ten number. They also identify any residual mode-activating material from the previous session: Am I carrying anything from the last session that might affect how I respond to this group today? If the answer is yes, the supervision domain described in the Front Matter's Note on Clinical Supervision is where that material belongs before the next session begins.

5.4 Documentation in Trauma-Informed BPD Groups

Documentation in BPD group settings carries the same dual requirement as in addiction group settings from Book 1, and one additional component specific to BPD treatment.

The first requirement is group-level regulatory state: the collective arousal level across the session, significant shifts in that level, and the facilitator's clinical response to those shifts.

The second requirement is session-content versus session-process distinction: what was discussed versus what the discussion produced relationally, and the regulatory state at session close compared to session open.

The BPD-specific third requirement is mode tracking: which modes were most active in the session, which group members were in which modes at significant clinical moments, and what facilitation responses were offered and with what apparent effect. Mode tracking in the clinical record supports continuity of care, informs supervision, and provides the longitudinal data about individual clients that makes the gradual movement toward Healthy Adult functioning visible over time.

The Relational Update

The cumulative clinical mechanism through which consistent, regulated, non-retaliatory facilitation responses to testing behavior and mode activation gradually update the client's developmental relational template, providing the experiential data that the adversity history never provided.

Apply it by treating every response to testing behavior as the primary clinical intervention of BPD treatment, not as a management challenge to be survived.

Key Insight Box

In BPD group treatment, how the facilitator responds to testing and mode activation matters more than any skill or psychoeducation delivered.

5.5 Apply This in Practice

Quick Win First

After your next BPD group session, take two minutes to identify one moment in which you experienced a pull toward an unhelpful response, either rescue, withdrawal, defensiveness, or retaliation, and consider what mode the client was expressing when the pull arose. The identification of the pull and its mode source is the beginning of the regulatory work that makes sustainable BPD facilitation possible.

When to Use This

The Relational Update framework applies to every session in the curriculum. It is most acutely applicable in the following moments: when testing behavior escalates during Module B sessions; when a client directly challenges the facilitator's competence or motives; when a client's vulnerability is so acute that the pull toward reassurance or rescue is strong; and when devaluation of the curriculum itself appears, particularly in clients with prior DBT experience.

Steps for Use

Step 1: Develop and practice the specific language for each mode response before the sessions in which those modes are most likely to appear: Modules B and C carry the highest mode activation potential.

Step 2: Complete the pre-session regulatory check before every session. If your zero-to-ten number is above five, take a specific regulatory action before entering the room.

Step 3: After every high-activation session, complete the post-session debrief: what did the session produce in the clients, what did it produce in you, and what mode dynamics were most active?

Step 4: Bring all three supervision domains to your supervisor consistently, including the countertransference domain, which is the domain most frequently omitted and most frequently predictive of boundary erosion in BPD treatment.

When It Does Not Work

The Relational Update mechanism is slow. It operates across many sessions, not within any individual one. Facilitators who expect visible relational change within Module A or Module B timeframes will be disappointed and at risk of the discouragement that leads to premature clinical pessimism about the population. The mechanism requires consistency over time, and its effects become visible most reliably in the transition from Module B to Module C and across Module D.

5.6 Case Study: Morgan Vale

Opening: Morgan Vale had been facilitating BPD groups for two years when she was assigned a co-facilitator for a new IOP cycle: Dakota, a licensed counselor with strong DBT training but no prior BPD group facilitation experience. The clinical director had paired them specifically because Dakota's DBT competence complemented Morgan's group facilitation experience.

The first four sessions went well by any observable measure. Then Session 5, the ACE framework session, produced the response that neither facilitator had fully anticipated: a group member named Skyler accused Morgan directly of "not really caring about any of us" and challenged Dakota to "admit that this whole thing is just a program that doesn't actually work."

Dakota looked at Morgan. Morgan looked at Skyler. The room was quiet.

Resolution: Morgan said: "You are testing whether we are going to leave or react or pretend that didn't happen. None of those. What you just said tells me something is happening for you right now that matters. What is it?"

This case illustrates the clinical architecture that makes Relational Update possible: the splitting was directed at the facilitator pair simultaneously, testing both poles, and the response that held the room was the one that named the testing behavior as clinical information rather than managing it as a problem.

Dakota's post-session reflection was that the moment had required the most deliberate regulatory self-management they had ever experienced in a clinical setting. The pull toward defensiveness had been strong. What replaced it was the pre-session consultation in which Morgan had specifically anticipated that Module B's ACE content might produce exactly this kind of relational escalation, and in which they had planned their response together before the session began.

Teaching Points

Pre-session consultation between co-facilitators is the preparation that makes in-session Relational Update possible. Morgan and Dakota's prepared response was not a performance. It was the outcome of deliberate clinical planning.

Naming the testing behavior as clinical information, rather than responding to its manifest content, is the specific facilitation move that the Relational Update depends on. Skyler did not need to be told that the accusation was wrong. She needed to experience a response that was different from what her developmental history had produced.

The post-session debrief that Morgan and Dakota conducted was as clinically significant as the session itself. Dakota's identification of the pull toward defensiveness, examined in that debrief, became the focus of the next supervision session and the foundation for the regulatory practice that made the subsequent sessions progressively more manageable.

Reader Mirror Moment

If the moment Morgan and Dakota navigated feels familiar, either as something you have managed or as something you have not known how to manage, the dynamics it represents are universal in BPD group facilitation. The Angry/Impulsive Child and the Punitive Parent modes, directed outward at the facilitator, are the most activating relational experiences in this work. The difference between the facilitation that helps and the facilitation that harms is often not skill or knowledge. It is the quality of the pre-session preparation, the availability of co-facilitation support, and the post-session supervision that makes the regulatory work sustainable.

Timeline: The Development of Clinical Competency in Trauma-Informed BPD Group Facilitation

Stage	Primary Task	Common Challenge	Required Support
Novice (0-6 months)	Holding the frame; delivering content; managing acute crises	Splitting, testing behavior, pull toward rescue or rejection	Observation, co-facilitation, weekly supervision with all three domains
Developing (6-18 months)	Recognizing mode activation in real time; beginning relational use of response	Mode conflation with behavior; inconsistent frame maintenance	Co-facilitation; supervision with countertransference focus
Competent (18-36 months)	Using the relational field deliberately; mode-specific facilitation responses	Facilitator fatigue; secondary traumatization from high-activation content	Peer consultation; supervision; personal regulatory practice
Proficient (3+ years)	Therapeutic use of the relational update across the full curriculum arc	Subtle frame erosion; over-identification with specific modes	Ongoing supervision; consultation team; personal therapy as indicated

The five clinical foundation chapters of Book 3 have built the theoretical and practical infrastructure for the thirty session plans that follow. Chapter 1 established that BPD is the developmental outcome of specific adversity, not a character defect. Chapter 2 described the neurobiological mechanism through which that adversity produces the specific symptom picture of BPD. Chapter 3 identified the gaps in standard DBT that a trauma-informed architecture addresses and the conditions under which DBT skills fail to generalize. Chapter 4 introduced the schema mode framework that maps the internal states DBT skills are designed to regulate. Chapter 5 established that the facilitator's relational presence is itself the primary treatment mechanism in BPD group work.

Part Two begins with the session plans. Everything in Part One is active in every session, not as content that clients are required to know but as the clinical understanding that determines how the facilitator holds the room, responds to the behavior, and makes the consistent, regulated, non-retaliatory relational choices that gradually update the developmental template the adversity produced.

"Holding the room without reactivity, across every mode the client brings, is not a support for the treatment. It is the treatment."

Part Two: The 30 Session Plans

Four modules across 30 sessions, adaptable to 12-week IOP, 8-week PHP, and rolling admissions formats.*

Chapter 6.0: How to Use a Session Plan

Each of the 30 session plans in this curriculum follows a consistent 14-component structure. The components in order are: Session Overview (the clinical rationale for this session in two to three sentences); Learning Objectives (three to four measurable outcomes); Time Allocation table (90-minute and 60-minute versions); Materials and Preparation; Facilitator Notes (clinical considerations and population-specific guidance); Opening Ritual and Check-In; Psychoeducation Component with facilitator talking points; Experiential Exercise or Skills Activity with full instructions; Group Processing and Discussion with facilitated questions; Closing Grounding Practice; Take-Home Reflection; and Handout Reference.

The session plan is not a script. It is a scaffold that requires clinical judgment to hold appropriately. This is particularly true in BPD treatment, where the relational dynamics described in Chapter 5 can shift the session's clinical center of gravity in ways that content delivery alone cannot address. The facilitator who knows the session plan well enough to adapt it is delivering better treatment than the facilitator who follows it precisely while the group's relational field reorganizes around them.

The opening ritual is the first clinical act of every session and its clinical function in BPD treatment extends beyond regulation. Feet on floor. Weight in chair. Orienting scan. Zero-to-ten check-in. This ritual is the co-regulatory signal and the attachment signal: I am regulated, this space is predictable, we begin the same way we always begin. For clients whose developmental history includes environments that were unpredictable and unsafe, the absolute consistency of the opening ritual is clinically irreplaceable. Any deviation from it, however small and however justified by content pressures, disrupts the attachment signal that the ritual provides.

The mode check-in is added to every session from Session 12 onward. In BPD treatment, the zero-to-ten arousal scale is supplemented from Module B by a brief mode identification: which of the five modes most described in Chapter 4 is most active right now? The mode check-in takes thirty additional seconds and provides the clinical data that transforms regulatory monitoring into schema-level awareness.

The closing grounding practice carries an additional function in BPD treatment. In BPD groups, session endings are small relational losses, and for clients whose developmental history includes significant abandonment experiences, each session ending activates the abandonment schema to some degree. The closing practice explicitly acknowledges the ending, provides regulatory grounding for the transition, and frames what continues after the session closes. The closing should never be abbreviated, regardless of content pressure. In the author's clinical observation, groups that are consistently well-closed are groups that arrive at the next session more regulated.

The Facilitator Notes within each session plan are required reading before the session, not during it. They contain the clinical considerations most essential for safe delivery. Sessions 2, 5, 10, 11, 12, 13, 14, and all Module C sessions carry the highest activation potential and require the most careful advance reading.

Chapter 7.0: Module A Overview: Safety and Dialectical Foundation

Module A spans Sessions 1 through 8. Its clinical purpose in Book 3 is distinct from Module A in Books 1 and 2, though its function is structurally identical: to build the conditions under which the pattern recognition work of Module B and the skills training of Module C become clinically possible.

The BPD-specific challenge of Module A is that the population it serves has, in many cases, extensive prior treatment exposure and frequently enters Module A with the expectation that they already have the foundation. Chapter 3 addressed the clinical reality that prior DBT exposure does not guarantee the regulatory foundation this curriculum requires. Module A makes no assumption about prior treatment. It builds from the first session as if the foundation is not yet in place, because in the majority of cases the specific foundation this curriculum requires, ACE-informed developmental understanding, somatic regulatory practice, mode-aware monitoring, and the attachment experience of a predictably safe group, is in fact not yet in place.

Sessions 1 and 2 establish the group container and the biosocial theory in ACE-informed language. Sessions 3 and 4 build the regulatory and dialectical foundations: the Window of Tolerance as a personalized monitoring tool and Wise Mind as the organizing DBT concept that connects acceptance and change. Session 5 delivers the ACE framework in BPD-specific terms. Session 6 delivers radical acceptance as a clinical concept that is frequently misunderstood as passivity or approval. Session 7 builds the stabilization network. Session 8 integrates the module's work and prepares the group for Module B.

The Module A clinical stance is dialectical architect: building the container and the dialectical ground simultaneously. The facilitator who delivers Module A primarily as psychoeducation and misses the relational architecture, the attachment signal of the consistent ritual, the warmth of the mode-aware response, and the non-retaliatory reception of testing behavior, delivers accurate content and incomplete treatment. The relational architecture is not an addition to the clinical work of Module A. It is the clinical work.

Module A: Safety and Dialectical Foundation

Sessions 1 through 8 | Clinical Focus: Establishing the therapeutic container, psychoeducation about BPD and its developmental origins, and the foundational regulatory and dialectical practices that Module C depends on*

Session 1: Welcome to the Group: Creating Safety With BPD in the Room

Module: A: Safety and Dialectical Foundation

Phase: Establishing the Container

Session Number: 1 of 30

Session Overview

Session 1 establishes the specific safety conditions that BPD presentations require in a group context. Its primary clinical purpose is relational and regulatory: the group's first experience of an environment that is predictably warm, consistently boundaried, and explicitly organized around their safety. The group agreement built in this session is the curriculum's first clinical intervention and its first relational update: evidence that this treatment is designed differently from what testing behavior expects.

Learning Objectives

By the end of Session 1, group members will be able to:

1. Identify at least three group norms and explain the clinical rationale for each, including the specific disclosure limit that applies to this group.

2. Complete the zero-to-ten arousal scale check-in and identify their number at session open and close.

3. Complete the orienting practice and describe one thing they noticed in the room.

4. Articulate, in their own words, the difference between what this group is and what prior treatment may have been.

Time Allocation

Component	90-Minute Format	60-Minute Format
Opening Ritual and Check-In	10 min	10 min
Psychoeducation: What This Group Is	20 min	15 min
Experiential: The Group Agreement	30 min	20 min
Group Processing	20 min	10 min
Closing Grounding	10 min	5 min

Materials and Preparation

- Handout 1A: Our Group Agreement (Appendix C, page C-1)

- Handout 1B: The Zero-to-Ten Arousal Scale (Appendix C, page C-2)

- Whiteboard or flip chart and markers

- Chairs in a circle with every seat having a direct sight line to the door

- Arrive ten minutes early to set up, complete a self-regulatory check, and place Handout 1A face-down at each seat

Facilitator Notes

Enter the room with deliberate calm. Chapter 5 established that the facilitator's regulatory state is the primary clinical instrument in BPD treatment. Session 1 is the first opportunity for the group's nervous systems to register that this environment will be different. A facilitator who enters the room with visible anxiety, over-preparation performance, or excessive energy communicates the wrong signal. Enter slowly. Speak at a volume slightly lower than feels necessary. Allow silence to be present before filling it.

The group agreement is the first relational update. Build it with the group rather than presenting it from a prepared list. The clinical non-negotiables, confidentiality, disclosure limits, no substance use, zero-to-ten monitoring, mutual respect, and the one specifically BPD-relevant addition (no graphic descriptions of self-harm in group settings) must be introduced with clinical rationale, not as rules. The rationale for each is the de-shaming explanation: these protections exist because everyone in this room matters, and the protections are designed to make that mattering possible across the full course of the program.

Disclosure limits in BPD groups carry an additional specification. Beyond the general disclosure limit from Chapter 5 of Book 1 (impact rather than specific event content), BPD groups specifically require that graphic descriptions of self-harm methods, severity, or frequency not be shared in group. The clinical rationale is specific and must be delivered directly: graphic self-harm content in group settings produces contagion effects in a population that already carries elevated self-harm rates, and the protection is for everyone in the room including the person who would share it. This limit should be introduced with warmth and specificity in Session 1 and referenced when needed in subsequent sessions.

Testing behavior should be expected in Session 1. For many clients with BPD, the first session of any new treatment program is a test: will this be different from the last time? A client who arrives skeptical, who challenges the group agreement, who presents with visible wariness or resistance, is gathering clinical data, not being disruptive. The facilitator's non-defensive, warm, direct response to every test is the data that matters.

Court-mandated and involuntary participants. When the group includes members who are court-mandated or attending under external pressure, this should be acknowledged without creating a hierarchy between voluntary and involuntary participants. Every person arrives with some mixture of choice and constraint. What matters is what happens from here.

Opening Ritual and Check-In (10 minutes)

Facilitator script:

"Before we start, I want us to take a moment to arrive together. We will begin every single session with the same practice, and I want to do it carefully the first time so you know what it is and why we do it.

Feel your feet on the floor. Not think about them. Actually feel them. The weight of your feet against the ground. [Pause 10 seconds.]

Notice whether you can feel the chair under you. [Pause 5 seconds.]

Now look around the room slowly and notice three things you can see. Just notice them. [Pause 10 seconds.]

This is called orienting. Your nervous system settles when it knows where it is. We do this every time we meet because consistency is the thing that makes a group safe.

[Distribute Handout 1B.] This is the zero-to-ten arousal scale. Zero means completely flat: not quite here, disconnected. Ten means completely flooded: overwhelmed, unable to think. Most of us are somewhere in the middle.

Take fifteen seconds and locate yourself right now. You do not need to share it. Just notice where you are."

Psychoeducation Component (20 minutes)

Talking Point 1: What this group is

"This group is a structured program that we will move through together in a specific sequence over the coming weeks. The sequence is deliberate and the structure is clinical, not administrative. What we have learned about how nervous systems that have been shaped by significant adversity actually change tells us they need predictability, safety, and a specific kind of consistent experience before they can work with the material that recovery requires. Every element of how this group is structured, including this opening practice, is there for a clinical reason.

I will tell you the reason for each element. If something about how this group works doesn't make sense to you, ask me. You deserve to understand why this is designed the way it is."

Talking Point 2: What this group is not

"This is not a group where you tell your full story. I want to say that clearly because it is probably different from what some of you have expected or experienced in prior treatment.

What happened in your past is real and it matters enormously to the clinical work we are doing. But the specific details of traumatic experiences belong in your individual therapy, not in this room. What belongs here is what it is like to be you in your life right now, in your current relationships, and in your current recovery. That is not a lesser version of this work. For most people, it is the version that actually changes things.

I'll explain this in more detail in the group agreement work. What I want you to know right now is that this limit is not about what you deserve to share. It is about what this group can safely hold."

Talking Point 3: The clinical foundation of this group

"This program is built on a specific understanding of borderline personality disorder, and I want to tell you what it is from the very first session.

The core idea is this: the emotional intensity, the relational instability, the fear of being abandoned, the difficulty knowing who you are, the history of relationships that swing between closeness and collapse, these are not evidence that something is fundamentally wrong with you. They are the predictable developmental outcomes of specific experiences. Your nervous system was built in a specific environment, and it learned exactly what that environment required it to learn.

That does not excuse any particular behavior. It does change the question. Instead of 'what is wrong with this person,' we ask 'what did this person's nervous system learn, and what does it need to learn now?' That is a different question, and it leads somewhere different."

Experiential Exercise: The Group Agreement (30 minutes)

"We are going to build our group agreement together. Not from a list I prepared. From what you actually need in order to do this work.

First question: What would you need in this room, from the people in this room, to feel safe enough to show up fully? Take thirty seconds before anyone speaks. [Pause.] I'll write down everything you offer."

[Write every contribution. Common themes: confidentiality, no judgment, permission to pass, no unsolicited advice, privacy.]

"Now: Is there anything you need from yourself in order to actually use this group? What commitment would you need to make to your own participation?"

[Write contributions.]

"Now I want to add three things that are clinically non-negotiable, and I'll explain exactly why each one is here.

The first is confidentiality. What is shared here stays here, including the names and identities of the people in this room. This is not just a rule. It is the condition under which genuine sharing is possible.

The second is about how we share. In this group we share the impact of our history on our lives, not the specific details of traumatic events. This includes a specific limit that is especially important in this group: we do not share graphic descriptions of self-harm, including methods, severity, or frequency. The reason is specific: hearing those descriptions can activate something in other people in this room who are carrying their own histories with self-harm. That activation does not help anyone, including the person sharing. What belongs here is the pain and the meaning, not the graphic content.

The third is participation: you are always in charge of your own experience. Passing is always available. What I ask is that you stay present in the room while we are here, even in silence."

[Build the full agreement. Read it back. Invite additions. Have every member indicate agreement.]

"This document belongs to all of us. I will bring it to every session."

Group Processing and Discussion (20 minutes)

1. "What was it like to build that agreement together, rather than being handed one?"

2. "Was there anything in the agreement that you found yourself reacting to?"

3. "The limit about graphic self-harm content: did that land as a protection or as a restriction? I want to know what you actually think."

4. "On the zero-to-ten scale: where are you now compared to when you walked in? What, if anything, shifted?"

5. "If you are willing: what is one thing you're hoping this group will give you that prior treatment did not?"

Closing Grounding Practice (10 minutes)

"We're going to close every session the same way we opened it. Feet on floor. [Pause.] Weight in chair. [Pause.] Look around the room. Notice it is the same room you walked into.

One breath slightly slower than usual. Not dramatically. Just slightly.

Zero-to-ten. Notice where you are now.

The consistency of this closing is part of the treatment. Every time we end this way, we are practicing the specific thing that recovery from what you've been through requires: the ability to complete something and still be here."

Take-Home Reflection

Once a day between now and our next session, take thirty seconds and locate yourself on the zero-to-ten scale. Notice the number. You do not need to do anything with it. Just notice. That noticing is already the beginning of what this curriculum is built on.

Handout Reference

Handout 1A: Our Group Agreement (Appendix C, page C-1)

Handout 1B: The Zero-to-Ten Arousal Scale (Appendix C, page C-2)

Session 2: The Biosocial Theory: What BPD Is and Where It Comes From

Module: A: Safety and Dialectical Foundation

Phase: Establishing the Container

Session Number: 2 of 30

Session Overview

Session 2 delivers the biosocial theory of BPD in ACE-informed, accessible language. The clinical purpose of this session is foundational to everything that follows: clients who understand the developmental explanation for their BPD presentation have a qualitatively different relationship to their diagnosis, to the skills they are being asked to learn, and to the therapeutic work ahead. The session introduces the emotional sensitivity and invalidating environment framework that Linehan's biosocial theory provides and extends it with the specific ACE research that makes it empirically concrete.

Learning Objectives

By the end of Session 2, group members will be able to:

1. Describe the biosocial theory of BPD in their own words, including both the emotional sensitivity and invalidating environment components.

2. Name at least two specific ways that the adversity history they carry connects to the BPD presentation they experience.

3. Distinguish between the BPD explanation the biosocial theory provides and the character-defect explanation that prior experience or prior treatment may have implied.

4. Locate themselves on the zero-to-ten scale at session open and close and notice what, if anything, shifted.

Time Allocation

Component	90-Minute Format	60-Minute Format
Opening Ritual and Check-In	10 min	10 min
Psychoeducation: The Biosocial Theory	30 min	20 min
Experiential: My BPD History Narrative	25 min	20 min
Group Processing	15 min	5 min
Closing Grounding	10 min	5 min

Materials and Preparation

- Group Agreement displayed or distributed

- Handout 2A: The Biosocial Theory and My History (Appendix C, page C-3)

- Whiteboard: two overlapping circles. Left: EMOTIONAL SENSITIVITY. Right: INVALIDATING ENVIRONMENT. Overlap: BPD DEVELOPS HERE.

Facilitator Notes

The biosocial theory is the primary de-shaming intervention of Module A. Deliver it with clinical precision and genuine warmth. The two components, emotional sensitivity and invalidating environment, must be named separately before being connected. Many clients have spent years believing that their emotional intensity is a defect. The specific clinical move of naming emotional sensitivity as a trait, not a defect, one that in other environments is associated with empathy and attunement, is often received as a significant shift.

Expect a range of responses. Some clients will experience the biosocial theory as profound relief. Some will experience it as denial of personal responsibility. Some will respond with anger at the environments that produced the invalidation. All three responses are clinically appropriate and should be received without pushing toward relief. The anger response in particular, addressed in Chapter 1, is the appropriate emotional response to understanding that the adversity was real and the shame was learned. Receive it as clinical information.

The emotional sensitivity component requires specific care. Do not conflate emotional sensitivity with fragility or weakness. High emotional sensitivity is a temperamental characteristic that carries genuine adaptive value in validating environments. The clinical challenge is that it is the combination of high sensitivity and an invalidating environment that produces the BPD presentation, not either component alone. Make this combinatorial logic explicit and return to it at any point in the session where a client appears to be hearing the biosocial theory as blaming their sensitivity.

Opening Ritual and Check-In (10 minutes)

Facilitator script:

"Feet on floor. [Pause.] Weight in chair. [Pause.] Three things you can see. [Pause.] Zero-to-ten check-in. Notice your number.

From the take-home: anyone who noticed their zero-to-ten number during the week. Not the numbers themselves. What was it like to notice?"

[Receive one or two brief responses.]

Psychoeducation Component (30 minutes)

Talking Point 1: The two components of the biosocial theory

"[Point to the diagram.] Marsha Linehan, who developed DBT, spent years working with people who received the BPD diagnosis and who had been told, explicitly or implicitly, that their disorder was evidence of a character problem. She proposed a different explanation.

She called it the biosocial theory, and it has two components.

The first is emotional sensitivity. Some people are born with a nervous system that is more emotionally responsive than average. They feel things more quickly, more intensely, and for longer than most people around them. This is not a character defect. It is a biological fact, like having a more sensitive immune system or a more sensitive digestive system. In the right environment, high emotional sensitivity is the basis for empathy, attunement to others, and the specific quality of relational presence that many people in this room have been told is 'too much.'

The second is an invalidating environment. An invalidating environment is one that consistently communicates to the emotionally sensitive child that their emotional responses are wrong, excessive, inappropriate, or evidence of a personal failure. Not occasionally, as every parent does at some point. Consistently. As a pattern. The child who is told 'stop being so dramatic' enough times, who learns that expressing distress produces punishment or contempt or abandonment, who discovers that the most reliable response to their emotional experience is that it will be dismissed or criticized, grows up unable to trust their own internal states.

[Point to the overlap.] BPD develops in the overlap: a person with high emotional sensitivity who grew up in an environment that consistently invalidated that sensitivity. Neither component alone is sufficient. Together, they produce exactly the presentation that BPD describes."

Talking Point 2: What invalidation actually means

"I want to be specific about what an invalidating environment looks like, because many people in BPD treatment have grown up in environments that were invalidating without anyone using that word or without the invalidation looking like obvious abuse.

An invalidating environment does not require dramatic cruelty. It requires consistent dismissal of the child's internal experience. It can look like: a parent who responds to distress with 'you're being ridiculous'; a household where emotional expression is treated as weakness; a caregiving environment so disrupted by the caregiver's own difficulties, addiction, mental illness, or absence, that the child's emotional needs consistently go unmet; or the specific form of emotional abuse where the child is told that their perception of events is wrong, that the thing that upset them did not happen the way they experienced it.

In each of these cases, the emotionally sensitive child learns the same lesson: my internal experience cannot be trusted. And without the ability to trust their internal experience, the child cannot develop the stable sense of self, the reliable emotional regulation, and the secure relational template that the BPD presentation reflects the absence of."

Talking Point 3: The ACE connection

"The research we looked at in Chapter 1 of the clinical text, and that I want to bring into this room today, is specific about which childhood experiences are most strongly associated with BPD.

Emotional abuse, the consistent communication that your emotional experience is wrong, excessive, or shameful, shows the strongest independent association with BPD of any ACE category. Emotional neglect, the absence of attunement and care, shows the second strongest. Sexual abuse shows particularly strong association with BPD when it co-occurs with substance use disorder.

What this research tells us is that the biosocial theory is not just a clinical framework. It is an empirically supported description of what many, perhaps most, people in this room actually experienced. The invalidating environment was not a vague background condition. It was specific, it was measurable, and its effects are documented with a precision that changes what treatment needs to address."

Experiential Exercise: My BPD History Narrative (25 minutes)

[Distribute Handout 2A.]

"I want you to spend fifteen minutes with the handout. It asks you to do two things.

First: look at the two components of the biosocial theory and write, honestly, whether each one fits your experience. Not whether you were officially diagnosed with emotional sensitivity or whether your environment meets a clinical threshold for invalidating. Whether, in your own experience, these components describe something recognizable.

Second: if the biosocial theory fits, what does it mean for how you understand your BPD diagnosis? Does it change anything? Does it produce any feeling? Does it meet resistance?

Write whatever comes. There are no right answers and nothing you write will be shared without your permission."

[After fifteen minutes:]

"Let's share briefly. Not the full narrative. One thing: does the biosocial theory fit your experience, and what does it produce in you when you consider that it might?"

[Receive contributions. After each, reflect the clinical precision without analyzing or elaborating. The session's clinical product is in the speaking, not in the facilitator's response to it.]

Group Processing and Discussion (15 minutes)

1. "For anyone who found the biosocial theory immediately recognizable: what was that recognition like?"

2. "For anyone who found resistance to it: what got in the way? I'm not asking you to agree with it. I'm asking what the resistance tells you about how you have understood your diagnosis."

3. "The emotional sensitivity component: does it feel different to hear that named as a trait rather than a defect? What, if anything, shifts?"

4. "Zero-to-ten. Where are you now?"

Closing Grounding Practice (10 minutes)

"Feet on floor. [Pause.] Weight in chair. [Pause.] Look around the room. [Pause.]

What you heard today is the theoretical foundation of this entire curriculum. Your BPD is not evidence of something fundamentally wrong with you. It is the evidence of a nervous system that developed in a specific environment and learned exactly what that environment required.

Zero-to-ten. One slightly slower breath."

Take-Home Reflection

Between sessions: spend five minutes holding this question, without pressure to answer it: does the biosocial theory explain anything about your history that you have previously explained in terms of personal deficiency? Just hold it. Write whatever comes, or nothing.

Handout Reference

Handout 2A: The Biosocial Theory and My History (Appendix C, page C-3)

Session 3: The Window of Tolerance: Emotion Dysregulation Explained

Module: A: Safety and Dialectical Foundation

Phase: Regulatory Foundation

Session Number: 3 of 30

Session Overview

Session 3 introduces the Window of Tolerance as the primary regulatory monitoring tool of the curriculum, adapted for the three BPD-specific modifications established in Chapter 2: the narrower window, the higher relational reactivity, and the slower return to baseline. The session gives clients a personalized, somatic, and behaviorally specific description of their own window's edges, which is the regulatory self-monitoring foundation on which Module C's skills training will depend.

Learning Objectives

By the end of Session 3, group members will be able to:

1. Describe the Window of Tolerance in their own words, including both poles and the functional differences between being inside and outside the window.

2. Identify at least two personal signs of being above the window and two of being below it, using their own somatic and behavioral language.

3. Name at least one relational cue that reliably moves them outside the window and describe what happens in their body when it does.

4. Demonstrate the orienting practice and describe one sensory element of the present environment they noticed.

Time Allocation

Component	90-Minute Format	60-Minute Format
Opening Ritual and Check-In	10 min	10 min
Psychoeducation: The Window of Tolerance for BPD	25 min	20 min
Experiential: My Window Map	25 min	20 min
Group Processing	20 min	5 min
Closing Grounding	10 min	5 min

Materials and Preparation

- Group Agreement displayed or distributed

- Handout 3A: My Window of Tolerance Map (Appendix C, page C-4)

- Whiteboard: Window of Tolerance diagram with three BPD annotations. Two horizontal lines creating a band. Above: HYPERAROUSAL. Inside: WINDOW OF TOLERANCE (add note: "where skills work"). Below: HYPOAROUSAL. Along the left margin: three BPD arrows labeled "narrower," "more reactive to relational cues," and "slower return to baseline."

Facilitator Notes

The three BPD-specific Window modifications must be named explicitly. Clients who have encountered the Window of Tolerance in prior DBT training may have learned a version without the BPD-specific modifications. The clinical value of this session depends on clients leaving with a personalized, specific, behaviorally accurate map of their own window, not with an abstract understanding of the general concept.

Relational cues as primary window activators. For BPD presentations, the most reliable window activators are relational in nature: changes in the facilitator's tone, perceived disconnection from other group members, ambiguous interpersonal signals, the approach of session endings. Standard Window of Tolerance presentations emphasize situational stressors. In BPD treatment, relational cues must be named as the primary activating category.

The slower return to baseline has direct clinical implications for this session. Some group members will enter Session 3 still activated from Session 2's biosocial theory content. The opening ritual check-in should include a brief acknowledgment of this: "Some of you may be carrying something from last session. That's expected. Let's check in before we proceed."

Opening Ritual and Check-In (10 minutes)

Facilitator script:

"Feet on floor. [Pause.] Weight in chair. [Pause.] Three things you can see. [Pause.] Zero-to-ten check-in.

Session 2 introduced the biosocial theory. Some of you may still be processing it. Before we begin today's content, one sentence from anyone: what are you carrying in from the week?"

[Receive one or two brief responses only. Do not extend this check-in into full group processing.]

Psychoeducation Component (25 minutes)

Talking Point 1: The window and how it works

"[Point to the diagram.] This is called the Window of Tolerance, and you will hear about it in every session of this curriculum because it is the most useful monitoring tool we have for understanding what is happening in your nervous system in real time.

The window is the zone of arousal in which your nervous system can function adaptively. Inside the window, you can think clearly, tolerate distress without acting on it, use skills you have learned, and be present in relationships. The thinking brain is online. You have options about how to respond.

Above the window is hyperarousal: too much activation. The nervous system is in a threat response. Fight, flight, freeze, or fawn. The thinking brain goes partly offline. Skills that are available inside the window become harder to access. The emotions are intense and feel permanent.

Below the window is hypoarousal: too little activation. The nervous system has shut down to protect itself from an activation it cannot process. Flatness, numbness, dissociation, the specific quality of being present in a room without quite being there. The thinking brain is offline for a different reason, but the result is similar: skills are not accessible.

Skills training works inside the window. DBT asks you to learn skills that require the thinking brain. That is why building the window, widening it and making it more stable, is the work of Module A. The skills of Module C depend on it."

Talking Point 2: The three BPD-specific modifications

"[Point to the annotations.] For people with BPD, the Window of Tolerance has three specific characteristics that are not universal across clinical populations.

The first is that the window tends to be narrower. This means you move outside the window more quickly and with less provocation than people whose developmental history included more consistent co-regulation and safety. This is not a personality trait. It is the developmental outcome of a nervous system that did not get the regulatory architecture that consistent, safe, attuned caregiving builds.

The second is that the window is more reactive to relational cues specifically. A change in tone, a perceived slight, a moment of disconnection, a session ending, these move the window more reliably than they do for people without BPD histories. Your nervous system was trained in an environment where relational cues mattered intensely and where getting them wrong had significant consequences. It is doing exactly what it was trained to do.

The third is that the return to baseline after window exceedance is slower. Once your nervous system goes above the window, it takes longer to come back than for most people. This means that skills failure in crisis is not evidence of insufficient learning. It may be evidence of a nervous system that has gone above the window and has not yet returned to the zone where skills are accessible."

Experiential Exercise: My Window Map (25 minutes)

[Distribute Handout 3A.]

"Take fifteen minutes to map your personal window. The handout asks three things.

In the hyperarousal section: what does being above your window feel like for you specifically? What happens in your body, your thoughts, your behavior? What would someone else notice about you if they saw you above the window?

In the hypoarousal section: what does being below your window feel like? What does the flatness or the absence feel like from the inside?

In the window section: what does being inside the window feel like? What is present, physically and emotionally, when you are there? How often are you there, roughly?

And one BPD-specific addition: name at least one relational cue that reliably moves you outside your window. What happens in your body when that cue arrives?"

[After fifteen minutes, invite sharing:]

"Let's share the relational cue. For anyone willing: what is one relational event that reliably moves you outside the window, and what does your body do first?"

Group Processing and Discussion (20 minutes)

1. "Looking at your window map: where do you spend most of your time? Above the window, in it, or below it?"

2. "The relational cue: does recognizing that a relational event is moving your nervous system before your mind registers it as a threat change anything about how you understand your reactions in relationships?"

3. "The slower return to baseline: has there been a time when you knew you were above the window and also knew you could not come back down? What did that feel like?"

4. "Zero-to-ten. Where are you now?"

Closing Grounding Practice (10 minutes)

"Orienting practice together. Eyes open. Slow visual scan of the room. Three things you can see. [Pause 15 seconds.] Let your gaze settle on one of them. [Pause.] Feel your feet on the floor. [Pause.] Zero-to-ten."

Take-Home Reflection

Three times a day between sessions, take fifteen seconds and ask: where am I in my window right now? Note whether you can identify a relational cue that moved you there. One sentence: "I was above/below/in my window because ___."

Handout Reference

Handout 3A: My Window of Tolerance Map (Appendix C, page C-4)

Session 4: Wise Mind: The Dialectical Foundation

Module: A: Safety and Dialectical Foundation

Phase: Regulatory Foundation

Session Number: 4 of 30

Session Overview

Session 4 introduces Wise Mind, the core DBT concept that integrates emotional experience with rational assessment to produce a regulated, grounded state from which values-based response is possible. In the BPD context, Wise Mind is specifically introduced as the internal experience of the window: the zone in which both the emotional and rational aspects of the mind are present and in dialogue. The session establishes Wise Mind not as a theoretical concept but as a recognizable internal experience that the group will practice accessing throughout the curriculum.

Learning Objectives

By the end of Session 4, group members will be able to:

1. Define Wise Mind in their own words and distinguish it from Emotion Mind and Reasonable Mind.

2. Describe at least one recent experience that occurred in Emotion Mind, Reasonable Mind, and Wise Mind respectively.

3. Name the connection between Wise Mind and the Window of Tolerance from Session 3.

4. Practice the breathing space exercise and describe what, if anything, shifted in their internal experience.

Time Allocation

Component	90-Minute Format	60-Minute Format
Opening Ritual and Check-In	10 min	10 min
Psychoeducation: Wise Mind and the Three States	25 min	20 min
Experiential: Finding Wise Mind	30 min	25 min
Group Processing	15 min	5 min
Closing Grounding	10 min	5 min

Materials and Preparation

- Group Agreement displayed or distributed

- Handout 4A: Wise Mind: Finding the Balance (Appendix C, page C-5)

- Whiteboard: three overlapping circles. Left: EMOTION MIND (hot, intense, reactive). Right: REASONABLE MIND (cool, logical, distant). Center overlap: WISE MIND (integrated, grounded, responsive)

Facilitator Notes

Wise Mind requires personal experience, not conceptual understanding. Clients who have encountered Wise Mind in prior DBT training have often encountered it as a concept they can define but have not reliably accessed. The experiential exercises in this session are designed to produce a brief, genuine Wise Mind experience rather than an accurate definition of it. The experiential product is the clinical one.

The BPD-specific Emotion Mind presentation. In BPD presentations, Emotion Mind is not simply emotional reasoning. It is frequently the specific experience of a mode state, particularly the Vulnerable Child or Angry/Impulsive Child mode, organizing perception and behavior before Wise Mind is accessible. The connection between Emotion Mind and mode states, introduced briefly in Session 4 and elaborated in Session 12, is worth naming here: "When you are in Emotion Mind, you are often in a mode. The mode is organizing what you feel and how you see the situation."

The breathing space exercise. This exercise is not a standard mindfulness practice and should not be presented as such. It is a brief, specific three-step practice: one minute of settling breath, two minutes of noticing what is present without evaluating it, and one minute of returning to the room. Its function is to create the brief internal space in which Wise Mind is more accessible, not to produce relaxation.

Opening Ritual and Check-In (10 minutes)

"Feet on floor. [Pause.] Weight in chair. [Pause.] Three things you can see. [Pause.] Zero-to-ten check-in.

From the take-home: anyone who noticed their window position and a relational cue during the week. One observation."

[Receive one or two brief responses.]

Psychoeducation Component (25 minutes)

Talking Point 1: The three states of mind

"[Point to the diagram.] DBT describes three states of mind that most people experience at different times.

Emotion Mind is the state in which emotion is the primary driver of perception and behavior. In Emotion Mind, the emotion feels like the whole truth. It feels permanent and certain and total. Reason is available but feels irrelevant. Emotion Mind is not wrong, exactly: it is right about the emotion. It has its own logic. The problem is that it tends to take over the full picture.

Reasonable Mind is the state in which logic and analysis are primary. In Reasonable Mind, you can assess a situation accurately, plan effectively, and solve problems. The limitation is that it tends to dismiss or minimize emotional information that is clinically relevant. A person in Reasonable Mind can know that they are in pain without being able to feel that they are in pain.

Wise Mind is the overlap: the state in which both the emotional truth and the analytical capacity are present simultaneously and in dialogue with each other. In Wise Mind, you can feel the emotion and also assess it. You can honor what the emotion is pointing toward without being controlled by it. You can make decisions from values rather than from the urgency of the mode state."

Talking Point 2: Wise Mind and the Window of Tolerance

"There is a direct connection between Wise Mind and the Window of Tolerance from Session 3.

Wise Mind is most accessible when you are inside your window. Above the window, Emotion Mind tends to take over because the nervous system's threat activation has reduced the thinking brain's capacity. Below the window, Reasonable Mind can become overly dominant because the flatness of hypoarousal suppresses emotional access.

This is why the grounding practices you are building in Module A are not an optional warm-up to the real work. They are the regulatory prerequisite for Wise Mind. You cannot access Wise Mind from outside your window with any reliability. The window work makes Wise Mind accessible."

Talking Point 3: Wise Mind and BPD

"People with BPD presentations are not deficient in Wise Mind. They are, in many cases, operating with a narrower and more reactive window than average, which means that Emotion Mind, especially in the Vulnerable Child or Angry/Impulsive Child mode, tends to take over at lower thresholds than in the general population.

What this means is that building Wise Mind in BPD treatment is not about learning a new thing. It is about building the regulatory conditions that make Wise Mind reliably accessible in the situations where it matters most: in relational activation, in moments of perceived abandonment, and in the high-activation states that the curriculum's pattern recognition work in Module B will map."

Experiential Exercise: Finding Wise Mind (30 minutes)

"We are going to practice finding Wise Mind using the breathing space exercise. This is not a relaxation exercise. It is a brief, three-step practice for creating the internal conditions under which Wise Mind is more accessible.

Step one: settle. Take thirty seconds with one slightly slower breath. Not deep breathing. Just slightly slower than your natural breath. Feet on floor. Weight in chair. [Pause 30 seconds.]

Step two: notice. Take two minutes and notice what is present in your experience right now. Not evaluate it. Not solve it. Just notice: there is this emotion, and there is this thought, and there is this body sensation. No story about any of it. Just noticing. [Pause 2 minutes.]

Step three: return. Take thirty seconds and come back to the room. Look around. Three things you can see. Zero-to-ten. [Pause 30 seconds.]

Now: take five minutes to answer one question in the handout. In the three-minute practice you just did, was there a moment that felt closer to Wise Mind than Emotion Mind or Reasonable Mind? What did it feel like? If there was no moment, what did you notice instead?"

[After five minutes:]

"Let's share. Not whether you found Wise Mind. What the exercise produced, including nothing, which is information too."

[Facilitate sharing. Receive every response with equal clinical attention. The absence of a Wise Mind experience is as clinically useful as its presence.]

Group Processing and Discussion (15 minutes)

1. "Emotion Mind, Reasonable Mind, and Wise Mind: which state do you spend the most time in? What does that cost you?"

2. "The connection between Wise Mind and the window: does it make sense that building your window is building access to Wise Mind? What does that change about how you think about the regulatory work of Module A?"

3. "Zero-to-ten. Where are you now?"

Closing Grounding Practice (10 minutes)

"Feet on floor. [Pause.] Weight in chair. [Pause.] Look around the room. [Pause.] One slightly slower breath. [Pause.] Zero-to-ten."

Take-Home Reflection

Between sessions, practice the breathing space exercise once daily, not during a crisis. In a neutral moment. Notice what state of mind you find yourself in most often. One sentence: "In the breathing space practice today, I was mostly in ___ mind because ___."

Handout Reference

Handout 4A: Wise Mind: Finding the Balance (Appendix C, page C-5)

Session 5: The ACE Connection: Your History Is Not Your Diagnosis

Module: A: Safety and Dialectical Foundation

Phase: Regulatory Foundation

Session Number: 5 of 30

Session Overview

Session 5 delivers the ACE framework in the group setting, adapted specifically for BPD presentations. The session's clinical purpose is the central de-shaming reframe of the entire curriculum: moving clients from "my BPD is evidence of what is fundamentally wrong with me" to "my BPD is the developmental outcome of specific adversity experiences, and understanding that changes what treatment can offer." The session connects the biosocial theory from Session 2 to the specific ACE research from Chapter 1, making the general framework specific to each client's history.

Learning Objectives

By the end of Session 5, group members will be able to:

1. Name the ACE Study and describe its central finding regarding BPD in one to two accessible sentences.

2. Identify their own ACE score and name at least one specific connection between their adversity history and the BPD presentation they carry.

3. Describe the specific ACE type (emotional abuse or emotional neglect) most strongly associated with BPD and identify whether it appears in their own history.

4. Distinguish the de-shaming reframe from the elimination of personal responsibility, in their own words.

Time Allocation

Component	90-Minute Format	60-Minute Format
Opening Ritual and Check-In	10 min	10 min
Psychoeducation: ACE Research and BPD	20 min	15 min
ACE Questionnaire Administration	10 min	10 min
Reflection and Group Discussion	40 min	20 min
Closing Grounding	10 min	5 min

Materials and Preparation

- Handout 5A: Understanding ACEs: Your History and Your BPD (Appendix C, page C-6), including the ACE questionnaire

- Small envelopes for private ACE score recording (recommended)

- Whiteboard: "A developmental outcome, not a character defect"

- Pre-session mandatory reporting review: Session 5's questionnaire and group discussion may produce disclosures carrying mandatory reporting implications. Review your jurisdiction's requirements before facilitating this session.

- Pre-session coordination with individual therapists: clients whose ACE score or session response indicates significant activation should have individual follow-up available.

Facilitator Notes

Session 5 carries the highest activation potential of Module A. The ACE questionnaire covers all ten categories of childhood adversity, and completing it in a group setting can produce significant somatic and emotional activation for clients whose adversity has not been previously named in clinical language. The framing is the clinical intervention. The data is secondary.

Emotional abuse as the BPD-specific finding. The ACE research specific to BPD, described in Chapter 1, differs from the addiction-focused ACE research in one clinically important way: emotional abuse, not physical abuse or sexual abuse, shows the strongest independent association with BPD. This finding is often surprising to clients and clinicians alike, and its delivery requires specific care. Clients who experienced primarily emotional abuse may have spent years being told that their history "wasn't that bad" because it did not include physical or sexual abuse. The finding that emotional abuse is the strongest BPD predictor is the research evidence that directly addresses that dismissal.

Do not ask group members to share their scores. The group discussion focuses on the framework and its meaning for each client's self-understanding, not on specific numbers. Scores are private.

The anger response. As established in Chapter 1, the anger that often follows the ACE framework delivery in high-ACE clients is appropriate and clinically productive. Receive it without rushing toward resolution.

Opening Ritual and Check-In (10 minutes)

"Feet on floor. [Pause.] Weight in chair. [Pause.] Three things you can see. [Pause.] Zero-to-ten check-in.

Today's session covers material that many people find significant. Before we begin, I want to say that directly: today we are connecting your personal history to your BPD presentation in a way that many people have never had the opportunity to do. If at any point you notice your number going above seven, I want to know. That is not a reason to leave. It is clinical information."

Psychoeducation Component (20 minutes)

Talking Point 1: The ACE Study and what it established for BPD

"In 1995 and 1997, Kaiser Permanente and the Centers for Disease Control administered a questionnaire to over seventeen thousand adults, asking about ten categories of adverse childhood experience, and then tracked the relationship between those experiences and adult health and behavioral health outcomes.

The finding specific to BPD is remarkable in its magnitude. A 2020 meta-analysis of ninety-seven studies found that individuals with BPD are nearly fourteen times more likely to report childhood adversity than people without BPD. Fourteen times. The relationship is not marginal. It is among the strongest associations in all of personality disorder research.

What is equally important, and more specific to your presentations, is which adversity type shows the strongest independent relationship to BPD. It is emotional abuse: the consistent communication that your emotional experience is wrong, excessive, or a personal failure. Not physical abuse. Not sexual abuse. Emotional abuse."

Talking Point 2: Why emotional abuse is the strongest predictor

"The reason emotional abuse is the strongest BPD predictor connects directly to what we covered in Session 2.

Emotional abuse disrupts exactly the developmental processes that BPD treatment is later asked to rebuild: the capacity to trust your own emotional experience, the development of a coherent sense of self, and the relational template that treats closeness as potentially safe. A child who is consistently told that their emotions are wrong, excessive, or shameful cannot develop the stable internal identity that a validating environment would produce. The identity instability of BPD is not a personality defect. It is the developmental outcome of an environment that made stable internal identity impossible to build.

For many people in this room, this finding will resonate with a history that was minimized in prior treatment because it did not include dramatic physical or sexual abuse. The absence of dramatic physical events does not mean the absence of developmental injury. For the BPD presentation specifically, the emotional environment is often the most clinically significant adversity type."

Talking Point 3: Using the questionnaire

"We are going to complete the ACE questionnaire in a few minutes. Three things before we do.

First: completion is optional. If you completed it in your intake assessment, you do not need to do it again. If completing it would be too activating right now, you can choose to listen to the discussion without completing it.

Second: your score is private. I will not ask you to share it. What I will ask you to do, after you have scored it, is reflect on one thing: does this number help explain anything about your BPD that has felt confusing or unexplained?

Third: there is no right score and no bad score. The questionnaire does not measure how serious your BPD is. It measures specific categories of adversity. A low score does not mean your history is irrelevant. A high score does not mean recovery is impossible. It is information."

ACE Questionnaire Administration (10 minutes)

[Distribute Handout 5A.]

"Take ten minutes to complete the questionnaire privately. Record your score."

[Allow ten minutes of silent completion. Circulate quietly.]

"Now: before we discuss, I want to invite you to sit with your score for a moment. The question I want you to hold is: does this number help explain anything about your BPD presentation or your history with treatment?"

[Allow two minutes of quiet reflection.]

Reflection and Group Discussion (40 minutes)

1. "What was it like to complete the questionnaire? Not your score. The experience of completing it."

2. "The emotional abuse finding: for anyone who experienced primarily emotional adversity, what is it like to have that named as the strongest BPD predictor? Does it change anything about how you have understood your history?"

3. "The sentence on the whiteboard: 'A developmental outcome, not a character defect.' When you read it, what is your reaction? Does part of you believe it and part resist it?"

4. "Here is the accountability question: does understanding the developmental origins of your BPD presentation change your responsibility for how you act in your current relationships and in treatment? I want to hear what you actually think."

5. "Zero-to-ten. Where are you now?"

Closing Grounding Practice (10 minutes)

"These were significant things to sit with. We looked at your history not to dwell in it but to make sense of something that has often felt incomprehensible.

Feet on floor. [Pause.] Weight in chair. [Pause.] Look around the room. You are here, now, in this room. [Pause.] Zero-to-ten. One slightly slower breath."

Take-Home Reflection

Between sessions, hold this question: is there one connection between your adversity history and your BPD presentation that you made today that you want to carry forward in your self-understanding? Not to share with anyone else. For your own understanding.

Handout Reference

Handout 5A: Understanding ACEs: Your History and Your BPD (Appendix C, page C-6)

Session 6: Radical Acceptance: What It Is and What It Is Not

Module: A: Safety and Dialectical Foundation

Phase: Regulatory Foundation

Session Number: 6 of 30

Session Overview

Session 6 delivers radical acceptance as a clinical concept and a practical skill, addressed specifically in terms of the BPD presentations that most frequently distort it. Radical acceptance is among the most misunderstood concepts in DBT and among the most clinically essential: without it, the pattern recognition work of Module B becomes a catalogue of grievances rather than a clinical map, and the skills training of Module C becomes effort in service of a goal that the client does not actually believe is available to them.

Learning Objectives

By the end of Session 6, group members will be able to:

1. Define radical acceptance in their own words and distinguish it from approval of what happened, from passivity, and from giving up on change.

2. Identify at least one specific thing in their history or current situation that they have been fighting rather than accepting, and describe the cost of that fight.

3. Practice the acceptance breathing exercise and describe one thing they noticed.

4. Name at least one way that radical acceptance of the adversity history, distinct from approval of it, would change their relationship to their own BPD presentation.

Time Allocation

Component	90-Minute Format	60-Minute Format
Opening Ritual and Check-In	10 min	10 min
Psychoeducation: Radical Acceptance Defined	25 min	20 min
Experiential: What I Have Been Fighting	30 min	20 min
Group Processing	15 min	5 min
Closing Grounding	10 min	5 min

Materials and Preparation

- Group Agreement displayed or distributed

- Handout 6A: Radical Acceptance: What It Is and What It Is Not (Appendix C, page C-7)

- Whiteboard: two columns. WHAT RADICAL ACCEPTANCE IS / WHAT RADICAL ACCEPTANCE IS NOT

Facilitator Notes

The three most common radical acceptance distortions in BPD treatment. First: radical acceptance means approving of what happened. It does not. Accepting that something happened exactly as it happened, that it cannot be changed, is not the same as endorsing it. Second: radical acceptance means giving up. It does not. Acceptance is the prerequisite for effective change, not an alternative to it. Fighting against what cannot be changed consumes the regulatory resources that change requires. Third: radical acceptance means forgiving the people who caused harm. It does not. Forgiveness is a separate clinical process that belongs in individual therapy. Radical acceptance of the adversity is an internal shift in the client's relationship to the reality of what happened, not a relational shift toward the people who produced it.

Radical acceptance and BPD specifically. For BPD presentations, the most clinically significant application of radical acceptance is often the acceptance of the BPD diagnosis itself: the specific acceptance that the nervous system that produced this presentation is the one that developed in the specific adversity context described in Session 5, and that fighting against the BPD presentation as evidence of personal deficiency is consuming regulatory resources that recovery requires. This application should be named directly in the session.

Opening Ritual and Check-In (10 minutes)

"Feet on floor. [Pause.] Weight in chair. [Pause.] Three things you can see. [Pause.] Zero-to-ten check-in.

From the take-home: one sentence from anyone who made a connection between their ACE history and their BPD presentation that they have been carrying since Session 5."

[Receive one or two brief responses.]

Psychoeducation Component (25 minutes)

Talking Point 1: What radical acceptance is

"[Point to the columns on the whiteboard.] Radical acceptance is one of the most important and most misunderstood concepts in DBT. I want to define it precisely because the misunderstandings of it prevent it from being usable.

Radical acceptance means this: fully and completely acknowledging the reality of what is, exactly as it is, without fighting against it, without demanding it be different, and without the energy expenditure of ongoing resistance to what cannot be changed.

The word 'radical' means complete. Not partial acceptance, not grudging acknowledgment, but the full internal recognition that what happened happened, that it cannot be unhappened, and that continuing to fight against that reality produces suffering without producing change.

The reason it is a skill, and not just an attitude, is that it requires deliberate practice. The nervous system's default response to painful reality is resistance: this should not have happened, this should be different, I should not feel this way. Radical acceptance is the deliberate, practiced turning toward reality as it actually is."

Talking Point 2: What radical acceptance is not

"[Write as you speak.] Radical acceptance is not approval. Accepting that you were emotionally abused is not the same as saying the emotional abuse was acceptable. It was not. What happened to you was not acceptable. And it happened, and it cannot be changed, and fighting against the fact that it happened produces suffering without changing it.

Radical acceptance is not giving up. Acceptance is the prerequisite for effective change. As long as your regulatory resources are consumed by fighting against the reality of your history or your diagnosis, those resources are not available for the change that recovery requires. Acceptance frees the resources that fighting was using.

Radical acceptance is not forgiveness. The people who produced the adversity in your history are not the subject of this skill. Whether or how to forgive them is a clinical conversation that belongs in your individual therapy. Radical acceptance is about your relationship to the reality of what happened, not about your relationship to the people who produced it."

Talking Point 3: Radical acceptance and your BPD

"The specific application of radical acceptance that matters most in this curriculum is this: what would it mean to radically accept that you have a BPD presentation that is the developmental outcome of specific adversity?

Not to approve of the adversity. Not to be grateful for the diagnosis. Not to stop working to change the patterns it produced. But to accept, fully and completely, that this is the nervous system you have, that it was built in the environment it was built in, and that fighting against the existence of the BPD presentation is consuming regulatory resources that the skills work of Module C will need.

The clients in BPD treatment who spend the most energy fighting against their own diagnosis are often the clients for whom Module C's skills are least accessible. The fight against the diagnosis consumes the Wise Mind capacity that skills require."

Experiential Exercise: What I Have Been Fighting (30 minutes)

[Distribute Handout 6A.]

"Take fifteen minutes to work through the handout. It asks you to identify something in your history or your current situation that you have been fighting rather than accepting, and to estimate the cost of that fight in regulatory resources.

The question is not whether the thing you are fighting is worth being angry about. It may be genuinely worth being angry about. The question is whether the ongoing fight against its reality is serving you, and what those regulatory resources could be used for if they were not in the fight."

[After fifteen minutes:]

"Now the acceptance breathing exercise. Three breaths, each one slightly slower than the last. With each exhale, try to say internally: this is what is. Not this is good. Not this is fair. This is what is.

Notice what the practice produces. Then share: what is one thing you have been fighting, and what did the practice do to your relationship to it, even briefly?"

Group Processing and Discussion (15 minutes)

1. "The three distortions: approval, giving up, and forgiveness. Which one most frequently gets in the way of your access to radical acceptance?"

2. "Radical acceptance of the BPD diagnosis itself: what is your reaction to that specific application? What would it cost, and what might it free?"

3. "Zero-to-ten. Where are you now?"

Closing Grounding Practice (10 minutes)

"Feet on floor. [Pause.] Weight in chair. [Pause.] Look around the room. [Pause.]

Radical acceptance does not make things okay. It makes them real. And only what is real can be worked with.

Zero-to-ten. One slightly slower breath."

Take-Home Reflection

Between sessions, practice the acceptance breathing exercise once daily around one specific thing you have been fighting. Not the largest thing. A representative one. Notice what the practice produces, including nothing, which is information too.

Handout Reference

Handout 6A: Radical Acceptance: What It Is and What It Is Not (Appendix C, page C-7)

Session 7: Building Your Stabilization Network

Module: A: Safety and Dialectical Foundation

Phase: Regulatory Foundation

Session Number: 7 of 30

Session Overview

Session 7 builds the stabilization network: the inventory of safe people, safe places, safe activities, and regulatory practices that constitute each client's co-regulatory and self-regulatory resource base. In BPD treatment, this session carries specific clinical attention to the relational template complications that make building a stabilization network more complex for this population than for others: the specific difficulty of identifying safe people when the developmental history has taught the nervous system that safety and closeness do not coexist.

Learning Objectives

By the end of Session 7, group members will be able to:

1. Identify at least two safe people, one safe place, and two safe activities for their stabilization network map.

2. Describe the specific challenge that the BPD relational template creates for safe person identification and name one step toward addressing it.

3. Distinguish co-regulatory resources from activating relationships using the regulatory assessment criteria from the session.

4. Identify at least one recovery community or peer support resource that is potentially appropriate for their specific relational template pattern.

Time Allocation

Component	90-Minute Format	60-Minute Format
Opening Ritual and Check-In	10 min	10 min
Psychoeducation: Co-Regulation, BPD, and the Safe Person Problem	20 min	15 min
Experiential: Building the Stabilization Network	30 min	25 min
Group Activity: Sharing One Safe Thing	15 min	5 min
Closing Grounding	10 min	5 min

Materials and Preparation

- Group Agreement displayed or distributed
  - Handout 7A: My Stabilization Network (Appendix C, page C-8)
  - Whiteboard: three columns, SAFE PEOPLE / SAFE PLACES / SAFE ACTIVITIES

Facilitator Notes

The safe person identification challenge in BPD is specific and must be named directly. For clients whose developmental history has taught them that closeness precedes harm, that people who express care become dangerous when they know you fully, or that safety requires the performance of self that idealized relationships demand, the concept of a "safe person" may feel either inaccessible or suspicious. The clinical move is not to avoid this complexity but to name it and hold it: "Finding safe people is genuinely harder when your developmental history has taught you that safety and closeness do not go together. That is a real barrier, not a personal failure. Let's look at it directly."

The BPD relational template and the stabilization network. Session 15 of this curriculum (Module B) will address the relational template in full. Session 7 introduces the relevant concept in a practical and accessible form: some people in our relational world settle our nervous systems, and some activate them. The assessment criterion for a safe person in this session is regulatory, not evaluative: does this person's presence tend to move your zero-to-ten number lower, or higher?

Opening Ritual and Check-In (10 minutes)

"Feet on floor. [Pause.] Weight in chair. [Pause.] Three things you can see. [Pause.] Zero-to-ten check-in.

From the take-home: anyone who practiced radical acceptance around one specific thing this week. One observation."

[Receive one or two brief responses.]

Psychoeducation Component (20 minutes)

Talking Point 1: Why stabilization networks matter more for BPD

"Your nervous system does not regulate itself in isolation. The primary mechanism through which nervous systems regulate is co-regulation: the capacity of one regulated nervous system to influence another through proximity, voice, and presence. When you are in the presence of a calm, attuned person, your nervous system reads their regulatory state automatically and begins to adjust toward regulation. This is neurobiological, not metaphorical.

For BPD presentations, this co-regulatory mechanism is both more important and more complicated than for most other clinical populations. More important because the window is narrower and the return to baseline is slower, which means the regulatory resource of a co-regulating relationship provides more of the regulatory work the window cannot do internally. More complicated because the developmental history that produced the BPD presentation is a relational history: the adversity was in relationships, which means relationships carry both the greatest regulatory potential and the highest activation risk."

Talking Point 2: The safe person problem in BPD

"Here is the specific clinical challenge I want to name directly today.

For many people with BPD histories, the concept of a 'safe person' produces one of three responses: immediate identification of someone who is idealized (currently in the idealization phase of the idealization-devaluation cycle, which means the safety assessment is not yet reliable); confusion or absence (no one comes to mind because the developmental history taught that safety and closeness do not coexist); or guardedness (awareness that what starts as safe tends to become dangerous when you are fully known).

All three responses are clinically appropriate given the developmental history. And all three can make the stabilization network building feel either dishonest or impossible.

The assessment criterion I want to offer is this: not 'do I trust this person completely' and not 'is this relationship without complication.' The question is simpler and more regulatory: does this person's presence, on balance, tend to move my zero-to-ten number lower or higher? If lower, they are a potential co-regulatory resource. If higher, they are a potential activation risk, regardless of how much you care about them."

Experiential Exercise: Building the Stabilization Network (30 minutes)

[Distribute Handout 7A.]

"Take fifteen minutes to build your stabilization network. Three categories.

Safe people: not people you trust completely or people whose relationships are uncomplicated. People whose presence, on balance, tends to settle your nervous system rather than activate it. They do not need to understand your BPD. They need to have a regulatory effect.

Safe places: physical locations where your nervous system tends to settle. Not because good things happen there, but because threatening things don't.

Safe activities: things that produce a regulatory effect for your specific nervous system. Not things you think you should enjoy. Things that actually work.

And one additional column specific to this curriculum: one relationship or context that reliably activates your window. Not to eliminate those relationships. To know the difference when you enter them."

[After fifteen minutes:]

"Let's share briefly. One safe person or one safe place from your map. And if you found the safe person category difficult: what made it difficult?"

[Facilitate sharing. The disclosure that the safe person category was difficult is itself clinically significant and should be received with specific acknowledgment, not with problem-solving.]

Closing Grounding Practice (10 minutes)

"Feet on floor. [Pause.] Weight in chair. [Pause.] Look around the room. Notice that you are currently in a room where your zero-to-ten number is, for most of you, lower than it was when you arrived. This group is part of your stabilization network. [Pause.]

Zero-to-ten. One slightly slower breath."

Take-Home Reflection

Between sessions, use one item from your stabilization network: reach out to one safe person, go to one safe place, or do one safe activity. Notice whether it produces the regulatory effect you mapped it for. Bring the observation to Session 8.

Handout Reference

Handout 7A: My Stabilization Network (Appendix C, page C-8)

Session 8: Module A Review: Anchoring the Dialectical Foundation

Module: A: Safety and Dialectical Foundation

Phase: Integration and Transition

Session Number: 8 of 30

Session Overview

Session 8 is an integration and transition session: reviewing the clinical concepts and personal discoveries of Module A, completing the Stabilization Plan, and preparing the group for Module B's pattern recognition work. The session's clinical tone shifts from building and practicing to consolidating and anchoring. The facilitator's primary task is helping each client articulate, in their own words, what has genuinely shifted in their self-understanding across the eight sessions of Module A, and to identify the specific regulatory and conceptual resources now available that were not available at Session 1.

Learning Objectives

By the end of Session 8, group members will be able to:

1. Name the five clinical concepts introduced in Module A (biosocial theory, Window of Tolerance, Wise Mind, ACE framework, radical acceptance) and describe each in one to two sentences in their own language.

2. Identify at least two regulatory practices from Module A that have been personally useful and describe one real context in which each was applied.

3. Complete the Stabilization Plan with specific, personal entries in each section.

4. Describe, in their own words, what Module B will ask of them and why Module A's foundation was necessary before Module B could begin.

Time Allocation

Component	90-Minute Format	60-Minute Format
Opening Ritual and Check-In	10 min	10 min
Module A Concept Review	20 min	15 min
Stabilization Plan Completion	25 min	20 min
Group Processing: Module A Reflections	20 min	10 min
Closing Ritual: Looking Ahead to Module B	15 min	5 min

Materials and Preparation

- All previously distributed handouts available for reference

- Handout 8A: My Stabilization Plan (Appendix C, page C-9)

- Whiteboard: list all five Module A concepts before the session

- Coordinate with individual therapists before this session: Module B's pattern recognition work significantly increases activation, and clients who are medically unstable, recently discharged from inpatient care, or in early stages of medication adjustment should have individual support confirmed before the transition

Facilitator Notes

Session 8 is a moment of genuine recognition. Module A has asked significant things of this group: the building of new regulatory practices, the reception of the biosocial theory and the ACE framework, the practice of radical acceptance, and the beginning of trust in a group container. Each of those contributions deserves to be named. The recognition should be specific rather than generically warm. "You have built a regulatory foundation that most of you have not had available before" is more clinically useful than "you've worked so hard."

The Module B preview is a clinical act. Clients who understand why Module B follows Module A, who understand that pattern recognition work requires regulatory foundation rather than preceding it, arrive at Module B significantly more prepared for its higher activation content. The preview should be offered as an honest invitation rather than as a reassurance: "Module B will ask more of you than Module A has. It will ask you to look at the patterns that have been running your BPD presentation with enough precision that they become workable. That work requires everything we have built in Module A. You are ready for it now in a way you were not in Session 1."

Opening Ritual and Check-In (10 minutes)

"Feet on floor. [Pause.] Weight in chair. [Pause.] Three things you can see. [Pause.] Zero-to-ten check-in.

This is our eighth session together. The last session of Module A. I want to start with one question that I would like everyone to answer. Just one sentence.

What is one thing you know now about yourself, your BPD, or your nervous system that you did not have language for before Module A began?"

[Go around the room. Every member answers. These sentences are the module review.]

Module A Concept Review (20 minutes)

"[Point to the five concepts on the whiteboard.] Before we move to the Stabilization Plan, a brief review using your definitions rather than mine.

The biosocial theory. [Invite one or two definitions.] BPD develops when a person with high emotional sensitivity grows up in an environment that consistently invalidates that sensitivity, and the specific adversity type most strongly associated with BPD is emotional abuse and emotional neglect.

The Window of Tolerance. [Invite one or two definitions.] The range of arousal in which the thinking brain is online and skills are accessible, with the BPD-specific modifications of a narrower window, higher relational reactivity, and slower return to baseline.

Wise Mind. [Invite one or two definitions.] The integrated state in which emotional and rational information are both present and in dialogue, accessible within the window, and the organizing internal experience that Module C's skills training is designed to strengthen.

The ACE framework. [Invite one or two definitions.] The research establishing that BPD is fourteen times more likely in people with childhood adversity histories, with emotional abuse as the strongest predictor, and the de-shaming reframe that follows: a developmental outcome, not a character defect.

Radical acceptance. [Invite one or two definitions.] Full acknowledgment of reality as it is, distinct from approval or forgiveness, which frees regulatory resources from ongoing resistance to what cannot be changed and makes those resources available for the change that recovery requires."

Stabilization Plan Completion (25 minutes)

[Distribute Handout 8A.]

"Take twenty minutes to complete the Stabilization Plan. It has four sections.

Your Window of Tolerance signs: the specific somatic and behavioral signs of being above and below your window, using the language you developed in Session 3.

Your Wise Mind access practices: the specific things you have found that make Wise Mind more accessible for your specific nervous system.

Your stabilization network: the safe people, safe places, and safe activities from Session 7, with contact information for your safe people.

Your radical acceptance commitments: one specific thing you are practicing accepting right now, and what the practice produces.

Make it specific. Generic plans produce generic access. Specific plans produce genuine resources."

[Allow twenty minutes. Circulate. After twenty minutes, invite one element from each person's plan to be shared, so the group knows what each member has available.]

Group Processing: Module A Reflections (20 minutes)

1. "What is the most significant shift in your self-understanding after Module A?"

2. "What was the hardest element of Module A for you? Not the most activating. The one that required the most of you."

3. "Is there anything you needed from Module A that we did not get to? Even if the answer is that it belongs somewhere else in the curriculum."

4. "What are you most uncertain about as we move into Module B?"

Closing Ritual: Looking Ahead to Module B (15 minutes)

"In our next session, we begin Module B. I want to tell you what Module B is before we close.

Module B is about pattern recognition. Over the next eight sessions, we are going to build the BPD Pattern Map: a detailed map of the specific patterns that have been organizing your BPD presentation. The abandonment fear and what it drives. The splitting: idealization and devaluation as nervous system responses. The identity disturbance: who you are when the emotional state changes. The schema modes and how they organize what you feel and what you do. The impulsivity chain. The specific history and function of self-harm, understood as communication and regulation rather than as evidence of how damaged you are. The chronic emptiness and what the ACE research tells us about its origins.

Module B does not ask you to change any of these patterns. It asks you to see them. Clearly. With enough precision and enough compassion that they become workable.

You cannot work with what you cannot see. Module A built the conditions under which seeing is possible. Module B begins the seeing.

Feet on floor. [Pause.] Weight in chair. [Pause.] Look around the room. The people in it have been through eight sessions with you. They are part of what Module A built. [Pause.]

Zero-to-ten. One slightly slower breath. See you in Module B."

Take-Home Reflection

Between Module A and Module B: read your Stabilization Plan once. Notice what it feels like to have a document that describes, in your own language, what you have built and what you now have available. Whatever you notice, bring it to Session 9.

Handout Reference

Handout 8A: My Stabilization Plan (Appendix C, page C-9)

Module B: Understanding the BPD Pattern Map

Sessions 9 through 16 | Clinical Focus: Psychoeducation about BPD patterns, shame, core states, and relational dynamics. Increasing visibility without destabilization.

Chapter 8.0: Before the Pattern Can Change, It Has to Be Seen

Chapter Complexity Level: Intermediate

Prerequisites: Part One; Module A (Sessions 1 through 8); Stabilization Plan completed

Time Investment: 45 to 60 minutes plus eight complete session plan read-throughs

Opening

In the field testing of this curriculum, a client in the fifth session of Module B said something that has since organized how the curriculum's second module is introduced to every new facilitator.

She had been working through the abandonment fear session, mapping the behavioral chain it produced, and she stopped mid-exercise. "I've been doing this thing my whole life," she said, "and nobody ever called it a thing. It was just how I am."

That sentence is the clinical agenda of Module B.

Module A built the regulatory and dialectical foundation. Module B uses it to do the specific work that every prior treatment has deferred, circled, or missed: the precise, compassionate, developmentally grounded mapping of the specific patterns that BPD produces. Not their management. Not their elimination. Their visibility. Because only what is visible can be worked with.

The Pattern Map that Module B produces across eight sessions is the most clinically specific document any client in BPD treatment is typically asked to create. It covers the abandonment fear and the behavioral chain it drives, the splitting pattern and its nervous system origins, the identity disturbance and the adversity history that explains it, the five schema modes and how they organize behavior before any conscious decision is made, the impulsivity chain, the regulatory and communicative functions of self-harm, and the specific phenomenology of chronic emptiness. Seven layers. One map. The clinical product that makes Module C's skills training genuinely targeted rather than generically applied.

The counterintuitive claim of Module B: insight without precision is not a clinical asset. It can be a clinical liability. Many clients with BPD have spent years in treatment generating insight that never changed their presentation. The difference Module B is designed to produce is not more insight. It is more precision: a level of visibility specific enough that the pattern becomes workable rather than simply familiar.

8.1 The Architecture of Module B

Module B spans eight sessions organized around a single clinical product: the BPD Pattern Map completed in Session 16.

Session 9 maps the abandonment fear: its developmental origins, its somatic and behavioral activation pattern, and the specific behavioral chain it produces. Session 10 addresses splitting: the idealization-devaluation cycle as a nervous system pattern with developmental origins rather than a character defect. Session 11 addresses identity disturbance: the chronic instability of self-image that adversity makes inevitable and that recovery must systematically address. Session 12 delivers the schema mode mapping exercise: the identification of the five BPD-relevant modes as they operate in each client's specific presentation. Session 13 maps the impulsivity chain: the urge-to-act sequence that the BPD nervous system produces before the prefrontal cortex can engage. Session 14 addresses self-harm directly, as both communication and regulation, from a trauma-informed frame that removes shame without removing clinical accountability. Session 15 addresses chronic emptiness: the specific phenomenology and its connection to the emotional neglect that Chapter 1 identified as the second strongest ACE predictor of BPD. Session 16 completes the BPD Pattern Map and prepares the group for Module C.

8.2 The Clinical Stance for Module B

Module A's clinical stance was dialectical architect. Module B's clinical stance is compassionate mapper: helping clients see their own patterns with enough accuracy and enough compassion that the patterns become understandable rather than overwhelming.

The facilitation challenge specific to Module B is the tendency for each session's pattern content to activate the very pattern being described. Session 9 on abandonment fear tends to activate abandonment fears. Session 10 on splitting tends to activate splitting dynamics in the group. Session 12 on schema modes tends to activate mode states in the room. This is not a complication to manage. It is live clinical material, and Chapter 5's Relational Update principle applies: the facilitator's regulated, non-retaliatory, mode-aware response to whatever the session activates is as clinically significant as any content delivered.

Sessions 14 on self-harm and 15 on chronic emptiness carry the highest activation potential of Module B. Both should be scheduled on days when individual therapy is available for follow-up, and both require the most deliberate pre-session facilitator preparation and post-session debrief.

Named Concept: The BPD Pattern Map

The seven-layer clinical document that makes visible the abandonment fear, splitting pattern, identity disturbance, schema modes, impulsivity chain, self-harm function, and chronic emptiness that organize the BPD presentation, enabling the targeted skills application that Module C provides.

Apply it by treating the completed Pattern Map as the most clinically precise document the client has ever produced about their own presentation, and by sharing it with the individual therapist (with consent) before Module C begins.

Session 9: The Abandonment Fear: Origins, Activation, and the Behavior It Drives

Module: B: Understanding the BPD Pattern Map

Phase: Pattern Mapping

Session Number: 9 of 30

Session Overview

Session 9 opens Module B by mapping the abandonment fear: the first and most foundational pattern in the BPD presentation. The session delivers the developmental explanation for the abandonment fear, maps the specific somatic and perceptual signs of its activation, and traces the behavioral chain it produces. The clinical purpose is not to eliminate the fear but to give clients enough visibility into its activation and its behavioral consequences that intervention becomes possible before the behavioral chain has run to its endpoint.

Learning Objectives

By the end of Session 9, group members will be able to:

1. Describe the developmental origins of the abandonment fear in their own words, connecting it to the attachment history identified in their ACE profile.

2. Identify at least three specific somatic and perceptual signs that signal abandonment fear activation before behavior begins.

3. Map one personal abandonment fear chain from a recent episode, working from the perceptual cue through the somatic activation through the emotional state through the behavioral response.

4. Identify at least one point in their personal chain where earlier-stage awareness might create an intervention opportunity.

Time Allocation

Component	90-Minute Format	60-Minute Format
Opening Ritual and Check-In	10 min	10 min
Module B Orientation	10 min	5 min
Psychoeducation: The Abandonment Fear	20 min	15 min
Experiential: My Abandonment Chain	25 min	20 min
Group Processing	15 min	5 min
Closing Grounding	10 min	5 min

Materials and Preparation

- Group Agreement displayed or distributed; Stabilization Plans available for reference

- Handout 9A: My Abandonment Fear Chain (Appendix C, page C-10)

- Whiteboard: five-link chain. PERCEPTUAL CUE -> SOMATIC STATE -> EMOTIONAL ACTIVATION -> BEHAVIORAL RESPONSE -> CONSEQUENCE

Facilitator Notes

Module B orientation takes five to ten minutes at the start of Session 9. The transition from Module A's regulatory and dialectical work to Module B's pattern recognition work requires an explicit acknowledgment. The framing: "Module A built the foundation. Module B uses it to look clearly at the specific patterns that have been running your BPD presentation. Not to judge them. To see them precisely enough that they become workable."

The abandonment fear's perceptual component is the most clinically significant finding of this session. Research on BPD, particularly the neuroimaging research on amygdala reactivity from Chapter 2, establishes that individuals with BPD show heightened activation to neutral faces, reading them as threatening at significantly higher rates than non-BPD participants. This means the abandonment fear is activated by perceptual cues that the person across from the client may not be aware they are sending. Naming this explicitly de-shames the activation: "The perception is accurate given what your nervous system was trained to detect. The perception may or may not be accurate about the current situation."

Session 9 tends to activate abandonment fears during delivery. When the group discussion reaches the behavioral responses to abandonment fear, some group members will begin to exhibit those behaviors in the room: withdrawal, escalation, clinging, or testing. This is live clinical material. The facilitator's calm acknowledgment, rather than management, is the intervention: "I notice something just shifted in the room. The content we're covering has a way of activating what it is describing. Let's check in with our windows."

Opening Ritual and Check-In (10 minutes)

"Feet on floor. [Pause.] Weight in chair. [Pause.] Three things you can see. [Pause.] Zero-to-ten check-in.

Welcome to Module B. Before we begin today's content, I want to mark this transition. Module A asked you to build regulatory practices, understand the developmental origins of your BPD, and accept the reality of what happened. That work was preparation. Module B is what it prepared you for: looking clearly at the specific patterns that have been organizing your BPD presentation.

One sentence from anyone: what are you carrying into Module B from the Stabilization Plan work?"

[Receive one or two brief responses.]

Psychoeducation Component (20 minutes)

Talking Point 1: What the abandonment fear actually is

"The abandonment fear is the most foundational and most consistently painful feature of BPD. Before we look at what it produces in behavior, I want to say something about what it actually is.

The abandonment fear is not irrationality. It is not weakness or excessive sensitivity or evidence of being too much. It is the specific adaptive response of a nervous system that grew up in an environment where the availability of attachment figures was genuinely unpredictable or genuinely conditional. A child whose caregiver might be present or absent, warm or cold, available or dangerous, on an unpredictable schedule learns an adaptive response: monitor constantly, detect signs of withdrawal early, and respond to even small cues of disconnection with urgency, because in the original environment, disconnection had significant consequences.

That nervous system learned exactly the right lesson for the environment it was in. The clinical challenge is that the lesson was learned so thoroughly that it continues to organize perception and behavior in adult environments where the consequences of disconnection are usually not the same."

Talking Point 2: The five-link abandonment chain

"[Point to the chain.] The abandonment fear operates as a chain, and like the trigger chain from Book 1, it initiates below conscious awareness. By the time the behavior appears, the chain has usually been running for minutes, sometimes hours.

Link one is the perceptual cue: the specific sensory or relational input that the nervous system registers as a potential abandonment signal. This can be a change in tone, a missed text reply, a moment of distraction in someone's attention, a session ending, a facilitator running five minutes late. Many of these cues would not register as significant to a nervous system not calibrated to abandonment threat.

Link two is the somatic state: the body's immediate response to the perceptual cue before the mind has named it. Chest tightening, stomach dropping, a quality of cold activation, a specific urgency in the limbs. This is the earliest intervention point and the one most clients have never had language for.

Link three is the emotional activation: the somatic state acquires an emotional definition. Terror of being alone. Rage at being dismissed. Grief that feels permanent. Shame that feels like confirmation of unworthiness.

Link four is the behavioral response: the action the emotional state drives. The frantically checking calls. The escalation designed to produce a response at any cost. The withdrawal that preempts the rejection. The self-harm that converts unbearable emotional pain into a physical state that feels more manageable.

Link five is the consequence: what the behavioral response produces, including the responses from others that confirm or disconfirm the abandonment prediction, and the behavioral shame that frequently follows."

Experiential Exercise: My Abandonment Chain (25 minutes)

[Distribute Handout 9A.]

"Take fifteen minutes to map one abandonment fear chain from a recent episode. Work backward from link five toward link one, because link five is the only link you have reliable conscious access to.

You know the behavior. That is link five. What was the emotional state that preceded the behavior? What was the somatic state before the emotion had a name? And can you identify anything in the environment, any perceptual cue, that preceded the somatic state?

Leave blank what you cannot access. Blank is information about where the chain is running below conscious awareness."

[After fifteen minutes:]

"Let's share. Not the behavior itself. The earlier links. What is the earliest link in the chain you were able to access?"

[Facilitate sharing. Reflect each contribution with attention to the specific link identified.]

Group Processing and Discussion (15 minutes)

1. "What was the most surprising element of mapping the chain? Was there a link you did not expect to find?"

2. "The perceptual cue: does recognizing that the abandonment fear can activate from a minor relational cue, one the other person was not aware of sending, change how you understand your reactions in relationships?"

3. "Where in your chain does intervention feel most possible right now?"

4. "Zero-to-ten. Where are you now?"

Closing Grounding Practice (10 minutes)

"Feet on floor. [Pause.] Weight in chair. [Pause.] Look around the room. [Pause.] What you mapped today is not a flaw. It is a map. You cannot work with what you cannot see.

Zero-to-ten. One slightly slower breath."

Take-Home Reflection

Between sessions: when you notice the abandonment fear activating in real time, identify the earliest link you can access. One sentence: "The earliest link I noticed was ___."

Handout Reference

Handout 9A: My Abandonment Fear Chain (Appendix C, page C-10)

Session 10: Splitting: Idealization and Devaluation as Nervous System Patterns

Module: B: Understanding the BPD Pattern Map

Phase: Pattern Mapping

Session Number: 10 of 30

Session Overview

Session 10 addresses splitting: the alternation between idealization and devaluation that is among the most visible and most relationally damaging features of BPD presentations. The session reframes splitting from a moral or characterological failure to a specific nervous system response to relational threat, maps the developmental origins of the pattern, and gives clients the first vocabulary for observing it in themselves in real time. The session is the most relational of Module B and tends to produce live splitting dynamics in the group room during delivery.

Learning Objectives

By the end of Session 10, group members will be able to:

1. Describe splitting as a nervous system response to relational threat rather than as a character defect, connecting it to the abandonment fear chain from Session 9.

2. Identify the somatic and perceptual signs that typically precede an idealization or devaluation shift in their own experience.

3. Name at least one current or recent relationship in which the splitting pattern is most active.

4. Add the splitting layer to their developing BPD Pattern Map.

Time Allocation

Component	90-Minute Format	60-Minute Format
Opening Ritual and Check-In	10 min	10 min
Psychoeducation: Splitting as a Nervous System Response	25 min	20 min
Experiential: My Splitting Pattern	25 min	20 min
Group Processing	20 min	5 min
Closing Grounding	10 min	5 min

Materials and Preparation

- Group Agreement displayed or distributed

- Handout 10A: My Splitting Pattern Map (Appendix C, page C-11)

- Whiteboard: horizontal line. Left: IDEALIZATION ("all good"). Right: DEVALUATION ("all bad"). Arrow below pointing left and right: "Splitting moves rapidly between poles"

Facilitator Notes

Session 10 is the most relational session of Module B and requires the most careful preparation. Splitting is a live relational dynamic, not merely a historical pattern, and its description in group frequently produces its activation. Clients who are currently in an idealization phase with the facilitator may become defensive of the facilitator during the session. Clients who are in a devaluation phase may escalate or disengage during the delivery of content that is describing their own pattern. The facilitator's regulated, non-defensive presence throughout is the Relational Update principle in its most direct application.

The developmental explanation for splitting is clinically essential. Splitting as a cognitive defense, the explanation drawn from object relations theory, describes the mechanism but not the origin. The developmental explanation this curriculum uses is more clinically useful for the de-shaming reframe: a child who experienced a caregiver as unpredictably alternating between warmth and harm could not hold "sometimes safe and sometimes dangerous" as a coherent experience. The nervous system responded by separating the two states into non-overlapping categories: all good (safe) and all bad (dangerous). This categorization protected the child by providing clear threat-and-safety signals. In adulthood, the same categorical processing applies to people who are not actually all good or all bad, producing the idealization-devaluation cycle.

Live splitting in the group room is clinical data. If splitting appears in the session, between group members or directed at the facilitator, the clinical response names it without shaming and uses it as live illustration: "I notice something just happened in this room that might be an example of what we've been discussing. Let's look at it carefully."

Opening Ritual and Check-In (10 minutes)

"Feet on floor. [Pause.] Weight in chair. [Pause.] Three things you can see. [Pause.] Zero-to-ten check-in.

From the take-home: anyone who noticed the abandonment chain activating in real time this week. The earliest link they could identify."

[Receive one or two brief responses.]

Psychoeducation Component (25 minutes)

Talking Point 1: What splitting is and what it is not

"Splitting is not a moral failing. It is not evidence of cruelty or manipulation or an inability to see people accurately. It is a specific nervous system response to relational complexity that was adaptive in the developmental environment in which it formed.

Here is the developmental explanation. A child who grows up with a caregiver who is sometimes warm and available and sometimes cold, absent, or harmful has a specific cognitive challenge: how do you hold a person who is sometimes safe and sometimes dangerous as a single coherent object? The mature nervous system learns to hold complexity: people are mixed, relationships contain both positive and negative qualities, someone can disappoint you and still be worth keeping in your life.

A nervous system that developed under chronic relational unpredictability or harm cannot reliably build this complexity. Instead, it processes people in categorical terms: all good or all bad, idealized or devalued, completely safe or completely threatening. These categories are not deliberately constructed. They are the automatic output of a nervous system that learned to categorize rather than integrate, because integration required a tolerance for relational ambiguity that the developmental environment did not permit."

Talking Point 2: How splitting operates in adult relationships

"[Point to the whiteboard.] In adult relationships, splitting produces the specific pattern that many people with BPD recognize: the intensity of idealization, the specific quality of "this person is the one," the sense that the relationship is extraordinary and the person is perfectly attuned; followed, often without warning, by the collapse into devaluation: the sense that the person was never safe, that the idealization was foolish, that this person is now the source of all that is wrong.

The shift between poles is not arbitrary. It is triggered by the same abandonment cue from Session 9: a perceptual signal that the person is withdrawing, that safety is threatened, that the "all good" category no longer holds. The nervous system's categorical processing cannot accommodate partial safety. When the safety signal is interrupted, the category shifts.

The consequence for relationships is the pattern many people with BPD describe with significant shame: relationships that begin with extraordinary intensity and collapse into rupture in ways that feel to both parties as if the person they are in relationship with has been replaced by someone else. Which, from the mode perspective in Chapter 4, is partly accurate: the shift from Vulnerable Child reaching for the idealized other to Angry/Impulsive Child responding to perceived devaluation is a mode shift that changes how the person in the relationship is perceived and how the client relates to them."

Talking Point 3: The somatic signature of splitting

"One of the most clinically useful things to know about splitting is that it has a somatic signature, a physical pattern that appears before the shift in perception becomes conscious. Common somatic signs that a splitting shift is beginning include: a sudden change in the quality of warmth in the chest, a quality of cooling or hardening, a change in visual perception where details that were previously filtered out become suddenly prominent, and the specific sense of "something is wrong" that appears before the cognitive formulation of what is wrong.

These somatic signs, like the abandonment chain's somatic early warning signals, are the earliest accessible intervention point. A client who can detect the physical beginning of a splitting shift has a brief window in which Wise Mind is still available before the mode shift narrows the perceptual field."

Experiential Exercise: My Splitting Pattern (25 minutes)

[Distribute Handout 10A.]

"Take fifteen minutes to work through the Splitting Pattern Map. It asks you to identify three things.

First: a current or recent relationship in which the idealization-devaluation pattern has been most active. Not necessarily the most painful one. The most recognizable one.

Second: the specific cue that most reliably triggers the shift from idealization to devaluation. Is it a specific type of behavior from the other person? A specific type of relational absence? A specific mode activation in yourself?

Third: the somatic signature of the shift. What happens in your body when the splitting shift begins? Not what you think or feel. What your body does."

[After fifteen minutes:]

"Let's share. Specifically, the somatic signature. For anyone willing: what does the beginning of a splitting shift feel like in your body?"

Group Processing and Discussion (20 minutes)

1. "The developmental explanation: does it change how you understand your splitting pattern? Does it produce any different feeling about it than you had before?"

2. "Is there a relationship in your current life where you can identify which pole you are currently in, idealization or devaluation? What does it feel like to name that?"

3. "The somatic signature: did anyone find a physical sign they had not previously been able to identify? What did it feel like to locate it?"

4. "Zero-to-ten. Where are you now?"

Closing Grounding Practice (10 minutes)

"Feet on floor. [Pause.] Weight in chair. [Pause.] Look around the room. [Pause.] The splitting pattern was a reasonable response to an unreasonable relational environment. Today you added a layer to the map.

Zero-to-ten. One slightly slower breath."

Take-Home Reflection

Between sessions: notice once when the somatic signature of a splitting shift begins. Not to stop it. To notice it. One sentence: "The splitting shift started with ___."

Handout Reference

Handout 10A: My Splitting Pattern Map (Appendix C, page C-11)

Session 11: Identity Disturbance: Who Am I When the Emotions Change?

Module: B: Understanding the BPD Pattern Map

Phase: Pattern Mapping

Session Number: 11 of 30

Session Overview

Session 11 addresses identity disturbance: the chronic instability of self-image that is among the most defining and least discussed features of BPD presentations. The session connects identity instability to the developmental mechanism established in Sessions 2 and 5: a child whose emotional experience is consistently invalidated cannot develop the stable internal identity that a validating environment produces. The session gives clients language for the specific quality of not-knowing-who-I-am that the BPD presentation carries, and introduces the values-based identity direction that Module D will build.

Learning Objectives

By the end of Session 11, group members will be able to:

1. Define identity disturbance in their own words, connecting it to the biosocial theory and the ACE research from Module A.

2. Describe at least two specific manifestations of identity instability in their own experience, using the vocabulary the session provides.

3. Distinguish the mode-based understanding of identity shifts from the experience of "having no identity," naming the modes that produce the shifting rather than the absence.

4. Identify at least one value or quality that persists across mode states as a potential anchor for values-based identity work.

Time Allocation

Component	90-Minute Format	60-Minute Format
Opening Ritual and Check-In	10 min	10 min
Psychoeducation: Identity Disturbance and Its Origins	25 min	20 min
Experiential: My Identity Map	25 min	20 min
Group Processing	20 min	5 min
Closing Grounding	10 min	5 min

Materials and Preparation

- Group Agreement displayed or distributed

- Handout 11A: My Identity Map (Appendix C, page C-12)

- Whiteboard: IDENTITY DISTURBANCE = Unstable self-image + Shifting values and goals + Chronic sense of inner emptiness

Facilitator Notes

Identity disturbance is the most existentially activating topic in Module B. Where the abandonment fear and splitting sessions activate relational pain, the identity session activates something more fundamental: the specific quality of not knowing who you are, which is both more private and more distressing than most clients expect when they encounter it in a clinical context. The facilitator's tone in this session should be its most grounded and most warmly precise.

The mode-based reframe is the primary clinical contribution of Session 11. Many clients with BPD experience their identity instability as absence: "I have no self," "I don't know who I am," "I become whoever I need to be in each relationship." The mode-based reframe offers a different account: the experience of having no stable self is not the absence of a self. It is the experience of multiple mode-states that each carry a different implicit self-concept, shifting between them so rapidly and with so little internal witness that the experience is one of absence rather than multiplicity. What Module D builds is not a new identity. It is the Healthy Adult observer capacity that can hold all the modes and choose from values rather than from any single mode's implicit self-concept.

Opening Ritual and Check-In (10 minutes)

"Feet on floor. [Pause.] Weight in chair. [Pause.] Three things you can see. [Pause.] Zero-to-ten check-in.

From the take-home: anyone who noticed the somatic signature of a splitting shift this week. One sentence."

[Receive one or two brief responses.]

Psychoeducation Component (25 minutes)

Talking Point 1: What identity disturbance actually means

"The DSM-5 describes BPD as including 'identity disturbance, manifested as a markedly and persistently unstable self-image or sense of self.' That description is accurate and clinically insufficient.

What identity disturbance actually feels like, from the inside, is one of several things. Some people experience it as genuine absence: 'I don't have a self, I become who people need me to be.' Some experience it as instability: 'I am completely different with different people, and I don't know which one is the real me.' Some experience it as chronic inauthenticity: a sense that every version of themselves is performed rather than genuine. And some experience it as the specific quality of feeling real only in extreme emotional states: intensity, crisis, or the early period of a new relationship, and unreal in the ordinary, undramatic stretches of daily life.

All of these are identity disturbance. All of them have the same developmental explanation."

Talking Point 2: How adversity prevents stable identity formation

"Stable identity develops through a specific developmental process: the child has an emotional experience, the caregiver reflects it back accurately and with warmth, and the child gradually builds an internal record of 'this is what I feel, this is what it means, this is who I am in the world.' Over thousands of such interactions, the child develops a coherent sense of self that persists across emotional states.

In an invalidating environment, this process is disrupted at the reflection step. The emotional experience arrives. The caregiver communicates that the experience is wrong, excessive, or shameful. The child cannot build a reliable internal record because the record is being consistently overwritten by the caregiver's contradictory message. The result is what the DSM-5 describes as identity disturbance: not the absence of inner experience, but the absence of a coherent internal framework for interpreting and integrating that experience.

This is why emotional abuse, which attacks exactly this reflective process, shows the strongest association with BPD: it systematically disrupts the developmental mechanism through which identity forms."

Talking Point 3: The mode-based understanding of identity shifting

"The mode framework from Chapter 4 offers an account of identity disturbance that is more clinically specific than 'having no self.'

When the Vulnerable Child mode is active, the implicit self-concept is: I am someone who is in pain and in need of care, who is fundamentally alone, whose needs are too large for anyone to meet. When the Angry/Impulsive Child is active, the implicit self-concept is: I am someone who has been wronged and who will not tolerate being treated this way. When the Detached Protector is active, the implicit self-concept is: I am someone who does not need anyone and is fine. When the Punitive Parent is active, the implicit self-concept is: I am someone who deserves what they get.

These are not four different people. They are four mode-states, each carrying a different implicit self-concept, that shift rapidly enough that the experience from the inside is one of not having a coherent self at all. What Module D builds is the Healthy Adult observer who can hold all four modes, recognize each one as a historical emotional state rather than a final truth, and choose behavior from values that persist across mode shifts."

Experiential Exercise: My Identity Map (25 minutes)

[Distribute Handout 11A.]

"Take fifteen minutes with the Identity Map. It asks three things.

First: which of the four experiences of identity disturbance, absence, instability, inauthenticity, or reality only in extremity, is most recognizable to you? Describe it in your own language.

Second: using the mode framework, which mode-state carries the implicit self-concept that is most painful? What does that mode-state tell you about who you are?

Third: is there any quality, value, or characteristic that appears consistently across mode-states? Something that you recognize as your own regardless of which mode is active? Write whatever comes, including nothing."

[After fifteen minutes:]

"Let's share. The last question: is there anything that persists across the mode shifts? For anyone willing."

Group Processing and Discussion (20 minutes)

1. "The developmental explanation for identity disturbance: does it change how you understand the experience of not knowing who you are?"

2. "The mode-based reframe: the idea that identity disturbance is not absence of self but rapid mode-shifting. Does that fit your experience? What does it open up, if anything?"

3. "The question about what persists: what was it like to look for something consistent, and what did you find?"

4. "Zero-to-ten. Where are you now?"

Closing Grounding Practice (10 minutes)

"Feet on floor. [Pause.] Weight in chair. [Pause.] Look around the room. You are here, and you are the same person who arrived at this session. Whatever shifts in mode today, the person who showed up persists. [Pause.]

Zero-to-ten. One slightly slower breath."

Take-Home Reflection

Between sessions: when you notice a mode shift, ask one question: what does this mode-state tell me about who I am? Notice whether the answer feels like truth or like one mode's version of the truth.

Handout Reference

Handout 11A: My Identity Map (Appendix C, page C-12)

Session 12: Schema Modes in BPD: Mapping the Inner Cast

Module: B: Understanding the BPD Pattern Map

Phase: Pattern Mapping

Session Number: 12 of 30

Session Overview

Session 12 delivers the schema mode mapping exercise: the clinical translation of Chapter 4's theoretical framework into a personalized, specific map of each client's five BPD-relevant modes and how they organize behavior in the client's specific presentation. The session is the most clinically sophisticated exercise of Module B and requires facilitators to have read Chapter 4 carefully and to be familiar with all five modes before delivering the session.

Learning Objectives

By the end of Session 12, group members will be able to:

1. Name the five BPD-relevant schema modes and describe each in accessible, personal language rather than clinical terminology.

2. Identify which modes are most active in their own presentation and describe how each expresses itself in their behavior and self-concept.

3. Describe the developmental origin of at least two of their own active modes, connecting each to the adversity history identified in Sessions 2 and 5.

4. Add the schema mode layer to their developing BPD Pattern Map.

Time Allocation

Component	90-Minute Format	60-Minute Format
Opening Ritual and Check-In	10 min	10 min
Psychoeducation: The Five Modes in Your Presentation	25 min	20 min
Experiential: My Mode Map	30 min	25 min
Group Processing	15 min	5 min
Closing Grounding	10 min	5 min

Materials and Preparation

- Group Agreement displayed or distributed

- Handout 12A: My Mode Map (Appendix C, page C-13)

- Handout 12B: The Five BPD Modes in Plain Language (Appendix C, page C-14): reference card for the five modes in non-clinical, accessible descriptions

- Whiteboard: five columns. VULNERABLE CHILD | ANGRY/IMPULSIVE CHILD | DETACHED PROTECTOR | PUNITIVE PARENT | HEALTHY ADULT

Facilitator Notes

Session 12 activates mode states in the room. When the Punitive Parent mode is described, group members who carry a strong Punitive Parent will often show signs of Punitive Parent activation: self-attacking statements, minimization, withdrawal. When the Detached Protector mode is described, some group members will shift into visible Detached Protector activation: a quality of intellectual engagement combined with emotional flatness. The facilitator should name these activations with clinical warmth when they are clearly visible: "I notice something happening in the room right now. Let's check our windows before we continue."

Use accessible, non-clinical language throughout. Chapter 4 establishes the clinical vocabulary. Session 12's clinical task is translation: helping clients access mode awareness from the inside rather than defining it from the outside. The facilitator should avoid terms like "schema mode activation" or "object relations" in the group room. Use: "the part of you that is in pain," "the part that shuts down," "the part that judges you," "the part that is angry," and "the part that holds all of this with more perspective."

The Healthy Adult mode requires specific care in delivery. Some clients will experience the Healthy Adult description with skepticism or despair: "That's not something I've ever felt." The clinical response is not reassurance. It is accuracy: "The Healthy Adult mode is not something most people with BPD have had reliable access to. It is what treatment is building. The fact that it feels unfamiliar or inaccessible right now is information about where the work is, not about what you are capable of."

Opening Ritual and Check-In (10 minutes)

"Feet on floor. [Pause.] Weight in chair. [Pause.] Three things you can see. [Pause.] Zero-to-ten check-in. And one addition we are adding from today's session onward: one brief mode check. Which of the five modes feels most present right now, even if you do not yet have all the vocabulary? Just a first instinct."

[Receive brief check-ins. Do not elaborate or analyze. The mode check-in is a practice, not a diagnostic moment.]

Psychoeducation Component (25 minutes)

"[Point to the five columns. Deliver each mode in accessible, non-clinical language.]

The Vulnerable Child is the part of you that carries the original pain. The terror of being alone. The grief of what was never there. The longing for care and connection that the adversity history made genuinely difficult to find. When this part is running the room, you are in pain and reaching for care, often in ways that the people around you cannot fully meet.

The Angry/Impulsive Child is the part of you that holds the rage at what was done. The entitlement to have needs met that were never met. The urgency that acts before the thinking brain can catch up.

When this part is running the room, you are explosive or escalating or doing things before you've decided to do them.

The Detached Protector is the part of you that learned to survive by becoming unreachable. It is not indifference. It is the specific emotional distance that protected you when being emotionally present was genuinely dangerous. When this part is running the room, you are here but not fully here. Present but not available.

The Punitive Parent is the part of you that took the harsh, contemptuous, or dismissive voice of the adversity environment and turned it on yourself. When this part is running the room, you are telling yourself that you deserve what you have, that the pain is your fault, that you should not be struggling.

The Healthy Adult is what treatment is building: the part of you that can recognize all of the other modes, hold them with some compassion, and choose behavior from what you value rather than from what the mode demands. This is the goal. It is not where most people with BPD presentations are at the start of treatment, and its unfamiliarity is not evidence of its impossibility."

Experiential Exercise: My Mode Map (30 minutes)

[Distribute Handout 12A and 12B.]

"Take twenty minutes to build your Mode Map. Handout 12B gives you accessible descriptions of each mode. For each mode, I want you to do two things: identify how active this mode is in your own presentation, rating it one to three, and describe in one to two sentences how it specifically expresses itself in your behavior or self-concept.

For the two modes you rate highest, add one sentence about where in your developmental history this mode likely came from."

[After twenty minutes:]

"Let's share. Specifically, the mode you rated highest and one sentence about how it expresses itself. Not the full narrative. The most recognizable expression."

[Facilitate sharing. Receive each mode identification with clinical precision. After each: "That expression of the ___ mode is clearly visible in what you described. What does naming it as a mode rather than as who you are produce?"]

Group Processing and Discussion (15 minutes)

1. "What was it like to map the modes? Was there a mode you found easier to identify than expected, or harder?"

2. "The Detached Protector: for anyone who recognized it in themselves, what did naming it produce? Did it feel different from the other modes to identify?"

3. "The Healthy Adult: what is your response to it being the goal rather than where you currently are?"

4. "Zero-to-ten. Where are you now?"

Closing Grounding Practice (10 minutes)

"Feet on floor. [Pause.] Weight in chair. [Pause.] Look around the room. [Pause.] The modes you mapped today are not who you are. They are the internal cast that has been organizing how you experience yourself. Naming them is the beginning of being able to work with them from the outside.

Zero-to-ten. One slightly slower breath."

Take-Home Reflection

Between sessions, use the mode check-in once daily: which mode is most present right now? One sentence. Do not analyze. Just notice.

Handout Reference

Handout 12A: My Mode Map (Appendix C, page C-13)

Handout 12B: The Five BPD Modes in Plain Language (Appendix C, page C-14)

Session 13: The Impulsivity Chain: Understanding Urge-to-Act Sequences

Module: B: Understanding the BPD Pattern Map

Phase: Pattern Mapping

Session Number: 13 of 30

Session Overview

Session 13 maps the impulsivity chain: the specific urge-to-act sequence that the BPD nervous system produces before the prefrontal cortex can engage, connecting it to the mode activation and regulatory collapse sequence from Chapter 2. The session's clinical purpose is to give clients enough visibility into the impulsivity sequence that intervention becomes possible at the earliest accessible link rather than only at the behavioral endpoint.

Learning Objectives

By the end of Session 13, group members will be able to:

1. Describe the impulsivity chain in their own words, naming at least four of the five links and their sequence.

2. Map one personal impulsivity episode, identifying the specific mode that was active at link two and the somatic state at link three.

3. Identify at least one point in their personal chain where earlier-stage awareness might create an intervention opportunity.

4. Connect the impulsivity chain to the regulatory collapse sequence from Chapter 2 and name one specific regulatory practice that addresses the gap.

Time Allocation

Component	90-Minute Format	60-Minute Format
Opening Ritual and Check-In	10 min	10 min
Psychoeducation: The BPD Impulsivity Chain	25 min	20 min
Experiential: My Impulsivity Chain	30 min	25 min
Group Processing	15 min	5 min
Closing Grounding	10 min	5 min

Materials and Preparation

- Group Agreement displayed or distributed

- Handout 13A: My Impulsivity Chain (Appendix C, page C-15)

- Whiteboard: five-link chain. TRIGGER -> MODE ACTIVATION -> REGULATORY COLLAPSE -> URGE STATE -> IMPULSIVE ACTION

Facilitator Notes

The BPD impulsivity chain is distinct from the addiction trigger chain in Book 1. While the structural logic is similar, the BPD impulsivity chain has a BPD-specific second link: mode activation. In the addiction model, the trigger leads directly to a somatic state. In the BPD model, the trigger activates a mode, which produces a specific somatic and cognitive state organized by the mode's implicit self-concept and emotional logic. Facilitators who have also used Book 1 should make this distinction explicit when it is relevant.

The regulatory collapse link requires specific attention. The impulsivity of BPD is not primarily motivational. It is the specific behavioral expression of a nervous system operating above the Window of Tolerance with the prefrontal cortex partly offline. Framing impulsivity as regulatory collapse rather than as insufficient self-control is the de-shaming move that changes how clients understand their own behavior and how they approach the skills work that addresses it.

Opening Ritual and Check-In (10 minutes)

"Feet on floor. [Pause.] Weight in chair. [Pause.] Three things you can see. [Pause.] Zero-to-ten check-in. And mode check: one word for which mode is most present right now."

[Receive brief check-ins.]

Psychoeducation Component (25 minutes)

Talking Point 1: The impulsivity chain

"[Point to the chain.] The impulsivity of BPD is not primarily a problem of motivation or character. It is the specific output of a nervous system that, under specific conditions, reaches a behavioral decision point with the thinking brain partly offline. Understanding the five-link sequence makes this visible.

Link one is the trigger: the perceptual, relational, or somatic input that initiates the chain. Often a relational cue, connected to the abandonment chain from Session 9.

Link two is mode activation: the trigger activates one of the BPD modes from Session 12. Most commonly the Angry/Impulsive Child or the Vulnerable Child, which are the two modes with the highest behavioral urgency. The mode carries its own implicit self-concept and emotional logic, which organizes what happens next.

Link three is regulatory collapse: the mode's emotional urgency exceeds the nervous system's current regulatory capacity, moves the window above the tolerance threshold, and begins to take the prefrontal cortex offline. This is the point at which skills that are available inside the window become progressively less accessible.

Link four is the urge state: the specific quality of urgency and narrowed perception that the regulatory collapse produces. Time feels compressed. Options feel limited or absent. The urge to act feels immediate and necessary. This is not a decision. It is the output of a nervous system operating in regulatory crisis.

Link five is the impulsive action: the behavior that the urge state drives. Whatever the specific behavior, it has a regulatory function: it does something to the urge state that the nervous system cannot do any other way in that moment."

Talking Point 2: Where intervention is possible

"The reason mapping this chain matters is that intervention is possible at multiple links, and each earlier link offers more time and more prefrontal capacity than the later ones.

At link one, if the trigger is recognizable before it activates the mode, Wise Mind is still fully available.

At link two, if the mode activation can be identified, naming the mode creates the brief observational distance from which Module C's skills may still be accessible.

At link three, if the regulatory collapse is caught early, grounding practices can interrupt the window exceedance before the prefrontal cortex is significantly offline.

At link four, the urge state itself, very few interventions are reliably available. The thinking brain has largely exited. Distress tolerance skills from Module C, specifically the TIPP skill, work at this link by directly addressing the physiological state.

At link five, after the action, the clinical work is not prevention but self-compassion and analysis: understanding what the action was doing for the nervous system, and what alternative the Pattern Map and Module C's skills can offer next time."

Experiential Exercise: My Impulsivity Chain (30 minutes)

[Distribute Handout 13A.]

"Take fifteen minutes to map one impulsivity episode, working backward from link five.

You know the action. Write it. Now: what was the urge state before the action? What did the urgency feel like, specifically, in your body? What mode was most active at that point? What triggered the mode? Can you identify the perceptual or relational trigger that initiated the chain?

Leave blank what you cannot access. The blank spaces are the earliest links running below conscious awareness."

[After fifteen minutes, facilitate sharing:]

"For anyone willing: what mode was active at link two, and what was the urge state like at link four?"

Group Processing and Discussion (15 minutes)

1. "The regulatory collapse framing: does it change how you understand the impulsivity? What is different about seeing it as a nervous system process rather than a motivation or character issue?"

2. "What is the earliest link in the chain you were able to identify? And what would it mean for your recovery to be able to intervene at that link?"

3. "Zero-to-ten. Where are you now?"

Closing Grounding Practice (10 minutes)

"Feet on floor. [Pause.] Weight in chair. [Pause.] Look around the room. [Pause.] One slightly slower breath. Zero-to-ten."

Take-Home Reflection

Between sessions: when you notice an impulsivity episode, identify the mode that was most active. One sentence: "The mode at link two was ___."

Handout Reference

Handout 13A: My Impulsivity Chain (Appendix C, page C-15)

Session 14: Self-Harm as Communication and Regulation: A Trauma-Informed View

Module: B: Understanding the BPD Pattern Map

Phase: Pattern Mapping

Session Number: 14 of 30

Session Overview

Session 14 is the most clinically sensitive session of the entire curriculum. It addresses self-harm directly: not as the behavior to be eliminated, which standard treatment addresses, but as the specific communicative and regulatory function it serves in the BPD presentation, from a trauma-informed frame that removes shame without removing clinical accountability. This session is where the de-shaming work of the curriculum's entire first two modules meets its most clinically significant application.

Learning Objectives

By the end of Session 14, group members will be able to:

1. Distinguish non-suicidal self-injury from suicidal behavior in their own words, using the clinical distinction the session provides.

2. Name at least two specific functions that self-harm serves for their nervous system, using regulatory and communicative language.

3. Identify the self-harm episode's position in the impulsivity chain from Session 13, naming the mode active and the regulatory state present.

4. Name at least one alternative regulatory resource that addresses the same function as the self-harm, and describe the barriers to accessing it.

Time Allocation

Component	90-Minute Format	60-Minute Format
Opening Ritual and Check-In	10 min	10 min
Psychoeducation: Self-Harm as Function	25 min	20 min
Experiential: My Self-Harm Function Map	25 min	20 min
Group Processing	20 min	5 min
Closing Grounding (extended)	10 min	5 min

Materials and Preparation

- Group Agreement displayed or distributed; individual therapist contacts confirmed before session

- Handout 14A: My Self-Harm Function Map (Appendix C, page C-16)

- Review the program's self-harm protocol and crisis pathway before this session

- Pre-session regulatory check: facilitators should complete a full self-regulatory assessment before entering the room for Session 14

- No content in this session involves graphic descriptions of self-harm methods; the group disclosure limit from Session 1 applies in full

Facilitator Notes

Session 14 is a required reading session for clinical supervisors. Before any facilitator delivers Session 14 independently, the clinical supervisor should have reviewed the session plan, confirmed the facilitator's readiness, and confirmed the individual crisis pathway that is available during and after this session.

The clinical distinction between NSSI and suicidal behavior must be delivered precisely and then held across the rest of the session. Non-suicidal self-injury is behavior that produces physical harm without suicidal intent, most commonly functioning as a regulatory strategy or a form of communication. Suicidal behavior involves intent to die. In BPD populations, both occur, and the clinical response to each is different. The facilitator must be clear: "We are discussing NSSI today, not suicidal behavior. If anything that comes up in or after this session involves thoughts of ending your life, that is a different clinical conversation that needs to happen individually and immediately."

The group disclosure limit is most critical in Session 14. No group member shares specific methods, severity, or frequency of self-harm in the group setting. The session is about function and meaning, not content.

Opening Ritual and Check-In (10 minutes)

"Feet on floor. [Pause.] Weight in chair. [Pause.] Three things you can see. [Pause.] Zero-to-ten check-in. Mode check: one word.

Today's session addresses self-harm directly. I want to name that before we begin. The session is about what self-harm does for the nervous system, not the specific details of what, how, or how often. The group's disclosure limit from Session 1 applies in full today: no graphic content.

If anything that comes up in or after today's session involves thoughts of ending your life, I need to know about it. That is a different conversation that happens individually.

I am also asking you to check in with your window throughout this session. If your number goes above seven, tell me."

Psychoeducation Component (25 minutes)

Talking Point 1: The clinical distinction

"Non-suicidal self-injury, NSSI, is behavior that produces physical harm to the body without the intent to die. It is one of the most consistent features of BPD presentations: research suggests between 69 and

80 percent of individuals with BPD engage in NSSI at some point. Suicidal behavior, including suicidal ideation with intent, plan, or means, is different in kind and requires a different clinical response.

This distinction matters not because NSSI is less serious than suicidal behavior but because conflating them prevents the clinical examination of what NSSI is actually doing for the nervous system that produces it. If NSSI is treated only as a behavior to be stopped, the regulatory and communicative functions it serves are left unaddressed, and the nervous system reaches for the next most reliable tool it has, which is often the same behavior."

Talking Point 2: What self-harm does

"Research and clinical observation consistently identify several specific functions that NSSI serves for the nervous systems that use it.

The regulatory function is the most consistent: NSSI produces a rapid shift in autonomic state. The specific mechanism varies by the type of NSSI, but the common outcome is a shift away from the flooding or emptiness that preceded the behavior toward a state that feels more manageable. For nervous systems in regulatory crisis, at link four of the impulsivity chain, NSSI works, in the narrow, immediate, regulatory sense of doing something to the state that could not otherwise be addressed.

The communicative function is equally common: NSSI communicates to others, and sometimes to the self, what verbal communication has not been able to convey. For clients whose emotional expression was chronically invalidated in development, the body's evidence may feel like the only communication that will be taken seriously. 'I tried to tell you I was in pain. You didn't hear. Now you can see it.'

The dissociation regulation function appears in presentations where NSSI is used to interrupt dissociative or hypoarousal states: the physical sensation grounds the person in their body, interrupts the flatness of the Detached Protector mode, and produces presence where there was absence.

The self-punishment function reflects the Punitive Parent mode: NSSI as the enactment of the belief that pain is deserved. This function carries the most shame and the most direct connection to the adversity history, as it is frequently the internalized voice of the abusive or invalidating environment turned against the self."

Talking Point 3: The cost and the clinical task

"Understanding the function of self-harm is not the same as endorsing it. The behavior has real costs: physical health consequences, the shame cycle it produces, the impact on relationships, and the clinical risk of escalation.

The clinical task is specific: understand the function, find what it provides that the nervous system cannot otherwise access, and build an alternative that addresses the same regulatory or communicative need without the harm. That building is part of Module C's distress tolerance work and Module D's identity and relational work. Today's session maps the function. Module C builds the alternative."

Experiential Exercise: My Self-Harm Function Map (25 minutes)

[Distribute Handout 14A.]

"Take fifteen minutes with the Function Map. It asks you to identify the function of self-harm in your own presentation using the four categories from the psychoeducation: regulatory, communicative, dissociation-interrupting, or self-punishing. More than one function may apply.

For each function you identify: describe in general terms what the behavior does for your nervous system. Not the specific behavior. What state it produces, and what state it is responding to.

For each function, identify one alternative that might address the same need. Even if the alternative is not reliably available yet. Even if it seems insufficient. Write what comes."

[After fifteen minutes:]

"Let's share, carefully. Not the behavior and not the specific details. One function and one alternative you identified, however tentative."

[Facilitate sharing. Receive each function identification with clinical acknowledgment. After each: "That function is real. It has been the best tool available for what it addresses. The work ahead is building something that does the same job with less cost."]

Group Processing and Discussion (20 minutes)

1. "The functional framing: does it change how you hold the behavior? What, if anything, does naming the function as real produce?"

2. "The communicative function: for anyone who recognized it, what have you been trying to communicate that other forms of communication have not reached?"

3. "The alternative you identified: what makes it hard to access in the moment when the function is most needed?"

4. "Zero-to-ten. Check carefully today. If anyone is above seven, name it."

Closing Grounding Practice (extended, 10 minutes)

"This session asked you to look at something that carries a great deal of shame. You looked at it from the inside, with enough compassion to see what it was doing rather than only judging that it happened.

Feet on floor. [Pause, fifteen seconds.] Feel the full weight of your body in the chair. [Pause.] Look around the room. Notice the people in it. [Pause.]

Individual follow-up is available this week for anyone who wants it. I will reach out.

Zero-to-ten. One slightly slower breath."

Take-Home Reflection

Between sessions: when an urge to self-harm arrives, practice one thing: identify the function. Not to stop the urge or to act on it. Just name what the urge is trying to do for your nervous system. One sentence: "The urge is trying to ___."

Handout Reference

Handout 14A: My Self-Harm Function Map (Appendix C, page C-16)

Session 15: Chronic Emptiness: The Phenomenology and the ACE Connection

Module: B: Understanding the BPD Pattern Map

Phase: Pattern Mapping

Session Number: 15 of 30

Session Overview

Session 15 addresses chronic emptiness: the specific phenomenological quality of inner hollowness, deadness, or absence that is among the most consistently reported and least clinically addressed features of BPD presentations. The session connects chronic emptiness to the emotional neglect history identified in Session 5, frames it as the developmental outcome of a nervous system that never reliably experienced the emotional attunement that fills the specific inner space emptiness describes, and begins the bridge to Module C's emotion regulation work.

Learning Objectives

By the end of Session 15, group members will be able to:

1. Describe the phenomenology of chronic emptiness in their own words, distinguishing it from depression, dissociation, and boredom.

2. Connect chronic emptiness to the emotional neglect history identified in their ACE profile, using the attunement-deprivation framework the session provides.

3. Name at least two behaviors or substances that they use to manage chronic emptiness and identify the specific quality of relief each provides.

4. Add the chronic emptiness layer to their developing BPD Pattern Map.

Time Allocation

Component	90-Minute Format	60-Minute Format
Opening Ritual and Check-In	10 min	10 min
Psychoeducation: What Chronic Emptiness Is	25 min	20 min
Experiential: Mapping the Emptiness	25 min	20 min
Group Processing	20 min	5 min
Closing Grounding	10 min	5 min

Materials and Preparation

- Group Agreement displayed or distributed; individual therapist contacts confirmed

- Handout 15A: Mapping My Chronic Emptiness (Appendix C, page C-17)

- Coordinate with individual therapists before this session

Facilitator Notes

Chronic emptiness is the most existentially activating topic in Module B after identity disturbance. Where Session 11 activated the grief of not knowing who you are, Session 15 activates the specific grief of the inner space that attunement was never able to fill. The facilitator's tone should be warmest and most grounded in this session.

Distinguish chronic emptiness from depression and dissociation. Many clients conflate them. Depression involves affective content: sadness, hopelessness, guilt. Hypoarousal involves deactivation: flatness, numbness, reduced responsiveness. Chronic emptiness is a specific phenomenological quality that many clients describe as the absence of inner substance: "There is nothing inside me," "I feel hollow," "I am a shell." It is not the absence of feeling. It is the absence of the specific internal richness that consistent emotional attunement produces during development.

The ACE connection to emotional neglect is the primary clinical contribution. Session 5 established that emotional neglect is the second strongest ACE predictor of BPD after emotional abuse. Session 15 explains why: the specific inner quality of being emotionally attended to, of having one's emotional experience reflected and valued by a caregiver, is the developmental mechanism through which the inner sense of self and the feeling of inner substance develop. Chronic neglect of that emotional experience produces the chronic emptiness that the BPD diagnostic criteria describe.

Opening Ritual and Check-In (10 minutes)

"Feet on floor. [Pause.] Weight in chair. [Pause.] Three things you can see. [Pause.] Zero-to-ten check-in. Mode check: one word.

From the take-home: anyone who noticed the function of a self-harm urge this week. One sentence, no content."

[Receive one brief response only.]

Psychoeducation Component (25 minutes)

Talking Point 1: What chronic emptiness actually is

"The DSM-5 criteria for BPD include 'chronic feelings of emptiness.' That criterion is among the most consistently reported by people with BPD and among the least clinically elaborated. Let me try to describe it more precisely.

Chronic emptiness is not depression. Depression has affective content: sadness, hopelessness, a sense of negative weight. Emptiness has the opposite texture: absence rather than negative presence, hollowness rather than heaviness, the sense of there being nothing inside where something should be.

Chronic emptiness is also distinct from dissociation or hypoarousal, though they can co-occur. Hypoarousal involves deactivation: the nervous system is flat. Emptiness involves a specific phenomenological quality that is often present even when the nervous system is not flat: the sense of inner hollowness that persists across emotional and arousal states.

The descriptions clients use most often are: 'There is nothing inside me.' 'I feel like a shell.' 'Other people seem to have something in them that I do not have.' 'When I am alone and not doing anything, there is this ___. I don't know what to call it. It is not nothing, but it is less than what other people describe.'"

Talking Point 2: The developmental explanation

"The developmental mechanism of chronic emptiness connects directly to the emotional neglect in the ACE framework.

When a child's emotional experience is consistently attended to, when the caregiver notices and reflects it with accuracy and warmth, the child gradually builds an internal world that has richness and substance: the felt sense of being known, of being seen, of having inner experience that matters. Over thousands of attunement moments, the child builds the specific inner quality that chronic emptiness is the absence of.

When emotional experience is consistently neglected, when the child's inner world is not noticed, not reflected, not considered, the developmental building process is interrupted. The child grows up with a nervous system that has the full range of emotional experience and without the inner sense of substance that attunement was supposed to produce. The emptiness is not a deficiency of emotion. It is the specific absence of the built structure that attunement would have created.

Emotional neglect shows the second strongest independent association with BPD of any ACE type. The chronic emptiness of BPD is, in this understanding, among the most direct developmental outcomes of what emotional neglect produces."

Talking Point 3: What emptiness drives

"Chronic emptiness drives behavior in two specific patterns that Module B's map should capture.

The first is filling: the use of substances, relationships, food, activity, or intensity to fill the inner space with something. The relief provided is real and temporary: whatever fills the emptiness provides the quality of inner substance that attunement never produced, briefly and artificially. The relief ends, the emptiness returns, and the filling behavior escalates.

The second is activation: the use of crisis, intensity, extreme emotion, or self-harm to feel something rather than nothing. For clients whose chronic emptiness co-occurs with dissociation or hypoarousal, activation behaviors serve a specific function: they produce the felt sense of being alive, present, and real that the emptiness state eliminates. The relief of feeling pain or anger or terror is preferable, for this nervous system, to the specific deadness of chronic emptiness."

Experiential Exercise: Mapping the Emptiness (25 minutes)

[Distribute Handout 15A.]

"Take fifteen minutes with the Emptiness Map. Three questions.

First: describe the quality of your chronic emptiness in your own language. Not the emotion words. The phenomenological texture. What does it feel like from the inside? Where does it live in your body, if it has a location?

Second: what do you use to fill it or to escape it? Not with judgment. With accuracy. At least two things.

Third: connect it to your history. When did you first notice this quality? And does the emotional neglect connection, the idea that attunement would have filled what is now absent, fit your experience?"

[After fifteen minutes:]

"Let's share carefully. One element from the map: the description of the emptiness's texture, or the connection to your history, or what you use to fill it. Whatever feels most accessible today."

Group Processing and Discussion (20 minutes)

1. "The distinction from depression and dissociation: does the specific phenomenological description of emptiness fit your experience? What does having that description do?"

2. "The attunement explanation: does it connect to your history? What is it like to understand the emptiness as the absence of something that was never provided, rather than as a deficiency in who you are?"

3. "The filling and activation behaviors: what does it feel like to see those behaviors as responses to the emptiness rather than as separate problems?"

4. "Zero-to-ten. Where are you now?"

Closing Grounding Practice (10 minutes)

"Feet on floor. [Pause.] Weight in chair. [Pause.] Look around the room. [Pause.] You are present in this room right now. Whatever the emptiness contains, the presence is also real.

Zero-to-ten. One slightly slower breath."

Take-Home Reflection

Between sessions, when you notice the emptiness, sit with it for thirty seconds without filling it or escaping it. Not to resolve it. To notice what it actually feels like from the inside, without the layer of behavior that usually follows it immediately.

Handout Reference

Handout 15A: Mapping My Chronic Emptiness (Appendix C, page C-17)

Session 16: Module B Review: My BPD Pattern Map

Module: B: Understanding the BPD Pattern Map

Phase: Integration and Transition

Session Number: 16 of 30

Session Overview

Session 16 is an integration and transition session: reviewing the seven layers of the BPD Pattern Map, completing the Pattern Map document, and preparing the group for Module C's DBT skills training through a trauma-informed lens. The session's tone shifts from pattern mapping to pattern integration: the clinical work is not new psychoeducation but the synthesis of seven sessions of visibility work into the most precise description of the BPD presentation's organization that any prior treatment has produced.

Learning Objectives

By the end of Session 16, group members will be able to:

1. Complete the BPD Pattern Map with specific entries in all seven layers.

2. Identify two or three patterns that appear consistently across multiple layers of their map, naming these cross-layer patterns as the primary targets for Module C's skills work.

3. Describe in their own words what changed in their self-understanding between Session 9 and Session 16.

4. Articulate what Module C will ask of them and why Module B's visibility work was necessary before Module C's skills training can be fully received.

Time Allocation

Component	90-Minute Format	60-Minute Format
Opening Ritual and Check-In	10 min	10 min
Module B Seven-Layer Review	15 min	10 min
BPD Pattern Map Completion	35 min	30 min
Group Processing: Module B Reflections	20 min	5 min
Closing Ritual: Looking Ahead to Module C	10 min	5 min

Materials and Preparation

- All Module B handouts available for reference

- Handout 16A: My BPD Pattern Map (Appendix C, page C-18)

- Whiteboard: list all seven layers before the session

- Coordinate with individual therapists before this session: the Pattern Map is the most clinically significant document clients produce in this curriculum and should be shared with the individual therapist, with client consent, before Module C begins

Facilitator Notes

Session 16 is the clinical culmination of Module B. The Pattern Map should receive the full thirty-five minutes allocated. Clients who do not complete it in session should complete it in individual therapy before Session 17 with support. The map is not a paperwork requirement. It is the clinical picture that determines which Module C skills are most immediately relevant to each client's specific BPD pattern organization.

The cross-layer patterns are the most important clinical product of Session 16. An abandonment fear that activates the Angry/Impulsive Child mode, drives the impulsivity chain, produces self-harm as its regulatory endpoint, and fills into the chronic emptiness that remains afterward, is a cross-layer pattern running at every level of the map simultaneously. Identifying these integrated patterns is what turns seven separate observations into a clinically unified picture of how the BPD presentation is organized.

The Module C preview is a clinical invitation. Clients who understand why the four DBT skill modules are delivered with the ACE-informed, mode-aware, somatic foundation of Modules A and B arrive at Module C significantly more able to receive the skills as clinically targeted rather than generically applied.

Opening Ritual and Check-In (10 minutes)

"Feet on floor. [Pause.] Weight in chair. [Pause.] Three things you can see. [Pause.] Zero-to-ten check-in. Mode check.

This is our sixteenth session together and the last session of Module B. Before we begin, one sentence from everyone.

What is one thing you know now about the patterns organizing your BPD that you did not have language for before Module B began?"

[Go around the room. Every member answers. Receive each with warmth and minimal elaboration. These sentences are the module review.]

Module B Seven-Layer Review (15 minutes)

"[Point to the seven layers.] Module B has mapped seven specific layers of the BPD presentation.

The abandonment chain: the five-link sequence from perceptual cue through somatic state through emotional activation through behavioral response through consequence, and the developmental calibration that makes the abandonment fear activate at low relational thresholds.

The splitting pattern: idealization and devaluation as the nervous system's categorical processing of relational complexity, driven by the abandonment chain and organized by mode activation.

The identity disturbance: the chronic instability of self-image as the developmental outcome of insufficient attunement during identity formation, expressed as the rapid mode-state shifts that produce the experience of having no stable self.

The schema modes: the five internal states, Vulnerable Child, Angry/Impulsive Child, Detached Protector, Punitive Parent, and Healthy Adult, that organize perception, self-concept, and behavior before conscious decision.

The impulsivity chain: the five-link urge-to-act sequence from trigger through mode activation through regulatory collapse through urge state through impulsive action.

The self-harm function: the communicative and regulatory functions of NSSI in the specific BPD presentation, mapped without shame and with clinical specificity about what the behavior is addressing.

The chronic emptiness: the phenomenological quality of inner hollowness produced by developmental emotional neglect, and the filling and activation behaviors it drives.

Seven layers. One map."

BPD Pattern Map Completion (35 minutes)

[Distribute Handout 16A.]

"Take thirty minutes to complete the BPD Pattern Map. Use all seven of your Module B handouts as reference. The map asks two things.

First: enter the key finding from each of the seven layers. Not everything you wrote in each handout. The most essential, most recognizable insight from each layer.

Second: identify two or three cross-layer patterns, things that appear in more than one layer simultaneously. An abandonment fear that drives the Angry/Impulsive Child mode that fuels the impulsivity chain that ends in self-harm is a cross-layer pattern. These integrated patterns are the primary targets for Module C.

This document belongs to you. It is not for anyone else unless you choose to share it."

[After thirty minutes, invite brief sharing:]

"For anyone willing: one cross-layer pattern you identified. The thing that appears in more than one layer of your map."

Group Processing: Module B Reflections (20 minutes)

1. "What is the most significant thing you have seen clearly in Module B that you had not seen before?"

2. "What has been the hardest thing to look at?"

3. "Looking at the Pattern Map as a whole: what does it tell you about why skills training alone, without this map, may not have fully reached the patterns your BPD is organized around?"

4. "What are you most uncertain about as we move into Module C?"

Closing Ritual: Looking Ahead to Module C (10 minutes)

"In Module C, which begins in our next session, we deliver the four DBT skill modules, the same skills that Marsha Linehan developed and that are the evidence-based core of BPD treatment.

But we deliver them with the Pattern Map you just completed as the clinical context. When we practice mindfulness in Sessions 17 and 18, you will know which mode is most active in the moment of practice. When we practice distress tolerance in Sessions 19 and 20, you will know which link of the impulsivity chain the skills are designed to interrupt. When we practice emotion regulation in Sessions 21 and 22, you will know which specific regulatory collapse sequence the skills are designed to address. When we practice interpersonal effectiveness in Sessions 23 and 24, you will know which relational template and which mode state the skills need to reach.

Module B made the map. Module C builds the skills. They are not the same work. But Module C's skills are more precisely targeted because Module B made the map first.

Feet on floor. [Pause.] Weight in chair. [Pause.] Look around the room. These people built this map with you. [Pause.] Zero-to-ten. One slightly slower breath. See you in Module C."

Take-Home Reflection

Between Module B and Module C: read your BPD Pattern Map once. Let it settle. Notice what it feels like to see your own patterns laid out clearly, without judgment, as a map rather than as an indictment. Whatever arises in response to that reading, bring it to Session 17.

Handout Reference

Handout 16A: My BPD Pattern Map (Appendix C, page C-18)

Module C: DBT Skills Through a Trauma Lens

Sessions 17 through 24 | Clinical Focus: The four DBT skill modules delivered with the ACE-informed, mode-aware, somatic architecture of Modules A and B as the targeting framework

Chapter 9.0: The Skills That the Map Makes Possible

The question Module C answers is not "which DBT skills do clients with BPD need?" That question has been answered by Marsha Linehan's foundational work across four decades of research. The four DBT skill modules, Core Mindfulness, Distress Tolerance, Emotion Regulation, and Interpersonal Effectiveness, are the evidence-based answer to that question, and Module C delivers them in their standard form.

The question Module C specifically answers is different: how do the DBT skills become genuinely accessible for clients whose adversity history has made the exact conditions required to use them the conditions most likely to be unavailable? A client whose window narrows sharply in the presence of relational threat cannot reliably access distress tolerance skills when relational threat is the trigger. A client whose Detached Protector mode activates under stress cannot observe their emotions nonjudgmentally because the mode exists to make emotional observation unavailable. A client whose nervous system learned that trusting internal experience leads to invalidation cannot practice checking the facts because the facts feel unreliable.

Module C addresses those specific access barriers by delivering each skill with three components that standard DBT training does not systematically include: the skill's relationship to the Window of Tolerance (when is it accessible and when is it not); the mode state most likely to block the skill (and the facilitation response that addresses the block); and the specific ACE-informed explanation for why the skill is difficult for this nervous system and why that difficulty is understandable rather than evidence of insufficient motivation.

9.1 The Module C Architecture

Module C spans Sessions 17 through 24, delivering the four DBT skill modules across two sessions each. The sequence mirrors Linehan's (2015) recommended sequencing: Mindfulness is foundational and therefore first, supporting all subsequent skills. Distress Tolerance provides the crisis survival layer for the high-activation states that Module B's pattern recognition work revealed. Emotion Regulation builds the longer-arc regulatory infrastructure. Interpersonal Effectiveness integrates the relational work that the Pattern Map's abandonment chain and splitting layer demand.

Each skill is delivered in the group with its Pattern Map connection made explicit. The facilitator does not merely teach the skill. They connect it to the map: "This is the TIPP skill. It addresses link three of the impulsivity chain, the regulatory collapse, by directly shifting the physiological state before the prefrontal cortex is fully offline. Look at your Pattern Map: where does regulatory collapse appear in your seven layers? That is where TIPP works."

That targeting move, Pattern Map to skill application, is the Module C clinical contribution that standard DBT training does not routinely provide.

9.2 The Regulatory Prerequisite Check Before Every Module C Session

Every Module C session begins with the opening ritual and the zero-to-ten check-in, as established in Module A. In Module C, this check-in carries a specific clinical decision: if the collective group window is above seven, the facilitator begins with somatic regulation rather than skills instruction.

This is not an optional adaptation. DBT skills require the prefrontal cortex, and the prefrontal cortex requires the window. A group that is above the window collectively cannot receive skills training with genuine access. The regulatory check before content is the clinical act that makes Module C skills delivery genuine rather than performative.

Session 17: Core Mindfulness I: What, How, and Why the Trauma-Affected Mind Resists It

Module: C: DBT Skills Through a Trauma Lens

Phase: DBT Skill Delivery: Core Mindfulness

Session Number: 17 of 30

Session Overview

Session 17 delivers the Core Mindfulness "What" skills, Observe, Describe, and Participate, within the specific clinical context that Module B established for each client. The session explicitly addresses why mindfulness is difficult for trauma-affected and BPD presentations rather than assuming that the difficulty reflects insufficient practice, framing the resistance as neurobiologically understandable and clinically addressable.

Learning Objectives

By the end of Session 17, group members will be able to:

1. Define the three "What" mindfulness skills (Observe, Describe, Participate) in their own words and describe the specific function of each.

2. Identify which of the three skills is most difficult to access in their BPD presentation, connecting the difficulty to a specific mode state or Pattern Map layer.

3. Complete a brief Observe practice and describe one thing they noticed, including whether any resistance arose and what it felt like.

4. Name the specific ACE-related mechanism that makes mindfulness access difficult for their nervous system and articulate why that difficulty is not evidence of inadequate effort.

Time Allocation

Component	90-Minute Format	60-Minute Format
Opening Ritual, Check-In, and Regulatory Assessment	12 min	12 min
Module C Orientation	8 min	5 min
Psychoeducation: Why Trauma-Affected Minds Resist Mindfulness	20 min	15 min
Experiential: The Three What Skills	30 min	20 min
Group Processing	10 min	5 min
Closing Grounding	10 min	3 min

Materials and Preparation

- Group Agreement displayed; BPD Pattern Maps available for client reference

- Handout 17A: Core Mindfulness: The What Skills (Appendix C, page C-19)

- Whiteboard: OBSERVE | DESCRIBE | PARTICIPATE

- Pre-session regulatory check: facilitators must complete their own window assessment before delivering mindfulness content to a BPD group. A facilitator above the window teaching mindfulness is a clinical contradiction.

Facilitator Notes

Module C orientation takes five to eight minutes at the start of Session 17. Explicitly bridge from Module B: "Module B made the map. Module C builds the skills. Every skill we deliver in the next eight sessions has a specific location on your Pattern Map. I will tell you that location at the start of each skill."

The three specific barriers to mindfulness in BPD presentations. First: the Detached Protector mode. Mindfulness requires gentle, nonjudgmental observation of internal experience. The Detached Protector's function is to make internal experience unavailable. When the Detached Protector is active, Observe produces nothing, and clients experience this as failure or further evidence of emptiness. The clinical response: "The nothing you find is the Detached Protector protecting you. That mode has a history and a function. It can be addressed." Second: the hypervigilant amygdala. Mindfulness asks the client to turn attention inward. For a nervous system trained to monitor the external relational environment for threat, turning attention inward feels both counterintuitive and unsafe. Third: the invalidation history. Being asked to observe internal experience nonjudgmentally runs directly against the internalized message from the adversity environment that internal experience is untrustworthy. The facilitator must name this directly.

Opening Ritual, Check-In, and Regulatory Assessment (12 minutes)

"Feet on floor. [Pause.] Weight in chair. [Pause.] Three things you can see. [Pause.] Zero-to-ten check-in. Mode check: one word.

Before we begin Module C, I need a collective window check. If anyone is above seven right now, say so. [Pause.] If the collective window is above seven, we ground before we continue.

[If window is within range:] Module B made the map. Today, Module C begins building the skills. Every skill connects to your Pattern Map, and I will make that connection explicit before each skill. Welcome to Module C."

Psychoeducation Component (20 minutes)

Talking Point 1: Mindfulness in DBT

"Core Mindfulness is the first skill module in DBT because it is foundational to every other skill. Marsha Linehan describes it as the skill that makes all other skills possible, because without the capacity to observe your own experience, you cannot detect when you need a distress tolerance skill, identify which emotion you are regulating, or notice what is happening in an interpersonal interaction before you respond.

The three What skills are Observe, Describe, and Participate. Observe means noticing what is present in your experience, sensorially and emotionally, without evaluating or modifying it. Describe means putting words on what you observe, applying language to internal experience without adding interpretation. Participate means engaging fully in what you are doing, fully present without self-conscious observation standing between you and the experience.

These three skills address your Pattern Map at Session 4's Wise Mind level: they are the practices through which the internal observational capacity that Wise Mind requires becomes reliable."

Talking Point 2: Why the trauma-affected mind resists mindfulness

"Mindfulness is specifically difficult for nervous systems shaped by the adversity histories in this room, and I want to name that directly rather than let the difficulty become evidence of failure.

The first barrier is the Detached Protector mode. Observe asks you to notice internal experience. The Detached Protector's entire function is to make internal experience unavailable. When you practice Observe and find nothing, or find a quality of flatness rather than actual observation, you are most likely in the Detached Protector. The mode is doing its job. The clinical task is not to force observation through the protection, but to address the protection with enough warmth that it gradually becomes less necessary.

The second barrier is the nervous system's trained threat monitoring. Your amygdala, calibrated as Chapter 2 described to monitor the external relational environment for threat signals, finds turning attention inward counterintuitive and, at the nervous system level, briefly unsafe. The external environment goes unwatched during inward attention, which the threat detection system registers as a vulnerability. This is not a flaw in your practice. It is accurate reporting from a nervous system doing exactly what it was trained to do.

The third barrier is the invalidation history directly. Observe asks you to notice your experience and trust that what you notice is real and worth noticing. Session 2's biosocial theory named exactly the developmental mechanism that makes this difficult: your environment taught you that your internal experience was wrong or untrustworthy. Being asked to observe it nonjudgmentally runs against a lesson learned across thousands of interactions. The difficulty is not evidence of insufficient effort. It is evidence of how thoroughly the adversity did its work."

Experiential Exercise: The Three What Skills (30 minutes)

[Distribute Handout 17A.]

"We are going to practice each of the three What skills briefly, and then connect each to your Pattern Map.

[OBSERVE, 5 minutes:] Eyes open or gently closed. For the next two minutes, practice Observe. Notice one thing in your sensory experience, something you can see, hear, feel, or sense in your body, without labeling it, evaluating it, or modifying it. Just noticing it as a phenomenon present in your experience. If your mind evaluates or wanders, notice that too. [Pause 2 minutes.] What did you observe? And what resistance, if any, arose?

[DESCRIBE, 5 minutes:] Now Describe. Take one observation from the Observe practice and put words on it. Not a story about it. Just a description: 'There is a sensation in my chest that I would describe as tight.' 'There is a thought present that sounds like concern.' One sentence that describes without interpreting. [Pause.] Share one description with the group if willing.

[PARTICIPATE, 5 minutes:] Participate is the hardest of the three for most people with BPD. For two minutes, bring full attention to this moment in this room, without self-monitoring, without watching yourself, without commentary on your own experience. Just here. Just now. [Pause 2 minutes.] What happened?

Now the Pattern Map connection. Look at your Map. Where does the inability to observe your own experience appear? In the impulsivity chain at link two, where mode activation precedes any awareness? In the self-harm chain, where the urge arrives without warning? In the abandonment chain, where the somatic state precedes consciousness? Identify one specific location on your map where Observe would produce an intervention opportunity if it were accessible."

Group Processing and Discussion (10 minutes)

1. "Which of the three What skills was most difficult? Can you name the specific barrier from the psychoeducation: Detached Protector, threat monitoring, or invalidation history?"

2. "The Pattern Map connection: where did you identify that Observe would create an intervention opportunity?"

3. "Zero-to-ten. Mode check."

Closing Grounding Practice (10 minutes)

"Feet on floor. [Pause.] Weight in chair. [Pause.] Three things you can see. [Pause.] Zero-to-ten."

Take-Home Reflection

Between sessions, practice Observe for two minutes once daily in a neutral moment, not in crisis. Notice what arises, including the specific form of resistance. One sentence: "The main barrier I notice in Observe practice is ___."

Handout Reference

Handout 17A: Core Mindfulness: The What Skills (Appendix C, page C-19)

Session 18: Core Mindfulness II: Wise Mind in Practice for Complex Trauma Clients

Module: C: DBT Skills Through a Trauma Lens

Phase: DBT Skill Delivery: Core Mindfulness

Session Number: 18 of 30

Session Overview

Session 18 delivers the Core Mindfulness "How" skills and deepens the Wise Mind practice introduced in Session 4, applying both to the specific mode states and Pattern Map layers identified in Module B. The session produces a more precise and personally calibrated Wise Mind practice than Session 4's introduction and establishes the daily mindfulness practice that Module C's subsequent skills will depend on.

Learning Objectives

By the end of Session 18, group members will be able to:

1. Define the three "How" mindfulness skills (Nonjudgmentally, One-Mindfully, Effectively) in their own words and identify a personal application of each.

2. Describe Wise Mind as an experiential state they have accessed at some point, connecting it to the window and mode conditions under which it was available.

3. Complete the Wise Mind body scan practice and locate one moment of Wise Mind access, however brief.

4. Name one specific mode state that most reliably blocks Wise Mind access and describe one facilitation response to that mode state.

Time Allocation

Component	90-Minute Format	60-Minute Format
Opening Ritual, Check-In, Regulatory Assessment	12 min	12 min
Psychoeducation: The How Skills and Mode-Aware Wise Mind	20 min	15 min
Experiential: Wise Mind Body Scan	30 min	20 min
Group Processing	18 min	8 min
Closing Grounding	10 min	5 min

Materials and Preparation

- Group Agreement displayed; BPD Pattern Maps available

  - Handout 18A: Core Mindfulness: The How Skills and Wise Mind (Appendix C, page C-20)

Facilitator Notes

The How skills are more practically actionable than the What skills for most BPD presentations. Nonjudgmentally addresses the Punitive Parent mode directly. One-Mindfully addresses the hypervigilant amygdala's tendency to split attention between internal experience and external threat monitoring. Effectively addresses the Detached Protector's intellectual engagement that produces accurate strategy without genuine presence. Name these mode connections explicitly.

The Wise Mind body scan is the most clinically significant practice in Sessions 17 and 18. Unlike the Wise Mind introduction in Session 4, which produced a brief experience of Wise Mind during low activation, Session 18's body scan is practiced with the Pattern Map as context: the client is asked to access Wise Mind not in a neutral moment but in relation to one specific layer of their map. This more targeted practice produces more clinically useful access and more accurate identification of the barriers.

Opening Ritual, Check-In, Regulatory Assessment (12 minutes)

"Feet on floor. [Pause.] Weight in chair. [Pause.] Three things you can see. [Pause.] Zero-to-ten. Mode check. Collective window assessment.

From the take-home: anyone who noticed the specific form of resistance in the Observe practice. One sentence."

[Receive one or two brief responses.]

Psychoeducation Component (20 minutes)

Talking Point 1: The How skills

"The three How skills describe the quality of attention that makes mindfulness clinically effective rather than merely technically correct.

Nonjudgmentally means observing without adding an evaluation layer: 'there is anger' rather than 'I shouldn't be angry,' 'there is a thought' rather than 'that is a stupid thought.' For BPD presentations, Nonjudgmentally is primarily a Punitive Parent intervention. The mode that turns self-evaluation into self-contempt is specifically addressed by the practice of removing the evaluative layer from observation.

One-Mindfully means bringing full attention to one thing at a time rather than splitting attention between the present task and monitoring for threat, planning, or ruminating. For BPD presentations, One-Mindfully addresses the hypervigilant amygdala's divided attention: the nervous system that is simultaneously attending to the present experience and monitoring the relational environment for abandonment signals cannot do either with genuine depth.

Effectively means doing what works in the current situation rather than what is right, fair, or satisfying in principle. For BPD presentations, Effectively is often the most challenging How skill because it runs against the Angry/Impulsive Child mode's insistence on justice and the Punitive Parent's preference for self-punishment over functional response. Effectively asks the question: 'What would actually serve my recovery goals in this moment?' rather than 'What do I feel like doing?' or 'What do I deserve?'"

Talking Point 2: Wise Mind with mode awareness

"The Wise Mind practice from Session 4 gave you a brief experience of the integrated state. Session 18 deepens that practice with a specific addition: mode awareness.

Most mindfulness instruction asks you to access Wise Mind from a neutral state. Your Pattern Map tells us that the states in which Wise Mind is most needed are not neutral: they are abandonment fear activations, splitting shifts, Punitive Parent escalations, and impulsivity chains.

Mode-aware Wise Mind practice adds one question to the standard practice: before you access Wise Mind, identify which mode is currently most active. Then access Wise Mind from the position of the Healthy Adult observer who can hold that mode with compassion rather than from the position of the mode itself.

This is different from standard mindfulness because it uses the internal cast of characters from your Pattern Map as the observational landscape. You are not observing undifferentiated experience. You are observing specific modes, with specific developmental histories, from the perspective of the part of you that is larger than any single mode."

Experiential Exercise: Wise Mind Body Scan (30 minutes)

[Distribute Handout 18A.]

"The Wise Mind body scan is a twelve-minute practice in three stages.

Stage one, four minutes: Start with the regulatory foundation. Feet on floor. Weight in chair. Orienting scan. Zero-to-ten. Allow the window to settle to its current position. Mode check: which mode is most active right now?

Stage two, four minutes: Name the mode that is present without evaluating it. 'The Detached Protector is here.' 'The Vulnerable Child is here.' Use the Nonjudgmentally skill: no evaluation of the mode's presence, just accurate observation of what is here. Now ask: is there any part of the experience that is observing the mode rather than being the mode? Even very briefly?

Stage three, four minutes: Bring one layer of your Pattern Map into the observational field, the layer that is most active for you right now. Observe it from the position of the observer rather than from inside the layer. 'There is the abandonment fear.' 'There is the chronic emptiness.' One-Mindfully. Nonjudgmentally. Notice what Wise Mind says about that layer. Even one word. Even one sentence.

[After twelve minutes:]

Take five minutes to write on the handout: What mode was present? What, if anything, did you observe from outside the mode? What did Wise Mind offer about the Pattern Map layer you brought in?"

Group Processing and Discussion (18 minutes)

1. "The mode-aware practice: was it different from standard mindfulness? What did adding the mode identification do?"

2. "The Healthy Adult observer: did you access it, even briefly? What was it like if you did, or what blocked it if you didn't?"

3. "The Nonjudgmentally skill and the Punitive Parent: for anyone who noticed the evaluative layer arrive, what was it saying, and what happened when you named it as Punitive Parent rather than as truth?"

4. "Zero-to-ten. Mode check."

Closing Grounding Practice (10 minutes)

"Feet on floor. [Pause.] Weight in chair. [Pause.] Orienting scan. Zero-to-ten."

Take-Home Reflection

Daily practice target for Module C: two minutes of Wise Mind body scan, beginning with the mode check. Not in crisis. In ordinary moments. The ordinary practice is what makes extraordinary access possible.

Handout Reference

Handout 18A: Core Mindfulness: The How Skills and Wise Mind (Appendix C, page C-20)

Session 19: Distress Tolerance I: Crisis Survival Skills for ACE-Burdened Nervous Systems

Module: C: DBT Skills Through a Trauma Lens

Phase: DBT Skill Delivery: Distress Tolerance

Session Number: 19 of 30

Session Overview

Session 19 delivers the crisis survival layer of Distress Tolerance: TIPP, ACCEPTS, Self-Soothe, and the STOP skill, positioned explicitly as the skills that address links three and four of the impulsivity chain, the regulatory collapse and the urge state, when the window has been exceeded and the prefrontal cortex is partly offline. The ACE-burdened nervous system context is named at the start: these skills are more urgently needed and more difficult to access for this population than for others, and both facts require honest clinical acknowledgment.

Learning Objectives

By the end of Session 19, group members will be able to:

1. Name and describe the TIPP skill, identifying the specific physiological mechanism through which each component shifts the nervous system state.

2. Identify at least three ACCEPTS strategies that have personal regulatory value and describe the specific quality of relief each provides.

3. Locate the crisis survival skills at the specific links of the impulsivity chain they address, using their own Pattern Map as reference.

4. Complete at least one TIPP component and describe what the practice produced for their nervous system.

Time Allocation

Component	90-Minute Format	60-Minute Format
Opening Ritual, Check-In, Regulatory Assessment	12 min	12 min
Psychoeducation: Crisis Survival and the Impulsivity Chain	15 min	10 min
Experiential: TIPP Practice	20 min	15 min
Psychoeducation: ACCEPTS and Self-Soothe	15 min	10 min
Group Processing and ACCEPTS Personalization	18 min	8 min
Closing Grounding	10 min	5 min

Materials and Preparation

- Group Agreement displayed; BPD Pattern Maps available
  - Handout 19A: Crisis Survival Skills: TIPP, ACCEPTS, and Self-Soothe (Appendix C, page C-21)
  - Cold water available in the room or accessible immediately outside for Temperature component
  - Space for brief physical movement for Intense Exercise component

Facilitator Notes

TIPP is the most physiologically direct skill in the Module C curriculum. It works at link three of the impulsivity chain, the regulatory collapse, by directly shifting autonomic state before the prefrontal cortex is fully offline. The Temperature component, specifically cold water on the face or wrists, activates the mammalian diving reflex and produces measurable parasympathetic activation. Intense exercise burns through stress hormones. Paced breathing shifts the autonomic balance toward parasympathetic. Paired muscle relaxation addresses the somatic tension component of hyperarousal. Each component has a specific mechanism, and naming the mechanism is part of the clinical delivery.

The Pattern Map connection must be made explicit. Before teaching TIPP, ask: "Look at your Pattern Map. Where does link three, the regulatory collapse, appear? TIPP addresses that specific link. This skill is designed for the moment when you are above the window and moving toward urge state."

ACCEPTS and Self-Soothe address the state after TIPP, when autonomic activation has been reduced enough for cognitive distraction strategies to become accessible. They do not work above the window. Delivering them with the honest acknowledgment that they require the window to be partially accessible is more clinically useful than teaching them as universally available tools.

Opening Ritual, Check-In, Regulatory Assessment (12 minutes)

"Feet on floor. [Pause.] Weight in chair. [Pause.] Orienting scan. Zero-to-ten. Mode check. Collective window assessment.

Today we begin Distress Tolerance. Before we start, Pattern Map connection: look at link three of your impulsivity chain. The regulatory collapse. That is what these skills address. The skills of the next two sessions exist specifically because your nervous system can exceed the window and reach a state in which the thinking brain is partly offline. Today's skills work at that link."

Psychoeducation Component 1: Crisis Survival and the Impulsivity Chain (15 minutes)

Talking Point: The crisis survival principle

"Distress tolerance skills are not skills for feeling better in the long run. They are skills for surviving the short run without making things worse. The clinical purpose is specific: to get through the highest-activation moments of the impulsivity chain, the regulatory collapse and the urge state, without acting on the behavior that the urge is driving.

For ACE-burdened nervous systems, the crisis survival skills are more urgently needed and more difficult to access than for nervous systems without this history. More urgently needed because the window is narrower and the regulatory collapse arrives faster. More difficult to access because the same high-activation states that require the skills are the states in which the prefrontal cortex, the executive function that would implement the skills, is least available.

This is the clinical paradox that honest DBT facilitation must acknowledge: the skills that are needed most are accessible least in the moments of greatest need. The solution is not to pretend the paradox does not exist. It is to build the regulatory foundation, as Module A did, and to practice the crisis skills in low-activation contexts until they become accessible at moderate activation, then practice them at moderate activation until they become accessible at high activation. Graduated exposure to the skills in increasingly activating contexts is the generalization pathway."

Experiential Exercise: TIPP Practice (20 minutes)

[Distribute Handout 19A.]

"We are going to practice each TIPP component briefly. I want you to rate each from one to three for your nervous system: one means no effect, two means mild shift, three means clear shift.

Temperature: If you have access to cold water, run it over your wrists or splash your face for thirty seconds. If not, hold a cold water bottle or imagine the cold sensation with as much sensory specificity as you can. Notice what happens to your arousal level. [Pause.] Rate it.

Intense Exercise: Stand up. Sixty seconds of something that elevates your heart rate: marching in place, jumping jacks, or as vigorous a movement as the space allows. [Pause 60 seconds.] Sit back down. Notice your zero-to-ten. Rate it.

Paced Breathing: Exhale slightly longer than your inhale for six breaths. Not deep breathing. Slightly longer exhale. Count to four on the inhale, six on the exhale. [Pause.] Rate it.

Paired Muscle Relaxation: Tighten the muscles in your hands and arms for five seconds, then release. Tighten your legs for five seconds, then release. Notice the shift in somatic state after the release. [Pause.] Rate it.

Which component rated highest for your nervous system? That is your primary TIPP tool."

Psychoeducation Component 2: ACCEPTS and Self-Soothe (15 minutes)

"ACCEPTS provides cognitive distraction strategies for when autonomic activation has been reduced enough, through TIPP or other means, that the thinking brain can reengage.

The seven ACCEPTS categories: Activities that occupy attention. Contributing, doing something for someone else, which shifts the nervous system from self-focused threat processing to outward engagement. Comparisons, not to judge yourself favorably, but to access perspective. Emotions, deliberately accessing a different emotion through music, memory, or film. Pushing away, temporarily placing the distressing thought or feeling in a mental container. Thoughts, engaging the thinking brain in a different cognitive task. Sensations, using strong but safe sensory experience to shift the somatic state.

Self-Soothe with senses, using pleasant sensory input through sight, sound, smell, taste, touch, or movement, activates the parasympathetic system through a different pathway than TIPP: rather than forcefully shifting the autonomic state, Self-Soothe provides the nervous system with the sensory experience of safety and comfort."

Group Processing and ACCEPTS Personalization (18 minutes)

1. "Which TIPP component produced the highest rating? What specifically did you notice?"

2. "Which three ACCEPTS strategies do you anticipate being most accessible for your nervous system? What is it about each that fits your specific regulatory profile?"

3. "Pattern Map connection: which mode state makes ACCEPTS least accessible for you, and which mode state makes it most accessible?"

4. "Zero-to-ten. Mode check."

Closing Grounding Practice (10 minutes)

"Feet on floor. [Pause.] Weight in chair. [Pause.] Orienting scan. Zero-to-ten."

Take-Home Reflection

Between sessions, practice your highest-rated TIPP component once in a neutral or mildly activated moment. Not in crisis. The window must be partially accessible for the practice to build the generalization pathway.

Handout Reference

Handout 19A: Crisis Survival Skills: TIPP, ACCEPTS, and Self-Soothe (Appendix C, page C-21)

Session 20: Distress Tolerance II: Radical Acceptance and the IMPROVE Skill

Module: C: DBT Skills Through a Trauma Lens

Phase: DBT Skill Delivery: Distress Tolerance

Session Number: 20 of 30

Session Overview

Session 20 delivers the acceptance-oriented layer of Distress Tolerance: Radical Acceptance deepened from Session 6, the IMPROVE the Moment skill, and the Willingness versus Willfulness distinction. The session extends Module A's radical acceptance work into the specific activation contexts that Module B's Pattern Map revealed, making the acceptance practice contextually targeted rather than generically applied.

Learning Objectives

By the end of Session 20, group members will be able to:

1. Demonstrate Turning the Mind toward acceptance for one specific Pattern Map activation, describing what the practice produced.

2. Name the seven IMPROVE components and identify at least three with personal regulatory value for their specific nervous system.

3. Distinguish Willingness from Willfulness in their own words and identify at least one current situation in which Willfulness is consuming regulatory resources.

4. Connect the IMPROVE skill to a specific layer of their BPD Pattern Map, naming which mode state each IMPROVE component is most accessible from.

Time Allocation

Component	90-Minute Format	60-Minute Format
Opening Ritual, Check-In, Regulatory Assessment	12 min	12 min
Psychoeducation: Radical Acceptance Deepened	20 min	15 min
Experiential: Turning the Mind Practice	20 min	15 min
Psychoeducation: IMPROVE and Willingness	20 min	13 min
Group Processing	8 min	0 min
Closing Grounding	10 min	5 min

Materials and Preparation

- Group Agreement displayed; BPD Pattern Maps available

  - Handout 20A: Radical Acceptance and IMPROVE (Appendix C, page C-22)

Facilitator Notes

Radical Acceptance in Session 20 is a deepening, not a repetition, of Session 6. Session 6 introduced the concept and addressed the three common distortions (approval, giving up, forgiveness). Session 20 applies it to specific Pattern Map content: accepting the reality of the abandonment fear, accepting the developmental origins of the splitting pattern, accepting the chronic emptiness rather than filling it. These contextually targeted applications produce more genuine clinical access than abstract acceptance practice.

The IMPROVE skill addresses the middle of a distressing moment: after the acute autonomic activation of TIPP has reduced and before the situation has resolved. Its components work best within the window or at its edge. Connecting each component to the mode state most compatible with it is the Module C clinical contribution: Imagery is more accessible from Vulnerable Child than from Detached Protector. Meaning is more accessible from Healthy Adult. Prayer or spiritual practice varies by individual history and should be offered without clinical prescription.

Opening Ritual, Check-In, Regulatory Assessment (12 minutes)

"Feet on floor. [Pause.] Weight in chair. [Pause.] Orienting scan. Zero-to-ten. Mode check. Collective window assessment.

From the take-home: anyone who practiced their highest-rated TIPP component this week. One sentence about what happened."

[Receive one or two brief responses.]

Psychoeducation Component 1: Radical Acceptance Deepened (20 minutes)

Talking Point 1: Turning the Mind

"Session 6 introduced Radical Acceptance as the full acknowledgment of reality as it is, without fighting, without demanding it be different, without the ongoing energy expenditure of resistance to what cannot be changed.

Today we practice what DBT calls Turning the Mind: the deliberate, repeated, moment-to-moment act of choosing acceptance when the nervous system's default response is resistance. Turning the Mind is not a single decision made once. It is a decision made and then made again, every time the resistance reasserts itself.

The specific application for your Pattern Map is this: Radical Acceptance of the patterns themselves. Not approval of the adversity that produced them. Full acceptance that the abandonment fear is real, that it is organized exactly as your chain maps it, that it activates at the thresholds your history produced, and that fighting against its existence consumes the regulatory resources that Module C's skills need."

Talking Point 2: Willingness and Willfulness

"DBT distinguishes Willingness from Willfulness, and the distinction carries specific clinical weight for BPD presentations.

Willingness means being open to what is, participating in life as it actually is rather than as it should be, responding to the moment from Wise Mind and effective action. Willingness is not passivity. It is engaged participation in reality.

Willfulness means refusing to participate in what is, insisting on what should be, demanding that reality conform to preference. In BPD presentations, Willfulness most commonly appears in two places: the Angry/Impulsive Child mode's refusal to accept the limits of what relationships can provide, and the Punitive Parent mode's insistence that the client deserves what is happening to them, which is Willfulness applied against the self.

Identifying which mode state produces Willfulness in your specific presentation is the Pattern Map work. Choosing Willingness from that mode state is the Turning the Mind practice."

Experiential Exercise: Turning the Mind Practice (20 minutes)

[Distribute Handout 20A.]

"Choose one specific Pattern Map layer that you have been fighting rather than accepting. Not the most painful one. A representative one. The abandonment fear's activation at low thresholds, perhaps, or the chronic emptiness, or the identity instability.

For five minutes, practice Turning the Mind. Hold the specific Pattern Map layer in your observational field. Notice the resistance that arises, the 'this should be different,' the 'this is not fair,' the 'I cannot accept this.' Name the resistance as resistance. Then, once, turn: 'This is what is. I accept that it is.'

The turning is not permanent. The resistance will return. When it does, turn again. One turn at a time.

After five minutes, write on the handout: What did you turn toward acceptance? What was the resistance like? What happened in your body when you turned?"

[After writing:]

"Let's share. The specific layer you turned toward, and what the turn produced."

Psychoeducation Component 2: IMPROVE (20 minutes)

"IMPROVE the Moment provides seven strategies for making a distressing moment more tolerable without making it worse. Each component has a mode-compatibility note that your Pattern Map informs.

Imagery: access a safe or peaceful image or memory. Most accessible from Vulnerable Child seeking comfort, less accessible from Detached Protector.

Meaning: find one specific element of meaning in the current difficulty. Most accessible from Healthy Adult perspective.

Prayer: spiritual practice or connection to a value larger than the current moment. Varies widely by personal history and preference.

Relaxation: paired with the TIPP somatic practices. Address the body before addressing the cognition.

One thing in the moment: narrow attention to the single immediate sensory experience rather than the full weight of the situation.

Vacation: a brief mental or physical time-out from the distressing content. Not avoidance; a temporary pause that allows regulatory resources to rebuild.

Encouragement: self-talk that is accurate and compassionate. 'I can get through this moment.' Not false positivity. Accurate, specific, self-directed compassion."

Group Processing (8 minutes)

1. "The Turning the Mind practice: what was the most resistant part of the experience?"

2. "IMPROVE: which three components fit your nervous system most naturally, and which mode state are you in when they are most accessible?"

3. "Zero-to-ten. Mode check."

Closing Grounding Practice (10 minutes)

"Feet on floor. [Pause.] Weight in chair. [Pause.] Orienting scan. Zero-to-ten."

Take-Home Reflection

Practice Turning the Mind once daily toward one specific Pattern Map layer. One turn. Write what you turned toward and what happened.

Handout Reference

Handout 20A: Radical Acceptance and IMPROVE (Appendix C, page C-22)

Session 21: Emotion Regulation I: Understanding Emotions in a Dysregulated System

Module: C: DBT Skills Through a Trauma Lens

Phase: DBT Skill Delivery: Emotion Regulation

Session Number: 21 of 30

Session Overview

Session 21 delivers the foundational layer of Emotion Regulation: understanding and labeling emotions, identifying their functions, reducing emotional vulnerability, and building the self-knowledge of the dysregulated system that makes longer-arc regulation possible. The session connects the three-part BPD emotional profile from Chapter 2 to the practical skills of emotion identification and function analysis.

Learning Objectives

By the end of Session 21, group members will be able to:

1. Name the function of at least three primary emotions using the DBT functional analysis framework.

2. Identify the specific emotion present in one recent activation, distinguishing the primary emotion from the secondary emotion that followed it.

3. Describe the three-part BPD emotional profile (high sensitivity, high reactivity, slow return to baseline) in relation to one recent emotional episode.

4. Identify at least two personal emotional vulnerability factors and name one concrete step toward reducing each.

Time Allocation

Component	90-Minute Format	60-Minute Format
Opening Ritual, Check-In, Regulatory Assessment	12 min	12 min
Psychoeducation: Emotions in a Dysregulated System	20 min	15 min
Experiential: My Emotion Map	25 min	20 min
Psychoeducation: Reducing Vulnerability	15 min	8 min
Group Processing	8 min	0 min
Closing Grounding	10 min	5 min

Materials and Preparation

- Group Agreement displayed; BPD Pattern Maps available

- Handout 21A: Emotion Regulation: Understanding My Emotional System (Appendix C, page C-23)

Facilitator Notes

The primary versus secondary emotion distinction is clinically essential for BPD presentations. Many BPD presentations present visible anger or contempt as the primary emotion when the actual primary emotion is terror or grief. The secondary emotion, the one that is socially visible, frequently functions as the Angry/Impulsive Child mode's protection of the Vulnerable Child's primary pain. Identifying the primary emotion beneath the secondary one is the clinical move that makes emotion regulation possible: you cannot regulate what you cannot see, and the visible emotion is frequently not the one that needs regulation.

The three-part BPD emotional profile should be explicitly connected to Module A's window work. High sensitivity, high reactivity, and slow return to baseline are not abstract clinical concepts in Session 21. They are the specific emotional architecture that each client's zero-to-ten monitoring practice has been tracking since Session 1.

Opening Ritual, Check-In, Regulatory Assessment (12 minutes)

"Feet on floor. [Pause.] Weight in chair. [Pause.] Orienting scan. Zero-to-ten. Mode check. Collective window assessment.

Pattern Map connection for today: look at your map's abandonment chain, link three: the emotional activation. Emotion Regulation works at that link. Today we learn to identify what is actually there."

Psychoeducation Component 1: Emotions in a Dysregulated System (20 minutes)

Talking Point 1: The function of emotions

"DBT frames emotions as functional rather than merely experiential: emotions carry information and motivate adaptive behavior. Understanding the function of an emotion changes the clinical relationship to it from 'this emotion is a problem to be eliminated' to 'this emotion is information about something that matters.'

Fear signals danger and motivates avoidance or preparation. Anger signals a violation and motivates action toward change. Sadness signals a loss and motivates slowing down and seeking support. Shame signals a violation of a social standard and motivates repair or concealment. Guilt signals a violation of a personal value and motivates repair. Love signals closeness and motivates approach.

For BPD presentations, the functional framing is a direct extension of the de-shaming work of Modules A and B: the emotional intensity is not a character defect. It is a functional system that is highly sensitive and that has been calibrated by adversity to detect specific threat signals with high sensitivity. The emotions themselves carry accurate information. The problem is the calibration, not the system."

Talking Point 2: Primary and secondary emotions

"Every emotional experience has a structure: the primary emotion, which is the first affective response to the triggering event, and the secondary emotion, which is the emotional response to the primary emotion.

For BPD presentations, the visible emotion is often secondary, not primary. The pattern is common: a relational cue produces primary terror (abandonment fear activation, Vulnerable Child mode). The terror is experienced as intolerable. The Angry/Impulsive Child mode activates as protection, converting the terror into anger, which feels more powerful and more manageable than the vulnerability. What the environment sees is anger. What is actually happening is terror.

Emotion regulation in this context requires identifying the primary emotion beneath the protective secondary one. That identification is a mindfulness practice: Observe and Describe applied to the emotional layer of the Pattern Map."

Experiential Exercise: My Emotion Map (25 minutes)

[Distribute Handout 21A.]

"Take fifteen minutes with the Emotion Map. Choose one emotional episode from the past week. The one that felt most activated or most confusing.

First: name the visible emotion, the one you or others would describe if asked. This is likely the secondary emotion. What was it?

Second: underneath it, or before it arrived, was there a different emotion? More painful, more vulnerable, more fundamental? What was that?

Third: using the function framework, what was the primary emotion telling you? What did it detect? Was the detection accurate to the current situation, or was it calibrated to a historical one?

Fourth: where does this emotional episode appear on your Pattern Map?"

[After fifteen minutes, facilitate sharing of the primary versus secondary emotion distinction.]

Psychoeducation Component 2: Reducing Vulnerability (15 minutes)

"The PLEASE skills, Physical Illness, Eating, Avoiding Substances, Sleep, and Exercise, address the physical and behavioral vulnerability factors that lower the window and increase emotional reactivity.

For ACE-burdened nervous systems, these factors matter more than for average clinical populations because the window is already narrower. Insufficient sleep reduces the window further. Physical illness reduces prefrontal capacity. Substance use disrupts the regulatory architecture that Module A built. These are not lifestyle recommendations. They are the specific physical conditions under which the skills of Module C become or become unavailable.

Each PLEASE factor connects directly to your Pattern Map: identify which factors most reliably lower your window, and name one concrete action toward addressing each."

Group Processing (8 minutes)

1. "The primary versus secondary emotion: for anyone who found the primary emotion beneath the visible one, what was it?"

2. "Zero-to-ten. Mode check."

Closing Grounding Practice (10 minutes)

"Feet on floor. [Pause.] Weight in chair. [Pause.] Orienting scan. Zero-to-ten."

Take-Home Reflection

Once daily, name one primary emotion without moving immediately to the secondary. One sentence: "The primary emotion present right now is ___."

Handout Reference

Handout 21A: Emotion Regulation: Understanding My Emotional System (Appendix C, page C-23)

Session 22: Emotion Regulation II: Opposite Action, PLEASE, and Building Positive Experience

Module: C: DBT Skills Through a Trauma Lens

Phase: DBT Skill Delivery: Emotion Regulation

Session Number: 22 of 30

Session Overview

Session 22 delivers the active change layer of Emotion Regulation: Opposite Action, the full PLEASE skills practice, and Building Positive Experience. Each skill is connected to the mode states most likely to block it and the Pattern Map layers most directly addressed by it. The session establishes the longer-arc regulatory practices that Module D's identity and values work will build on.

Learning Objectives

By the end of Session 22, group members will be able to:

1. Define Opposite Action and demonstrate its application to one specific emotional episode, naming the primary emotion and the opposite action that would address it.

2. Identify their personal PLEASE vulnerability factors and name one specific, achievable change for each.

3. Describe the specific challenge that BPD's chronic emptiness creates for Building Positive Experience and name one approach that addresses that challenge.

4. Connect each skill to its Pattern Map location and identify which mode state most reliably blocks access to each.

Time Allocation

Component	90-Minute Format	60-Minute Format
Opening Ritual, Check-In, Regulatory Assessment	12 min	12 min
Psychoeducation: Opposite Action and Mode Awareness	20 min	15 min
Experiential: Opposite Action Practice	25 min	20 min
Psychoeducation: PLEASE and Building Positive Experience	18 min	8 min
Group Processing	5 min	0 min
Closing Grounding	10 min	5 min

Materials and Preparation

- Group Agreement displayed; BPD Pattern Maps available

- Handout 22A: Emotion Regulation: Opposite Action, PLEASE, and Building Positive Experience (Appendix C, page C-24)

Facilitator Notes

Opposite Action is the most clinically powerful and most mode-blocked of the Emotion Regulation skills. It works by directly contradicting the action urge of the primary emotion, which changes the emotional state through behavioral engagement. Fear's action urge is to avoid or withdraw; the opposite action is approach. Anger's action urge is to attack or escalate; the opposite action is gentle engagement. Shame's action urge is to hide or conceal; the opposite action is to share appropriately.

The mode-blocking issue is specific: Opposite Action requires the Healthy Adult observer to identify the primary emotion's action urge and then choose the opposite. The Angry/Impulsive Child mode cannot do this because the mode's action urge is the entire content of the mode state. The Punitive Parent mode cannot do this because it endorses the shame response's action urge to hide. Opposite Action is specifically a Healthy Adult skill, and its inaccessibility in mode states is not a failure of learning. It is accurate reporting of which internal resource must be built before the skill can be reliably used.

Building Positive Experience and chronic emptiness. The chronic emptiness from Session 15 creates a specific challenge for Building Positive Experience: the inner hollowness that emotional neglect produced means that positive experiences may not register or accumulate in the way they do for clients without that developmental history. The clinical approach is not to dismiss this report but to address it specifically: short-duration, somatic, present-moment positive experiences are more accessible than longer-duration, cognitively mediated ones. Brief, repeated, body-level positive engagement builds the inner substance more reliably than sustained positive activities that the emptiness state can absorb without registering.

Opening Ritual, Check-In, Regulatory Assessment (12 minutes)

"Feet on floor. [Pause.] Weight in chair. [Pause.] Orienting scan. Zero-to-ten. Mode check. Collective window assessment.

From the take-home: anyone who named a primary emotion this week. One sentence."

[Receive one brief response.]

Psychoeducation Component 1: Opposite Action (20 minutes)

Talking Point: The mechanism and the mode barrier

"Opposite Action works through a specific mechanism: behavioral change produces emotional change. When the action urge of the primary emotion is contradicted by the actual behavior, the nervous system updates the emotional state based on the new behavioral evidence. Fear followed by avoidance is reinforced. Fear followed by approach is gradually reduced.

The four primary emotion applications in BPD treatment: Fear, whose action urge is avoidance and whose opposite action is approach and engagement. Anger, whose action urge is attack and whose opposite action is gentle disengagement or gentle engagement. Guilt and shame, whose action urge is hiding and whose opposite action is appropriate disclosure and repair. Sadness, whose action urge is withdrawal and whose opposite action is engagement with the environment.

The mode barrier is specific. Opposite Action is a Healthy Adult intervention: it requires the internal observer to be present, to identify the primary emotion and its action urge, and to choose the opposite. When any of the four non-Healthy-Adult modes is fully activated, the observer is not available, and Opposite Action is not accessible. This is why the mindfulness work of Sessions 17 and 18 is prerequisite to Opposite Action: without the observer, the opposite action cannot be chosen."

Experiential Exercise: Opposite Action Practice (25 minutes)

[Distribute Handout 22A.]

"Take fifteen minutes to practice Opposite Action in writing, for one emotional episode from the past week.

Name the primary emotion. Name its action urge. What was the behavior the emotion wanted? Name the opposite action. What would directly contradict the action urge? And then: can you imagine doing the opposite action, even briefly, even partially? What would it feel like, and what mode would most need to be present for that to be possible?

This is not about having done the opposite action. It is about mapping what it would require."

[After fifteen minutes:]

"For anyone willing: the primary emotion, its action urge, and the opposite action that would address it."

Psychoeducation Component 2: PLEASE and Building Positive Experience (18 minutes)

"We reviewed the PLEASE skills in Session 21. Today I want to make them specific and actionable. The target is one specific, achievable change per PLEASE factor, calibrated to your current life rather than to an ideal one.

The chronic emptiness connection to Building Positive Experience is worth naming directly. If positive experiences have historically not registered or accumulated for your nervous system, the standard recommendation to 'schedule pleasant activities' may feel clinically naive. The modification for BPD presentations with chronic emptiness is this: start small and somatic. A two-minute sensory positive experience, warm water, a specific food, sunlight on skin, music that produces a physical response, builds the inner substance more reliably than a scheduled pleasant afternoon. The building is gradual and real, even when it does not feel dramatic."

Group Processing (5 minutes)

1. "Zero-to-ten. Mode check. One sentence about the Opposite Action practice."

Closing Grounding Practice (10 minutes)

"Feet on floor. [Pause.] Weight in chair. [Pause.] Orienting scan. Zero-to-ten."

Take-Home Reflection

Once between sessions: practice one two-minute somatic positive experience and notice whether anything registers. One sentence: "The positive experience I tried was ___, and what I noticed was ___."

Handout Reference

Handout 22A: Emotion Regulation: Opposite Action, PLEASE, and Building Positive Experience (Appendix C, page C-24)

Session 23: Interpersonal Effectiveness I: DEAR MAN and GIVE for Trauma-Affected Relational Systems

Module: C: DBT Skills Through a Trauma Lens

Phase: DBT Skill Delivery: Interpersonal Effectiveness

Session Number: 23 of 30

Session Overview

Session 23 delivers the DEAR MAN and GIVE skills from DBT's Interpersonal Effectiveness module, with specific trauma-informed adaptations for the abandonment-fear-organized and splitting-influenced relational systems that Module B's Pattern Map revealed. The session positions interpersonal effectiveness not as social skill training but as the relational layer of the Pattern Map work: skills for navigating the specific relational configurations that the BPD nervous system produces.

Learning Objectives

By the end of Session 23, group members will be able to:

1. Describe the DEAR MAN skill and apply it to one specific interpersonal request from their current life, naming the mode state most likely to interfere with each component.

2. Describe the GIVE skill and identify how it applies to at least one current relationship where maintaining the relationship is the primary goal.

3. Name the specific BPD relational complications that make DEAR MAN and GIVE more difficult for this population and describe one approach to each complication.

4. Connect both skills to their Pattern Map's abandonment chain and splitting layer.

Time Allocation

Component	90-Minute Format	60-Minute Format
Opening Ritual, Check-In, Regulatory Assessment	12 min	12 min
Psychoeducation: Interpersonal Effectiveness and the Relational Template	15 min	10 min
Psychoeducation: DEAR MAN with BPD Adaptations	20 min	15 min
Experiential: DEAR MAN Script Practice	25 min	18 min
Psychoeducation: GIVE	10 min	0 min
Group Processing	8 min	0 min
Closing Grounding	10 min	5 min

Materials and Preparation

- Group Agreement displayed; BPD Pattern Maps available
    - Handout 23A: Interpersonal Effectiveness: DEAR MAN and GIVE (Appendix C, page C-25)

Facilitator Notes

The BPD-specific DEAR MAN complications must be named before the skill is delivered. Standard DEAR MAN assumes: the person making the request can Describe the situation objectively (splitting makes this difficult when the devaluation mode has activated); the person can Express feelings without the Angry/Impulsive Child mode escalating; the person can Assert without the abandonment fear making any direct request feel catastrophically risky; and the person can stay Mindful without the abandonment fear activating during the conversation. Each of these complications connects directly to the Pattern Map, and naming them is both de-shaming and clinically precise.

GIVE is particularly complex in BPD presentations because the G (gentle) component conflicts with the Angry/Impulsive Child mode, the I (interested) component conflicts with the Detached Protector mode, and the V (validate) component requires the Healthy Adult observer to be present. The mode barriers to GIVE should be mapped explicitly before practice.

Opening Ritual, Check-In, Regulatory Assessment (12 minutes)

"Feet on floor. [Pause.] Weight in chair. [Pause.] Orienting scan. Zero-to-ten. Mode check. Collective window assessment.

Pattern Map connection: today's skills address the abandonment chain's behavioral response layer and the splitting pattern's relational expression. Look at your map. These skills are designed for exactly the relational terrain your map describes."

Psychoeducation Component 1: Interpersonal Effectiveness and the Relational Template (15 minutes)

"Interpersonal Effectiveness skills are organized around three questions: What do I want from this interaction? (Objectives effectiveness.) What is the state of this relationship? (Relationship effectiveness.) What do I think of myself after this interaction? (Self-respect effectiveness.) DEAR MAN addresses the first. GIVE addresses the second. FAST, in Session 24, addresses the third.

For BPD presentations, all three questions are complicated by the relational template from Session 15: the specific developmental template that organizes what relationships are expected to do, how safe closeness is, and what happens when needs are expressed. A relational template organized by emotional abuse expects that direct expression of needs produces contempt. A template organized by abandonment experiences expects that any request increases the risk of loss. These expectations are not cognitive distortions in the standard CBT sense. They are accurate predictions calibrated to the developmental environment. The skills of the next two sessions address how to act effectively despite those predictions, not how to eliminate them."

Psychoeducation Component 2: DEAR MAN with BPD Adaptations (20 minutes)

"DEAR MAN is the skill for getting what you need from an interaction. The seven components.

Describe: state the situation in objective behavioral terms. BPD adaptation: the Detached Protector can describe without emotional engagement, producing accuracy without presence. The Angry/Impulsive Child can describe with emotional activation that distorts the description. The Healthy Adult describes accurately and with appropriate emotional presence.

Express: name the impact on you in feeling language. BPD adaptation: for emotional experiences that have been consistently invalidated, expressing feelings directly carries the historical risk of contempt. Naming this risk explicitly before practice: 'This step feels dangerous because your history taught you it is.'

Assert: state clearly what you are asking for. One request, specific and behavioral. BPD adaptation: the abandonment fear makes direct assertiveness feel like a catastrophic risk. The Vulnerable Child mode may become inaudible. The Angry/Impulsive Child mode may become demanding. The Healthy Adult asserts.

Reinforce: name the benefit to the other person of meeting the request. This is not manipulation. It is the legitimate communication of shared interest.

Mindful: stay with the request without being derailed. BPD adaptation: the abandonment fear's hypervigilant threat detection scans for signs of withdrawal during the conversation. One sign of withdrawal can activate the impulsivity chain. The Mindful component requires maintaining the Wise Mind observer through the conversation's emotional terrain.

Appear confident: present the request assertively, regardless of whether you feel confident. BPD adaptation: the Vulnerable Child mode's physical presentation of distress and the Angry/Impulsive Child mode's presentation of threat both undermine the Appear component. The practice is somatic: feet on floor, eye contact appropriate to comfort level, steady voice.

Negotiate: be genuinely willing to find different ways to meet the need. BPD adaptation: the all-or-nothing categorical thinking of the splitting pattern makes negotiation genuinely difficult. A response that is 'not yes' is experienced as abandonment. Naming this explicitly before practice."

Experiential Exercise: DEAR MAN Script Practice (25 minutes)

[Distribute Handout 23A.]

"Take fifteen minutes to build a DEAR MAN script for one specific interpersonal request from your current life. Not the most charged relationship. A manageable one.

Write each component in your own language. After each component, note: which mode is most present when I think about delivering this component? And which mode would need to be present for this component to land as intended?"

[After fifteen minutes, invite pairs or the full group to practice one component aloud. The facilitator models the Healthy Adult delivery of at least one complete DEAR MAN sequence.]

Psychoeducation Component 3: GIVE (10 minutes)

"GIVE is the skill for maintaining the relationship when the relationship itself is the primary goal.

Gentle: no attacks, no threats, no judgments. Gentle is a Healthy Adult skill and the direct opposite of the Angry/Impulsive Child mode's action urge.

Interested: show interest in the other person's perspective. Interest is blocked by both the Detached Protector (unavailable) and the Angry/Impulsive Child (uninterested in other's perspective when activated).

Validate: acknowledge the other person's perspective as understandable given their experience. This is the interpersonal application of the nonjudgmental stance. For BPD presentations with significant Punitive Parent mode, extending validation to others while withholding it from the self is a common clinical finding.

Easy manner: lightly. Without the weight of every prior relational injury in the conversation."

Group Processing (8 minutes)

1. "The BPD adaptations: which specific complication is most recognizable for your relational template?"

2. "Zero-to-ten. Mode check."

Closing Grounding Practice (10 minutes)

"Feet on floor. [Pause.] Weight in chair. [Pause.] Orienting scan. Zero-to-ten."

Take-Home Reflection

Between sessions: practice one DEAR MAN request in a low-stakes interaction. Notice which mode was active when you attempted it.

Handout Reference

Handout 23A: Interpersonal Effectiveness: DEAR MAN and GIVE (Appendix C, page C-25)

Session 24: Interpersonal Effectiveness II: FAST Skills and Limits in BPD Relationships

Module: C: DBT Skills Through a Trauma Lens

Phase: DBT Skill Delivery: Interpersonal Effectiveness

Session Number: 24 of 30

Session Overview

Session 24 delivers the FAST skills for self-respect effectiveness and addresses limits in BPD relationships, connecting both directly to the splitting pattern and the identity disturbance from Module B. The session completes the four DBT skill modules and prepares the group for Module D's identity and relational work with the full Pattern Map and all four skill modules as the clinical foundation.

Learning Objectives

By the end of Session 24, group members will be able to:

1. Describe the FAST skill and identify at least two components most difficult to maintain in their specific relational template.

2. Define limits in BPD relationships using a regulatory rather than punitive frame, connecting limits to the self-harm function map and the stabilization network.

3. Complete the Module C skill integration review, identifying which skills are most accessible and which require the most continued practice.

4. Describe what Module D will ask of them and why the full Pattern Map and four skill modules are the foundation Module D requires.

Time Allocation

Component	90-Minute Format	60-Minute Format
Opening Ritual, Check-In, Regulatory Assessment	12 min	12 min
Psychoeducation: FAST and Self-Respect	20 min	15 min
Experiential: Limits as Self-Protection in BPD	25 min	20 min
Module C Skill Integration Review	20 min	8 min
Closing Ritual: Looking Ahead to Module D	13 min	5 min

Materials and Preparation

- Group Agreement displayed; all Module C handouts and BPD Pattern Maps available

- Handout 24A: FAST Skills and Limits (Appendix C, page C-26)

- Whiteboard: four columns for the Module C skill integration review: MINDFULNESS | DISTRESS TOLERANCE | EMOTION REGULATION | INTERPERSONAL EFFECTIVENESS

Facilitator Notes

FAST is the most identity-relevant skill of Module C. Fair (treat yourself fairly), no Apologies (do not apologize for existing or for your values), Stick to values (maintain values under pressure), and Truthful (do not lie to maintain a relationship). For BPD presentations with significant Punitive Parent mode, every component of FAST is actively undermined by the mode: the Punitive Parent treats the self unfairly, demands constant apology, abandons values under relational pressure, and lies to avoid the feared abandonment. FAST is therefore both the most challenging and the most therapeutically significant self-respect skill for this population.

Limits in BPD relationships require a regulatory frame, not a punitive one. Standard limits instruction in DBT and in general clinical practice is often experienced by BPD clients as punishment or rejection, particularly when the limits come from people they are currently idealizing. The regulatory frame from Book 1 applies here with specific BPD adaptation: limits are not rules imposed on others. They are the specific conditions under which the client's nervous system can maintain recovery. Framing limits as regulatory tools rather than as control mechanisms is the clinical move that makes limits-setting feel like self-care rather than cruelty.

Opening Ritual, Check-In, Regulatory Assessment (12 minutes)

"Feet on floor. [Pause.] Weight in chair. [Pause.] Orienting scan. Zero-to-ten. Mode check. Collective window assessment.

Pattern Map connection: today's FAST skills address the identity disturbance layer. And limits connect to the self-harm function map. Look at both layers before we begin."

Psychoeducation Component: FAST and Self-Respect (20 minutes)

Talking Point 1: The four FAST components

"FAST addresses self-respect effectiveness: how you feel about yourself after an interpersonal interaction, regardless of whether you got what you wanted or maintained the relationship.

Fair: treat yourself fairly, with the same standards you apply to others. For BPD presentations with significant Punitive Parent mode, fairness to the self is the most radical component of FAST: the mode systematically applies standards to the self that it would not apply to anyone else. Practice: when you would be compassionate toward another person in the same situation, apply the same standard to yourself.

No Apologies: do not apologize for your existence, your values, your needs, or the fact that you have a BPD presentation. This is distinct from genuine repair of genuine harm, which is appropriate and important. No Apologies addresses the specific pattern in which apology becomes the default relational position, the reflexive concession that precedes genuine engagement, organized by the fear that existence is imposition.

Stick to values: maintain your values under relational pressure. The splitting pattern makes this specifically challenging: when the idealization-devaluation cycle shifts, the values that felt clear in the idealization phase may feel arbitrary or wrong in the devaluation phase. The identity disturbance from Session 11 also contributes: values that feel genuinely one's own in Healthy Adult mode may feel like performances in Detached Protector or impositions in Punitive Parent mode. Identifying two or three values that persist across mode states, which Session 11 began, is the prerequisite for Stick to values being a genuine practice.

Truthful: do not lie to maintain a relationship, even through exaggeration or omission. For BPD presentations, the most common form of truthfulness failure is not deliberate deception but the Fawn mode's adaptive performance: becoming whoever the relationship needs rather than staying with the truth of your own experience. The no-Apologies and Stick-to-values components support Truthful by providing the relational ground from which truth can be spoken."

Experiential Exercise: Limits as Self-Protection in BPD (25 minutes)

[Distribute Handout 24A.]

"Take fifteen minutes with the limits section of the handout. Three categories.

Category one: relational limits. Not what behaviors you will not tolerate in others, but what relational conditions your nervous system needs to maintain recovery. Name two or three specific conditions. These are not demands. They are the regulatory requirements your Pattern Map reveals.

Category two: disclosure limits. What you share, with whom, and at what stage of trust. These connect directly to the abandonment chain: premature disclosure is one of the ways the Vulnerable Child mode's urgency overrides the Healthy Adult's judgment about relational timing.

Category three: self-harm limits. Using the self-harm function map from Session 14: what alternative regulatory resource addresses the same function without the harm? This is not a commitment to never self-harm. It is the commitment to having a prepared alternative available before the next urge arrives.

For each limit, write one sentence describing how you will maintain it when the abandonment fear or splitting shift makes maintaining it feel like rejection."

[After fifteen minutes, facilitate sharing of one limit from each client and the specific challenge to maintaining it.]

Module C Skill Integration Review (20 minutes)

[Write four skill module columns on the board.]

"We have covered all four DBT skill modules across Sessions 17 through 24. Before we close Module C, I want each of you to do a brief inventory.

In your handout, for each of the four modules: name the one skill you have found most accessible so far, and the one skill that has required the most from you. Then name the mode state most active when the accessible skill works, and the mode state most active when the difficult skill blocks.

This is your Module C access map. It tells your individual therapist exactly where the continued skills practice needs to go, and it tells us, as a group, what Module D needs to build on."

[After five minutes of individual completion, gather one observation from each client.]

Closing Ritual: Looking Ahead to Module D (13 minutes)

"Module C has delivered the four DBT skill modules with the Pattern Map as their targeting framework. You now have a set of skills whose access profile is specific to your BPD presentation, whose mode barriers are named, and whose Pattern Map locations are identified.

Module D uses all of it. Across six sessions, we will address identity beyond the diagnosis, relational repair, managing abandonment triggers after treatment, building a life organized around values rather than around managing the disorder, post-traumatic growth without forced optimism, and graduation.

Module D is the forward-facing work. Not recovery from BPD as the goal. A life that is genuinely yours, built from the values that persist across mode shifts, using the skills that Module C has built, with the regulatory foundation that Module A established and the clear-eyed map that Module B produced.

That is the goal. Module D builds it.

Feet on floor. [Pause.] Weight in chair. [Pause.] Look around the room. [Pause.] You have completed three modules together. Module D begins the fourth.

Zero-to-ten. One slightly slower breath."

Take-Home Reflection

Between Module C and Module D: review your Module C skill access map. Notice which skills are most available to you right now and which require the most continued practice. Bring both observations to Session 25.

Handout Reference

Handout 24A: FAST Skills and Limits (Appendix C, page C-26)

Module D: Identity, Relationships, and a Life Worth Living

Sessions 25 through 30 | Clinical Focus: Values-based identity construction, relational repair, post-treatment planning, post-traumatic growth, and graduation

Chapter 10.0: The Work the Map Was Always Pointing Toward

Three modules have been pointing toward this one.

Module A built the regulatory and dialectical foundation. Module B made the specific patterns organizing the BPD presentation visible with enough precision that they became workable. Module C delivered the four DBT skill modules with the Pattern Map as their targeting framework. Each of those modules was instrumental: building conditions for something larger.

Module D is what they were building conditions for.

The clinical agenda of Module D is not recovery from BPD. The BPD presentation does not disappear with treatment, and promising otherwise is a clinical misrepresentation that sets up the specific quality of treatment failure that the most experienced BPD clinicians know well: the client who has completed a full program and discovers that the patterns are still present, the abandonment fear is still there, the splitting still happens, and concludes that treatment failed. Treatment did not fail. The expectation was wrong.

The clinical agenda of Module D is something more specific and more honest: a life that is genuinely the client's own, built from the values that persist across mode shifts, organized around direction rather than around symptom management, and equipped with the regulatory foundation, the Pattern Map visibility, and the skills access that make genuine forward movement possible. The BPD patterns will recur. The difference is whether the client has the framework to understand them, the skills to interrupt them at earlier chain links, the relational resources to co-regulate through them, and the identity grounding to return to after them.

10.1 The Module D Architecture

Module D spans six sessions: shorter than Modules A, B, and C because it builds directly on everything that came before rather than introducing new conceptual frameworks. The sessions are organized as a forward arc: from identity to relationships to post-treatment planning to life direction to growth to graduation.

Session 25 addresses values and identity beyond the diagnosis, extending Session 11's identity disturbance mapping into the constructive work of identifying what persists across mode shifts and building a values-based identity direction that the mode states do not own. Session 26 addresses relational repair: the specific relationships that BPD behavior has damaged or ended, examined without minimization or catastrophization, with realistic frameworks for the repair that is possible and the loss that requires acceptance. Session 27 provides the abandonment trigger management framework for the post-treatment period: the specific calendar-based and relational planning that keeps the abandonment fear from organizing the months following discharge. Session 28 integrates ACT values work with DBT's central goal of building a life worth living, producing the specific forward direction that is this curriculum's equivalent of Book 1's Integration Map. Session 29 addresses post-traumatic growth without forced optimism: the genuine positive changes that can emerge from the struggle with BPD and its developmental origins, held without requiring the adversity to have been worth it. Session 30 is graduation.

10.2 The Module D Clinical Stance

Module A's clinical stance was dialectical architect. Module B's was compassionate mapper. Module C's was skilled navigator. Module D's clinical stance is honest witness: the facilitator who has walked through all thirty sessions with this group and can now speak truthfully about what was built, what remained difficult, what is genuinely available to each person as they leave, and what the work ahead looks like with honesty rather than reassurance.

The graduation session is the most relationally charged session of the curriculum. Chapter 5's Relational Update principle operates in every Module D session at its highest intensity: each session ending brings the program's ending closer, which activates the abandonment system in ways that the facilitator must name directly and respond to with the same regulated, non-retaliatory, consistent warmth that every prior session required. The ending of this program is itself the last clinical intervention of Module D: a modeled relational ending that is acknowledged, grieved appropriately, and metabolized rather than avoided.

Session 25: Values and Identity Beyond the Diagnosis

Module: D: Identity, Relationships, and a Life Worth Living

Phase: Identity Construction

Session Number: 25 of 30

Session Overview

Session 25 extends the identity disturbance work of Session 11 into the constructive direction: using the mode mapping from Session 12 and the values persistence question from Session 11 to build a values-based identity anchor that the mode shifts do not dissolve. The session's clinical purpose is specific and limited: not to eliminate identity instability but to identify what persists across mode shifts and to name that persistent element as the organizing center of a forward-looking identity that the BPD diagnosis does not own.

Learning Objectives

By the end of Session 25, group members will be able to:

1. Identify at least three values or qualities that persist across their mode states, distinguishing these from mode-specific values or role-based identities.

2. Describe the specific challenge that each of their most active modes presents to values-based identity and name one Opposite Action response to each challenge.

3. Write a two-to-three sentence identity statement that describes who they are beyond the BPD diagnosis, using values language rather than diagnostic language.

4. Connect the identity statement to the Healthy Adult mode as the internal observer from which values-based identity is organized.

Time Allocation

Component	90-Minute Format	60-Minute Format
Opening Ritual, Check-In, Regulatory Assessment	12 min	12 min
Module D Orientation	8 min	5 min
Psychoeducation: Identity Beyond the Diagnosis	20 min	15 min
Experiential: My Values and Identity Statement	30 min	23 min
Group Processing	10 min	0 min
Closing Grounding	10 min	5 min

Materials and Preparation

- Group Agreement displayed; BPD Pattern Maps and Module C Skill Access Maps available

- Handout 25A: My Values and Identity Statement (Appendix C, page C-27)

- Whiteboard: THE BPD DIAGNOSIS DESCRIBES A PATTERN. IT DOES NOT DESCRIBE A PERSON.

Facilitator Notes

Module D orientation takes five to eight minutes at the start of Session 25. Bridge explicitly from Module C: "Module C built the skills. Module D uses them for the specific purpose the whole curriculum has been pointing toward: building a life that is genuinely yours. Not a symptom-free life. A life organized around what you value rather than around managing what you fear."

The identity statement exercise requires specific facilitation care. Clients with significant Detached Protector mode may produce intellectually correct identity statements that feel empty even as they write them. Clients with significant Punitive Parent mode may produce identity statements that are undermined by self-contempt in the same sentence. The facilitator should watch for both and offer the mode-naming response: "I notice the Punitive Parent arrived while you were writing. What does the identity statement say when you write from the Healthy Adult instead?"

Values persistence is the clinical anchor. Many clients with BPD have genuinely never identified what persists across mode states because the mode shifts have been too rapid and the identity instability too chronic for anything to feel permanent. The clinical patience required in this exercise is the patience to sit with a client who says "I don't know what persists" and to offer the specific question that Session 11 introduced: "What quality or value is present in you, even in the hardest mode states? Even the Detached Protector is protecting something it values. What is it protecting?"

Opening Ritual, Check-In, Regulatory Assessment (12 minutes)

"Feet on floor. [Pause.] Weight in chair. [Pause.] Orienting scan. Zero-to-ten. Mode check.

Welcome to Module D. This is the final module of the curriculum and the six sessions we have been building toward since Session 1. Before we begin, I want to say something directly: the work ahead in Module D is the most personally significant work of the entire curriculum. It will also activate the program's ending, which activates the abandonment system for many of you. When that activation happens, name it. We will work with it here rather than outside the room."

Psychoeducation Component (20 minutes)

Talking Point 1: What the diagnosis does and does not describe

"The BPD diagnosis is a description of a pattern: a set of emotional, relational, and identity responses that your nervous system produces under specific conditions, with specific developmental origins, addressed by specific clinical interventions. The diagnosis describes the pattern accurately. It does not describe the person who carries it.

The clinical danger of a BPD diagnosis is specific: it is the only personality disorder diagnosis in common clinical use that is frequently experienced by the people who receive it as a description of who they fundamentally are rather than of how their nervous system responds. 'I am BPD' rather than 'I have a BPD presentation.' That conflation, the collapse of person and pattern, is the identity-level consequence of the invalidating environment's work: if your internal experience was consistently described as evidence of who you are rather than as a response to what happened to you, you will experience a diagnostic label the same way.

Module D begins with the correction: the BPD diagnosis describes a pattern. It does not describe you."

Talking Point 2: Values that persist

"Identity, understood as a stable and genuine sense of self, does not require the absence of mode shifts. It requires something that persists across mode shifts: a quality, a value, a characteristic that is recognizably yours regardless of which mode is running the room.

From Session 11, you were asked whether anything persists. From Session 12, you mapped the five modes and their specific self-concepts. The values persistence question now: what is present in you even inside the most painful mode states?

The Vulnerable Child mode values connection, even when it cannot find it. The Angry/Impulsive Child mode values fairness and care for needs, even when it expresses them destructively. The Detached Protector mode values safety, even when it achieves safety through disconnection. The Punitive Parent mode, most counter-intuitively, frequently reflects a value for honesty or standards, distorted by being turned against the self rather than applied with compassion.

The persistent value is not in spite of the mode. It is within the mode, distorted by the mode's historical emotional logic. Identifying the value beneath the mode state is the first step in the identity work: finding what is genuinely yours that the BPD patterns have been expressing in forms you have not been able to claim."

Experiential Exercise: My Values and Identity Statement (30 minutes)

[Distribute Handout 25A.]

"Take twenty minutes with the values inventory. Three tasks.

First: from your Pattern Map and mode map, identify three to five qualities or values that appear consistently across mode states. They may appear in distorted form in the painful modes. Look for the underlying value beneath the distortion.

Second: for each value, write one sentence describing how it expresses itself in your life when you are in Healthy Adult, even briefly. Not how you wish it expressed. How it actually does, in the moments when you are most genuinely yourself.

Third: write a two-to-three sentence identity statement. Not 'I am a person with BPD who is trying to recover.' Who you are, in values language, beyond the pattern. 'I am someone who ___.' What you care about. What you are building toward. What you want to be known for.

Do not show this to anyone unless you choose to."

[After twenty minutes, invite each group member to share one value from their list and one sentence from their identity statement if willing.]

Group Processing (10 minutes)

1. "What was it like to write an identity statement that was not organized around the diagnosis?"
2. "Which value surprised you to find, or felt most genuinely yours?"
3. "Zero-to-ten. Mode check."

Closing Grounding Practice (10 minutes)

"Feet on floor. [Pause.] Weight in chair. [Pause.] Orienting scan. [Pause.] The identity statement you wrote today is not final. It is a beginning. It will change as the Healthy Adult observer builds. What is already true is that the values you named are yours.

Zero-to-ten. One slightly slower breath."

Take-Home Reflection

Between sessions: read your identity statement once daily. Notice what mode receives it. If the Punitive Parent dismisses it, that is information about the work. If the Healthy Adult recognizes it, that is also information. One sentence: "When I read my identity statement today, the mode that received it was ___."

Handout Reference

Handout 25A: My Values and Identity Statement (Appendix C, page C-27)

Session 26: Relational Repair: Relationships Changed by BPD Behavior

Module: D: Identity, Relationships, and a Life Worth Living

Phase: Relational Work

Session Number: 26 of 30

Session Overview

Session 26 addresses relational repair: the specific relationships that BPD behavior has damaged or ended, examined with the full clinical framework of Modules A through C available as context. The session's clinical purpose is neither to require repair of all damaged relationships nor to require acceptance of all relational losses. It is to examine each relationship category honestly, using the Pattern Map and skills access that make honest examination possible without the shame-driven avoidance or escalation that prior treatment attempts may have produced.

Learning Objectives

By the end of Session 26, group members will be able to:

1. Identify at least two relationships that the BPD presentation has significantly affected, categorizing each using the repair-possible and repair-not-possible framework.

2. Apply the developmental explanation to the relational damage: name what Pattern Map layer was most active in producing the damage and what the behavioral chain looked like.

3. Complete one DEAR MAN repair script for one specific relationship where repair is both possible and genuinely wanted.

4. Practice radical acceptance toward at least one relationship where repair is not possible or not appropriate.

Time Allocation

Component	90-Minute Format	60-Minute Format
Opening Ritual, Check-In, Regulatory Assessment	12 min	12 min
Psychoeducation: Relational Repair with BPD	20 min	15 min
Experiential: My Relational Repair Map	30 min	23 min
Group Processing	18 min	5 min
Closing Grounding	10 min	5 min

Materials and Preparation

- Group Agreement displayed; BPD Pattern Maps available
    - Handout 26A: My Relational Repair Map (Appendix C, page C-28)
    - Whiteboard: two columns. REPAIR POSSIBLE | ACCEPTANCE NEEDED

Facilitator Notes

The relational repair session carries the group's highest cumulative relational activation of Module D. By Session 26, the group has been together for twenty-five sessions, and the topic of relationships damaged by BPD behavior intersects with both the group members' relational histories and, for some, their experience of this group relationship. The facilitator's regulated presence and the group's established container are the clinical holding for this material.

The shame component of relational damage in BPD requires direct address. Unlike relational damage in addiction recovery, where cultural frameworks for amends exist (particularly through twelve-step traditions), relational damage from BPD behavior does not have a widely recognized cultural container. The splitting-driven ruptures, the abandonment-driven escalations, the impulsivity chain's behavioral endpoint in a valued relationship, these produce a quality of relational shame that is frequently more isolating than addiction-related shame because there is no recognized amends process and no community of people who share the specific experience.

Opening Ritual, Check-In, Regulatory Assessment (12 minutes)

"Feet on floor. [Pause.] Weight in chair. [Pause.] Orienting scan. Zero-to-ten. Mode check.

Today we look at the relationships that the BPD patterns have most significantly affected. Before we begin, I want to name something directly: the relational damage that BPD behavior produces is real, and it carries a quality of shame that is often more isolating than other clinical presentations' relational consequences. If shame arrives today, name it. We have the framework to work with it."

Psychoeducation Component (20 minutes)

Talking Point 1: The two categories

"The relational repair work in BPD recovery falls into two categories, and it is essential to distinguish them before beginning any repair attempt.

Repair-possible relationships are those where: the other person is available and willing to engage; the relational damage is specific and nameable using Pattern Map language; a genuine repair offer, distinct from the Vulnerable Child mode's plea for reinstatement, is possible; and the relationship would genuinely support recovery if repaired rather than reactivating the patterns that damaged it.

Acceptance-needed relationships are those where: repair is genuinely not possible, because the other person is not available, not willing, or not safe; the relationship's value lies in its historical meaning rather than in its current potential; genuine acceptance of the loss is the clinical task rather than repair; or the relationship was itself organized around the BPD patterns in ways that repair would reinforce.

Neither category requires perfection of assessment. Many relationships contain elements of both. The clinical task is not to categorize perfectly but to approach repair attempts with the distinction active, because repair attempted in acceptance-needed relationships produces retraumatization rather than healing."

Talking Point 2: The developmental explanation in repair

"The developmental explanation that has organized this entire curriculum has a specific application in relational repair.

When you offer repair to a person whose relationship with you was significantly affected by your BPD patterns, the most honest and most effective repair offer includes the developmental explanation: not as excuse but as context. 'What happened in our relationship was partly organized by a pattern in me that I now understand differently than I did when it was happening. The abandonment fear that looked like attack. The splitting shift that looked like I had decided you were worthless. I am not asking you to excuse what happened. I am offering you an explanation that is more accurate than the one the behavior implied, and I am telling you what I am building now.'

This offer is not always received. The other person's capacity to receive it is their own clinical territory. What the offer does, regardless of reception, is the identity work: it gives the repair attempt the Healthy Adult foundation rather than the Vulnerable Child's plea or the Angry/Impulsive Child's negotiation."

Experiential Exercise: My Relational Repair Map (30 minutes)

[Distribute Handout 26A.]

"Take twenty minutes to build your Relational Repair Map. Three sections.

Section one: identify two or three relationships most significantly affected by your BPD patterns. For each, categorize: repair-possible or acceptance-needed? Note which Pattern Map layer was most active in producing the damage.

Section two: for one repair-possible relationship, write the beginning of a DEAR MAN repair script. Describe the impact of the pattern on the relationship. Express what the impact cost both people. Assert what you are offering, not what you are asking for. This is a repair offer, not a request for reinstatement.

Section three: for one acceptance-needed relationship, practice the Turning the Mind exercise from Session 20. Hold the loss. Name the resistance. Turn once toward acceptance. Write what the turn produced."

[After twenty minutes, invite sharing from each section, one element per person.]

Group Processing (18 minutes)

1. "The categorization: was there a relationship whose category surprised you? What determined the category?"

2. "The repair script: what mode was most active when you tried to write it? What would the Healthy Adult version sound like, compared to the Vulnerable Child version?"

3. "The acceptance turn: what is the hardest relational loss to accept, and what makes it hardest?"

4. "Zero-to-ten. Mode check."

Closing Grounding Practice (10 minutes)

"Feet on floor. [Pause.] Weight in chair. [Pause.] Orienting scan. [Pause.] The relational damage is real. So is the understanding you now have of what produced it. Both are true.

Zero-to-ten. One slightly slower breath."

Take-Home Reflection

Between sessions: hold one repair-possible relationship in mind. Not to act yet. To notice what mode activates when you consider the repair, and what the Healthy Adult would say about the timing.

Handout Reference

Handout 26A: My Relational Repair Map (Appendix C, page C-28)

Session 27: Managing Abandonment Triggers After Treatment

Module: D: Identity, Relationships, and a Life Worth Living

Phase: Post-Treatment Planning

Session Number: 27 of 30

Session Overview

Session 27 builds the post-treatment abandonment trigger management framework: the specific calendar-based, relational, and regulatory planning that addresses the predictable high-risk periods for abandonment activation after program completion. The session draws on the trauma anniversary and seasonal trigger work from Book 1, adapted for the abandonment-fear-specific patterns of BPD presentations, and produces the abandonment trigger calendar that is this curriculum's equivalent of Book 1's Trauma Calendar.

Learning Objectives

By the end of Session 27, group members will be able to:

1. Identify at least three predictable post-treatment abandonment trigger contexts: relational transitions, calendar periods, and situational patterns.

2. Build a personalized abandonment trigger calendar for the first twelve months after program completion.

3. Name at least two proactive regulatory and relational strategies for each high-risk period identified.

4. Identify at least one safe person from their stabilization network who can provide co-regulatory support during identified high-risk periods.

Time Allocation

Component	90-Minute Format	60-Minute Format
Opening Ritual, Check-In, Regulatory Assessment	12 min	12 min
Psychoeducation: Abandonment Triggers After Treatment	20 min	15 min
Experiential: My Abandonment Trigger Calendar	30 min	23 min
Group Processing	18 min	5 min
Closing Grounding	10 min	5 min

Materials and Preparation

- Group Agreement displayed; BPD Pattern Maps and Stabilization Plans available

- Handout 27A: My Abandonment Trigger Calendar (Appendix C, page C-29)

- A physical calendar or calendar template on the handout covering the next twelve months

Facilitator Notes

The program ending is itself the most immediate abandonment trigger this session addresses. The group has been together for twenty-six sessions. The ending of the program, three sessions from now, activates the abandonment system for virtually every client in a BPD group, and it activates it in ways that the group's earlier work has made more visible but not necessarily more comfortable. Naming this directly in Session 27 is both clinically honest and a relational update: "The ending of this program will activate your abandonment system. That is expected. It does not mean the program failed. It means you are human and you built something real here."

Post-treatment is the highest relapse risk period for BPD presentations. The research on treatment outcomes in BPD is consistent: the period immediately following the end of structured treatment is the period of highest risk for return to prior behavioral patterns, crisis admission, and self-harm. The calendar-based planning in this session directly addresses that risk by making the high-risk periods visible before they arrive and by building proactive regulatory strategies before the activation makes planning difficult.

Opening Ritual, Check-In, Regulatory Assessment (12 minutes)

"Feet on floor. [Pause.] Weight in chair. [Pause.] Orienting scan. Zero-to-ten. Mode check.

Three sessions remain after today. I want to name that directly. The end of this program will activate the abandonment system for most of you. That activation is itself one of the abandonment triggers we are planning for today. We will work with it in the room as it arrives."

Psychoeducation Component (20 minutes)

Talking Point 1: Why post-treatment is high-risk

"The end of structured treatment produces a specific cluster of abandonment activations for BPD presentations that standard discharge planning does not typically address.

The most immediate is the ending of the group itself. For most clients in a BPD group program, this group has been, for its duration, the most consistently safe and predictably warm relational environment they have experienced. Losing that environment activates the abandonment system directly, and it does so at a moment when the client is also losing the structured regulatory support, the daily or weekly session contact, and the co-facilitation by people who understand the Pattern Map.

The second cluster is relational transitions: returning to full-time work or caregiving, reengaging with relationships that were minimally available during treatment, or entering new relational contexts without the group container as regulatory backup.

The third cluster is calendar-based: the same seasonal, temporal, and anniversary-based triggers from the trauma calendar in Book 1, applied to BPD-specific activation patterns. Dates associated with major relational losses. Periods of year historically associated with family-of-origin contact. Seasons with sensory associations to the adversity environment."

Talking Point 2: Proactive planning

"The clinical principle this session applies is identical to the one Book 1's Session 29 established: the abandonment triggers that post-treatment will produce are largely predictable before they arrive, and planning for them before activation is possible produces regulatory resources that planning during activation cannot.

A client who knows, in advance, that the week following program completion will activate the abandonment system and has a proactive relational and regulatory plan prepared for that week has a different clinical trajectory than a client who encounters the same activation without preparation. The preparation does not eliminate the activation. It makes the activation legible and survivable rather than confirming the prediction that endings always end in loss."

Experiential Exercise: My Abandonment Trigger Calendar (30 minutes)

[Distribute Handout 27A.]

"Take twenty minutes to build your abandonment trigger calendar. Four sections.

Section one: the program ending. Specifically plan for the seven days following your last session. Who will you contact? What regulatory practices will you use? What do you need to have in place before the last session rather than after it?

Section two: relational transitions in the first six months. What relational shifts are coming after treatment? For each, identify the abandonment activation risk and one proactive relational strategy.

Section three: calendar-based trigger windows in the next twelve months. Mark periods that historically carry higher activation. For each, name one proactive plan: a safe person who will be more available, a regulatory practice you will increase, a preparation you will make in advance.

Section four: the return of the patterns. Not if, but when. The abandonment fear will activate again. The splitting shift will occur. The impulsivity chain will run. Write one sentence for that moment: 'When the pattern returns, I will remember ___.' What does the Healthy Adult want the activated mode state to hear?"

[After twenty minutes, facilitate sharing of section four specifically: "When the pattern returns, I will remember ___." Go around the room if time allows.]

Group Processing (18 minutes)

1. "The program ending as the first abandonment trigger: what activation did naming it produce, right now, in this session?"

2. "The calendar exercise: what period in the next twelve months is the highest-risk window, and what is one proactive strategy you named for it?"

3. "The message to the future activated self: what did you write, and what did writing it feel like?"

4. "Zero-to-ten. Mode check."

Closing Grounding Practice (10 minutes)

"Feet on floor. [Pause.] Weight in chair. [Pause.] Orienting scan. [Pause.] The preparation you built today is real. It does not guarantee a smooth path. It guarantees that the path is more visible than it was before.

Zero-to-ten. One slightly slower breath."

Take-Home Reflection

Between sessions: add any additional triggers to your calendar as they come to mind. And bring the calendar to your individual therapist before the last session of this program.

Handout Reference

Handout 27A: My Abandonment Trigger Calendar (Appendix C, page C-29)

Session 28: Building a Life Worth Living: ACT Values in a DBT Framework

Module: D: Identity, Relationships, and a Life Worth Living

Phase: Forward Direction

Session Number: 28 of 30

Session Overview

Session 28 integrates Acceptance and Commitment Therapy's values clarification with DBT's central goal of building a life worth living. The session extends Session 25's values and identity work into the practical direction of a life organized around values rather than around symptom management, producing the Life Worth Living document that is the forward-facing clinical product of the entire curriculum.

Learning Objectives

By the end of Session 28, group members will be able to:

1. Define "a life worth living" in terms specific to their own values and direction, distinct from symptom reduction as the primary goal.

2. Identify at least three life domains where values-based action is possible in the immediate post-treatment period.

3. Name one specific committed action per values domain, achievable in the first thirty days after program completion.

4. Distinguish values-based direction from pain-avoidance goals, and name at least one place in their current life where they are pursuing the former.

Time Allocation

Component	90-Minute Format	60-Minute Format
Opening Ritual, Check-In, Regulatory Assessment	12 min	12 min
Psychoeducation: ACT Values in DBT Context	20 min	15 min
Experiential: My Life Worth Living Document	35 min	28 min
Group Processing	13 min	0 min
Closing Grounding	10 min	5 min

Materials and Preparation

- Group Agreement displayed; identity statements from Session 25 available

- Handout 28A: My Life Worth Living Document (Appendix C, page C-30)

Facilitator Notes

The Life Worth Living concept requires honest clinical framing in BPD treatment. For many clients in BPD groups, the phrase "a life worth living" carries a specific weight that it does not carry in other clinical populations: for a population with a 10 percent suicide rate, the question of whether life is worth living has often been asked in crisis rather than in recovery. The facilitator should name this directly without dwelling on it: "DBT's goal of a life worth living is not a motivational slogan. For this population, it is a specific clinical commitment: the work ahead is building a life that answers that question with genuine conviction rather than with survival alone."

The values-versus-pain-avoidance distinction is the most practically significant clinical contribution of Session 28. A client who is sober to avoid consequences is organized around pain avoidance. A client who is sober because sobriety is required by the life they want to build is organized around values. The former is sustainable only while the threat remains real. The latter is self-sustaining. For BPD presentations, many of whose recovery behaviors have been motivated primarily by the fear of abandonment or the fear of hospitalization, the shift to values-based motivation is the most durable clinical change Module D can produce.

Opening Ritual, Check-In, Regulatory Assessment (12 minutes)

"Feet on floor. [Pause.] Weight in chair. [Pause.] Orienting scan. Zero-to-ten. Mode check.

Two sessions remain after today. Abandonment trigger check: where is your zero-to-ten, and is any of the activation connected to the program's ending? Name it if so."

[Receive brief check-ins. Acknowledge the program's ending activation if it appears without expanding on it.]

Psychoeducation Component (20 minutes)

Talking Point 1: The distinction

"The Acceptance and Commitment Therapy framework, which DBT has always been in dialogue with, makes a specific distinction that Session 28 applies: the distinction between pain-avoidance goals and values-based direction.

Pain-avoidance goals are organized around moving away from something: avoiding hospitalization, avoiding crisis, avoiding the relational consequences of BPD behavior. They require the threat to remain real to sustain motivation. When the threat recedes, as it tends to after successful treatment, the motivation organized around the threat recedes with it. This is why the period immediately after program completion is the highest-risk period: the pain is less acute, and the motivation organized around the pain loses some of its force.

Values-based direction is organized around moving toward something: what you care about, what you want to build, what kind of person you want to be and what kind of relationships you want to have. It does not require a threat to sustain. A values-based direction is self-sustaining because it is organized around what already matters rather than around what must be avoided."

Talking Point 2: DBT's life worth living

"DBT's concept of a life worth living is Linehan's specific articulation of the treatment's ultimate goal: not merely the reduction of suffering and the management of crisis, but the building of a life that contains genuine positive value. A life the client chooses to be in, not merely a life they are surviving.

For BPD presentations, this goal carries specific clinical meaning. The developmental adversity that produced the BPD presentation frequently also produced a specific deficit in the experience of genuine positive value: the chronic emptiness from Session 15, the identity instability that makes stable goals difficult to maintain, and the relational template that makes the positive experience of closeness so complicated. Building a life worth living for this population means building the specific infrastructure that the adversity failed to provide: genuine positive relational experience, a stable enough identity to organize around, and the regulatory capacity to tolerate positive experience without the nervousness that unfamiliar safety can produce."

Experiential Exercise: My Life Worth Living Document (35 minutes)

[Distribute Handout 28A.]

"Take twenty-five minutes to build your Life Worth Living Document. Four sections.

Section one: values and direction. From Session 25's identity statement and values inventory, name three to five values that will organize the life you are building. Not aspirational values. Values that are genuinely yours, even in their imperfect current form.

Section two: life domains. For at least three domains, name what values-based action looks like: relationships, work or purpose, health, creativity, community, or any domain that matters to you. One sentence per domain: 'In the domain of ___, a life organized around my values would include ___.'

Section three: committed actions. For each domain, one specific, achievable, observable action in the first thirty days after program completion. Not a resolution. A committed action: something you can do, that can be observed, that connects directly to the values domain.

Section four: the honest version. Complete this sentence: 'The life I am building is not ___ yet. But it is genuinely moving toward ___.' The honest version names both the current reality and the real direction. The Healthy Adult writes this section."

[After twenty-five minutes, invite each group member to share their honest version: the current reality and the real direction.]

Group Processing (13 minutes)

1. "The values-versus-pain-avoidance distinction: where in your current recovery are you primarily organized around pain avoidance, and where are you organized around values direction?"

2. "The honest version: what did it feel like to write both the 'not yet' and the 'genuinely moving toward'?"

3. "Zero-to-ten. Mode check."

Closing Grounding Practice (10 minutes)

"Feet on floor. [Pause.] Weight in chair. [Pause.] Orienting scan. [Pause.] The document you built today is the most forward-facing clinical work of the entire curriculum. It does not describe where you are. It describes where you are going.

Zero-to-ten. One slightly slower breath."

Take-Home Reflection

Between sessions: read the Life Worth Living Document once. Notice which mode receives each section. Notice whether the Healthy Adult can hold the document as genuinely yours, even briefly.

Handout Reference

Handout 28A: My Life Worth Living Document (Appendix C, page C-30)

Session 29: Post-Traumatic Growth in BPD Recovery: Growth Without Forced Optimism

Module: D: Identity, Relationships, and a Life Worth Living

Phase: Meaning and Integration

Session Number: 29 of 30

Session Overview

Session 29 addresses post-traumatic growth in the specific context of BPD recovery: the genuine positive changes that can emerge from the struggle with BPD and its developmental origins, held without requiring the adversity to have been worth it, the recovery to be complete, or the growth to be dramatic. The session uses the Tedeschi and Calhoun (2004) post-traumatic growth framework adapted for BPD presentations and explicitly rejects the forced optimism that makes post-traumatic growth presentations feel invalidating to clients who are still in significant pain.

Learning Objectives

By the end of Session 29, group members will be able to:

1. Define post-traumatic growth in the BPD context and distinguish it from false positivity, silver-lining thinking, and the forced optimism that the invalidation history makes especially activating.

2. Identify at least one genuine area of growth across the Tedeschi and Calhoun growth domains that is specifically connected to the recovery work of this curriculum.

3. Write one despite-structure sentence for each growth domain they identify: "Despite the cost of ___, I have found ___."

4. Name one area where growth is not yet visible and practice radical acceptance of that absence without Punitive Parent commentary.

Time Allocation

Component	90-Minute Format	60-Minute Format
Opening Ritual, Check-In, Regulatory Assessment	12 min	12 min
Psychoeducation: Post-Traumatic Growth Without Forced Optimism	20 min	15 min
Experiential: My Growth Domains	30 min	23 min
Group Processing	18 min	5 min
Closing Grounding	10 min	5 min

Materials and Preparation

- Group Agreement displayed; BPD Pattern Maps, identity statements, and Life Worth Living Documents available

- Handout 29A: Post-Traumatic Growth in BPD Recovery (Appendix C, page C-31)

Facilitator Notes

The forced optimism problem requires explicit clinical address. For clients whose developmental history included systematic invalidation of their emotional experience, being told that their suffering has produced positive change can re-enact the invalidation: "You have been through something terrible, and it has made you stronger" may be heard as "Your suffering was justified by its outcomes." The post-traumatic growth framework must be delivered with the specific framing that Session 21 of Book 1 established: growth without requiring the adversity to have been worth it. The adversity was not worth it. It happened. Growth can emerge from the struggle with what happened. Both of these things are true simultaneously.

The despite-structure sentence is the clinical form of this truth. "Despite the cost of the adversity, I have found ___" holds both poles: the cost is real and named; the growth is real and named; neither cancels the other. This dialectical structure, acceptance and change held simultaneously, is the last application of the curriculum's core philosophical principle before graduation.

Opening Ritual, Check-In, Regulatory Assessment (12 minutes)

"Feet on floor. [Pause.] Weight in chair. [Pause.] Orienting scan. Zero-to-ten. Mode check.

One session after today. Abandonment trigger check: where is your zero-to-ten, and what is present right now that connects to the program's ending?"

[Receive brief check-ins. Acknowledge the ending activation with warmth and without minimizing it.]

Psychoeducation Component (20 minutes)

Talking Point 1: What post-traumatic growth is and is not

"Tedeschi and Calhoun's post-traumatic growth framework identifies five domains in which genuine positive change can emerge from the struggle with significant adversity or difficulty.

I want to be precise about what this framework is and is not, because the invalidation history that most people in this room carry makes the forced optimism version of this framework genuinely activating.

Post-traumatic growth is not the claim that the adversity was worth it. The adversity was not worth it. The adversity that produced the BPD presentation in this room represents specific, real, and significant harm to specific children who deserved better. That is not redeemed by positive outcomes.

Post-traumatic growth is also not the claim that suffering inevitably produces strength. It does not. Suffering sometimes produces strength and sometimes produces damage, and both outcomes can occur in the same person in different domains.

Post-traumatic growth is a specific empirical observation: that in the struggle with significant adversity, some people in some domains experience genuine positive change that would not have occurred without the struggle. The change is real. The adversity was still not worth it. Both are true. This is the dialectical structure that this entire curriculum has been practicing."

Talking Point 2: The five growth domains

"Tedeschi and Calhoun identified five domains in which post-traumatic growth is commonly reported. For BPD presentations, each domain has a specific recovery-relevant application.

Personal strength: changed sense of one's own capacity, the recognition that you have survived and built something under conditions that would have been genuinely beyond some people. The specific application: you have completed this curriculum with a BPD presentation, an adversity history, and a pattern of treatment that may have previously failed you. The fact that you are in Session 29 is itself evidence of strength.

Relating to others: changed quality or depth in at least some relational connections. The specific application: the relational work of this curriculum, the group connection, the repair attempts of Session 26, the DEAR MAN and GIVE practices, represent relational learning that is different in quality from what was available before.

New possibilities: the opening of new directions that the pre-adversity or pre-recovery self would not have accessed. The specific application: the identity statement from Session 25 may describe a direction that the Detached Protector's protection or the Punitive Parent's contempt had previously made inaccessible.

Appreciation of life: a changed relationship to ordinary experience and its value. The specific application: the chronic emptiness work, the somatic positive experience practices, represent the beginning of this domain for many BPD presentations.

Spiritual or existential change: changed beliefs about meaning, purpose, or the structure of experience. This domain varies most widely by individual history and should be offered without clinical prescription."

Experiential Exercise: My Growth Domains (30 minutes)

[Distribute Handout 29A.]

"Take twenty minutes to complete the growth domain inventory. For each of the five domains: first, identify whether any growth is visible, even minimally. Second, if visible, write one despite-structure sentence: 'Despite the cost of ___, I have found ___.' Third, if not visible, write one sentence of radical acceptance: 'Growth in this domain is not yet visible, and that is the current reality.'

Do not manufacture growth where there is none. The honest absence is more clinically valuable than the performed presence."

[After twenty minutes, invite sharing of one despite-structure sentence per person.]

Group Processing (18 minutes)

1. "The forced optimism distinction: did the despite-structure feel different from the silver-lining framing? What was different about it?"

2. "The domain where growth was hardest to find: what makes that domain the most difficult?"

3. "The program is ending in one more session. What is one genuine thing that this group and this work have given you, stated in the despite-structure: 'Despite ___, I have found ___'?"

4. "Zero-to-ten. Mode check."

Closing Grounding Practice (10 minutes)

"Feet on floor. [Pause.] Weight in chair. [Pause.] Orienting scan. [Pause.] The growth you named today is real. The cost that produced it was also real. Both are true.

Next session is graduation. Come prepared to receive what this group has offered you, and to offer what you have built to the people in this room.

Zero-to-ten. One slightly slower breath."

Take-Home Reflection

Between sessions: read your despite-structure sentences once. Then read your Life Worth Living Document. Notice whether they connect. One sentence: "The connection between my growth and my direction is ___."

Handout Reference

Handout 29A: Post-Traumatic Growth in BPD Recovery (Appendix C, page C-31)

Session 30: Graduation: Carrying the Dialectic Forward

Module: D: Identity, Relationships, and a Life Worth Living

Phase: Closure and Forward Direction

Session Number: 30 of 30

Session Overview

Session 30 is the graduation session: the structured clinical closure of the thirty-session program. The session has four purposes: to acknowledge what was built across the curriculum; to metabolize the ending of the group rather than avoiding or minimizing it; to complete and sign the Continuing Care Plan that is each client's primary post-treatment planning document; and to mark the graduation as a forward-facing relational event, the model of a relational ending that is acknowledged, grieved appropriately, and held rather than abruptly cut.

Learning Objectives

By the end of Session 30, group members will be able to:

1. Name three specific things they built across the curriculum using the vocabulary of the curriculum: the Pattern Map layer, the skill, or the Healthy Adult capacity they developed.

2. Complete and sign the Continuing Care Plan with specific entries in each section.

3. Receive feedback from one other group member and offer feedback to one other group member using GIVE and FAST skills.

4. Name one thing they will carry forward from this group that they did not have before Session 1.

Time Allocation

Component	90-Minute Format	60-Minute Format
Opening Ritual, Check-In, Regulatory Assessment	12 min	12 min
Curriculum Review: What We Built	15 min	10 min
Continuing Care Plan Completion	20 min	20 min
Graduation Exercise: What I Carry Forward	25 min	13 min
Closing Ritual	18 min	5 min

Materials and Preparation

- Group Agreement displayed; all module documents available
  - Handout 30A: My Continuing Care Plan (Appendix C, page C-32)

- Individual contact information for each group member, if the group has established a peer support agreement

- Facilitator preparation: the closing ritual requires the facilitator to offer a brief, genuine, specific acknowledgment to each group member. Prepare these individually before the session. They should be specific to the person's work, naming one thing the facilitator observed that was specific to this client's contribution, struggle, or growth across the curriculum.

Facilitator Notes

The graduation session activates the abandonment system at its highest intensity of the curriculum. Every technique for managing this activation has been built across the prior twenty-nine sessions. The clinical task of Session 30 is not to prevent the activation but to provide the clinical model of how a relational ending can be held: acknowledged honestly, grieved genuinely, and completed with forward direction rather than avoidance or collapse.

The Continuing Care Plan is the most practically important document Session 30 produces. Its entries should be specific and achievable, not aspirational. Each section references a specific module's work: the stabilization plan from Session 8 for the regulatory section; the Pattern Map for the self-awareness section; the Module C skill access map for the skills section; the Life Worth Living Document from Session 28 for the direction section; and the abandonment trigger calendar from Session 27 for the high-risk period section.

The facilitator's specific acknowledgments are the most clinically significant facilitation act of Session 30. They should be offered in the closing ritual, not scattered throughout the session. They should be specific to the person's work, not generically warm. They should model the Healthy Adult's capacity to see another person clearly and to name what they see with accuracy and care. For many clients in this group, a specific, accurate, genuinely warm acknowledgment from a clinician who has known them across thirty sessions is an experience of being seen that their developmental history did not provide.

Opening Ritual, Check-In, Regulatory Assessment (12 minutes)

"Feet on floor. [Pause.] Weight in chair. [Pause.] Orienting scan. Zero-to-ten. Mode check.

This is the last session of the program. I want to name directly: the abandonment system is likely activated for most of you right now, at some level. That is expected, and it is appropriate. This group is ending. The work you built in it is not ending. The people in this room are not ending. The group container, this specific form of meeting, is ending.

We will name what this ending produces rather than manage it. Everything in this curriculum has been preparing for exactly this: a relational ending that we hold together rather than avoid."

Curriculum Review: What We Built (15 minutes)

"Before we close, a brief review of what this curriculum built across thirty sessions.

Module A built the regulatory and dialectical foundation: the Window of Tolerance as a monitoring tool, the zero-to-ten practice, the Stabilization Plan, Wise Mind, the ACE framework for your BPD presentation, radical acceptance, and the co-regulatory experience of a group that was consistently and predictably safe.

Module B built the Pattern Map: seven layers of visibility into the specific patterns organizing your BPD presentation, with enough precision that they became workable rather than simply familiar.

Module C built the skills: all four DBT skill modules, with the Pattern Map as their targeting framework and the mode barriers to each skill explicitly named and addressed.

Module D built the forward direction: values and identity beyond the diagnosis, relational repair, abandonment trigger planning, a life worth living document, post-traumatic growth without forced optimism, and this graduation.

What you built is yours. It does not live in this room. It lives in you."

Continuing Care Plan Completion (20 minutes)

[Distribute Handout 30A.]

"Take fifteen minutes to complete the Continuing Care Plan. Every section requires a specific entry, not a general aspiration.

The regulatory section: your top two regulatory practices and your highest-rated TIPP component.

The pattern awareness section: the one Pattern Map layer that is most active for your BPD presentation and the one earliest chain link at which you can currently intervene.

The skills section: the two skills from your Module C access map that are most accessible right now and the one skill that requires the most continued practice.

The direction section: one sentence from your Life Worth Living Document describing where you are going.

The high-risk period section: the highest-risk abandonment trigger window in the next twelve months from your Session 27 calendar, and one proactive plan for it.

The support section: your primary safe person and your primary individual therapist, with contact information.

Sign and date. This document belongs to you."

Graduation Exercise: What I Carry Forward (25 minutes)

"We are going to close with two exchanges.

First, one thing you carry forward. Go around the room. Each person names one thing they are leaving this program with that they did not have at Session 1. One sentence, using the curriculum's vocabulary: a Pattern Map layer that is now visible, a skill that now works when it did not before, a Healthy Adult moment that was not available before, or something the group gave you that you could not have gotten alone.

[Go around the room. Receive each contribution with specific acknowledgment: "That is a real thing you built."]

Second, one thing you offer. Each person offers one sentence to one other person in the room: something you observed in them across this curriculum that they may not have named for themselves. Use GIVE and FAST: gentle, validating, honest.

[Facilitate offering circle. The facilitator participates, offering their specific acknowledgment of each group member.]"

Closing Ritual (18 minutes)

"I want to close this program the same way we have closed every session: with the practice that was the first clinical act of Session 1 and has been the last clinical act of every session since.

Feet on floor. [Pause 15 seconds.] Weight in chair. [Pause.] Look around the room. [Pause.]

What you see is a group of people who have completed thirty sessions of the most demanding clinical work available in BPD treatment. They have mapped the patterns that organized their presentation with more precision than most treatment ever asked them to bring. They have built the regulatory foundation that makes skills accessible. They have learned four DBT skill modules with those patterns as the targeting framework. They have looked at their identity, their relational history, the growth that emerged from the struggle, and the life they are building.

The group is ending. The dialectic is not. Acceptance and change. Both are always necessary. Neither alone is sufficient. You learned that in the first week of Module A and you are carrying it into whatever comes next.

Zero-to-ten. One slightly slower breath. Go build the life.

[Wait in silence for one full minute before anyone moves.]"

Take-Home Reflection

There is no take-home reflection from Session 30. The program is complete. The work continues.

Handout Reference

Handout 30A: My Continuing Care Plan (Appendix C, page C-32)

Part Three: Appendices and Clinical Resources

Reproducible Client Handouts (1A through 30A)

All print-ready handouts for all modules. Formatted for sixth to eighth grade reading level. Camera-ready for photocopying or digital distribution. Includes colour-coded module headers and writing lines.

https://drive.google.com/file/d/1e_wumye4yIhsOmQcU93q8_xy8ltqaQfA/view?usp=sharing

Appendix A: ACE Questionnaire and BPD-Specific Scoring Guidance

A.1 About This Questionnaire

The ACE Questionnaire is adapted from the original Centers for Disease Control and Kaiser Permanente Adverse Childhood Experiences Study instrument (Felitti et al., 1998). It assesses ten categories of childhood adversity occurring before age 18. In this curriculum it is administered in Session 5 as a clinical tool for the de-shaming developmental reframe described in Chapters 1 and 2 and the Front Matter's Preface.

Facilitator administration guidance: Complete the questionnaire individually and privately. Do not ask group members to share their scores aloud. Scores are used for the client's own reflection on the developmental connections to their BPD presentation, not for group disclosure. If completing the questionnaire produces acute distress, individual therapist follow-up should be scheduled before the next group session. See Appendix D for crisis protocol.

A.2 The ACE Questionnaire

Before age 18, did you experience any of the following? Answer Yes or No for each.

#	Item	Yes	No
1	Did a parent or other adult in the household often swear at you, insult you, put you down, humiliate you, or act in a way that made you afraid you might be physically hurt?		
2	Did a parent or other adult in the household often push, grab, slap, or throw something at you, or ever hit you so hard that you had marks or were injured?		
3	Did an adult or person at least five years older than you ever touch or fondle you or have you touch their body in a sexual way, or attempt or actually have oral, anal, or vaginal intercourse with you?		
4	Did you often feel that no one in your family loved you or thought you were important or special, or that your family did not look out for each other, feel close to each other, or support each other?		
5	Did you often feel that you did not have enough to eat, had to wear dirty clothes, and had no one to protect you, or that your parents were too drunk or high to take care of you or take you to the doctor if you needed it?		
6	Were your parents ever separated or divorced?		
7	Was your mother or stepmother often pushed, grabbed, slapped, or had something thrown at her, or sometimes or often kicked, bitten, hit with a fist, or hit with something hard, or ever repeatedly hit over at least a few minutes, or ever threatened or hurt by a knife or gun?		
8	Did you live with anyone who was a problem drinker or alcoholic or who used street drugs?		
9	Was a household member depressed or mentally ill, or did a household member attempt suicide?		
10	Did a household member go to prison?		

My ACE Score (total Yes responses): ________ (This information is private)

A.3 BPD-Specific Scoring Guidance for Facilitators

Score of 0 to 2: Below the clinical average for BPD populations. If the client presents with BPD and reports a low ACE score, clinical caution is warranted: research consistently documents underreporting of emotional abuse and neglect, the two categories most strongly associated with BPD, in populations where those adversity types were so chronic they were experienced as normal. A low score does not indicate absence of adversity; it may indicate adversity that was never named as such. Session 5 group discussion should include space for this clinical reality.

Score of 3 to 5: Moderate adversity burden. Consistent with research on BPD populations; connects to biosocial theory content of Session 2. The specific categories endorsed are more clinically significant than the total score: emotional abuse (item 1) and emotional neglect (item 4) have the strongest independent associations with BPD symptoms and should be highlighted in the facilitator's Session 5 delivery.

Score of 6 to 10: High adversity burden. Research by Porter and colleagues (2020) found BPD individuals are 13.91 times more likely to report childhood adversity than non-clinical controls; this range is consistent with that finding. NESARC-III analyses (Fall, 2020) further establish that emotional abuse and emotional neglect are among the strongest independent predictors of BPD diagnosis. Clients in this range may experience the questionnaire completion itself as activating. Facilitators should monitor the collective window in Session 5 and be prepared to extend somatic regulation time before the group discussion.

Critical clinical note on Item 1 (emotional abuse): This item is the single most clinically significant ACE category for BPD presentations. Many clients answer No to this item not because they did not experience emotional abuse but because the chronic quality of the invalidation made it unrecognizable as abuse. The Session 5 psychoeducation on what emotional abuse looks like, including relentless dismissal, contempt for emotional expression, and systematic communication that the child's experience was wrong, is designed to help clients revisit this item with more clinical accuracy.

A.4 Connecting ACE Score to BPD Pattern Map

After Session 5, clients are invited to connect their specific ACE endorsements to the Pattern Map layers being built in Module B. The connection table below supports that work.

ACE Item	Most Directly Connected BPD Pattern Map Layer
Item 1: Emotional abuse	Abandonment chain (relational threat calibration); identity disturbance (invalidated self-concept); Punitive Parent mode (internalized critical voice); chronic emptiness (attunement disruption)
Item 4: Emotional neglect	Chronic emptiness (attunement deprivation framework); Vulnerable Child mode (unmet developmental needs); stabilization network deficits
Item 7: Domestic violence	Window of Tolerance narrowing; hypervigilant amygdala calibration; splitting (unpredictable environment produces categorical processing)
Item 8: Substance use in household	Relational template disruption; stabilization network deficits; impulsivity chain activation by unpredictability
Item 9: Mental illness in household	Window of Tolerance narrowing; identity disturbance (role reversal, parentification); Detached Protector mode development
Items 2, 3	Self-harm function map (dissociation-interrupting function); window narrowing; Vulnerable Child mode; relational template disruption

Appendix B: Screening Tools

B.1 About the Screening Tools in This Appendix

Appendix B contains four validated screening instruments used in BPD treatment programs alongside this curriculum. These instruments are not part of the curriculum's session plan structure but are recommended for program intake assessment and ongoing monitoring. Facilitators should review each instrument's scoring guidance and understand its clinical purpose before using it with clients.

Note on clinical authorization: These instruments should be administered and interpreted by licensed clinical professionals. Results should be integrated into the individual treatment plan and discussed with the supervising clinician. Scores on any instrument do not constitute a diagnosis and should not be communicated to clients in isolation from clinical context.

B.2 Zanarini Rating Scale for BPD (ZAN-BPD)

The ZAN-BPD is a nine-item clinician-administered instrument assessing the severity of BPD symptoms across four domains: affective disturbance, cognitive disturbance, impulsive disturbance, and interpersonal disturbance. It is recommended at intake, at Module B completion, and at program discharge to track symptom severity change across the curriculum.

Domain	Symptom Item	Score (0 to 4)
Affective	Inappropriate, intense anger or difficulty controlling anger	
Affective	Affective instability due to marked reactivity of mood	
Affective	Chronic feelings of emptiness	
Cognitive	Transient, stress-related paranoid ideation or severe dissociative symptoms	
Cognitive	Identity disturbance: markedly unstable self-image or sense of self	
Impulsive	Impulsivity in at least two areas that are potentially self-damaging	
Impulsive	Recurrent suicidal behavior, gestures, or threats, or self-mutilating behavior	
Interpersonal	Frantic efforts to avoid real or imagined abandonment	
Interpersonal	Pattern of unstable and intense interpersonal relationships	

Scoring: 0 = None; 1 = Mild; 2 = Moderate; 3 = Severe; 4 = Very severe. Total score range: 0 to 36. Scores of 9 or higher are associated with clinically significant symptom burden.

Interpretation guidance: At intake, a high score on affective items (1 and 2) with high emptiness (item 3) and identity disturbance (item 5) is the most common BPD presentation in IOP and PHP settings and is most directly addressed by the Module A through B curriculum sequence. High scores on impulsive items (6 and 7) require elevated clinical monitoring and should prompt review of Appendix D's self-harm protocol before Module B begins.

Reference: Zanarini, M. C., Vujanovic, A. A., Parachini, E. A., Boulanger, J. L., Frankenburg, F. R., & Hennen, J. (2003). Zanarini Rating Scale for Borderline Personality Disorder (ZAN-BPD): A continuous measure of DSM-IV borderline psychopathology. Journal of Personality Disorders, 17(3), 233-242.

B.3 Primary Care PTSD Screen for DSM-5 (PC-PTSD-5)

The PC-PTSD-5 is a five-item self-report screening tool for PTSD symptoms. It is included in this appendix because of the high prevalence of co-occurring PTSD in BPD presentations and the clinical significance of the BPD-PTSD overlap for this curriculum's delivery. Clients with probable PTSD alongside BPD require additional clinical planning before Module B's higher-activation sessions and may need modified pacing through Sessions 14 and 15.

In the past month, have you had any experience that was so frightening, horrible, or upsetting that you...

Item	Yes	No
1. Had nightmares about it or thought about it when you did not want to?		
2. Tried hard not to think about it or went out of your way to avoid situations that reminded you of it?		
3. Were constantly on guard, watchful, or easily startled?		
4. Felt numb or detached from others, activities, or your surroundings?		
5. Felt guilty or could not stop blaming yourself or others for the event or any problems the event may have caused?		

Scoring: Three or more Yes responses indicate a positive screen. A positive screen warrants referral for full PTSD assessment before Module B begins.

Clinical note for BPD-PTSD co-occurrence: The combination of BPD and PTSD in the same client produces a clinical presentation that requires careful consideration of session pacing. Sessions 14 (self-harm) and 15 (chronic emptiness) in Module B carry the highest PTSD activation risk in the curriculum. Facilitators working with clients who screen positive for PTSD should review the individual crisis pathway in Appendix D and coordinate individual therapist availability for the week of those sessions.

Reference: Prins, A., Bovin, M. J., Smolenski, D. J., Marx, B. P., Kimerling, R., Jenkins-Guarnieri, M. A., Kaloupek, D. G., Schnurr, P. P., Kaiser, A. P., Leyva, Y. E., & Tiet, Q. Q. (2016). The Primary Care PTSD Screen for DSM-5 (PC-PTSD-5): Development and evaluation within a veteran primary care sample. Journal of General Internal Medicine, 31(10), 1206-1211.

B.4 Patient Health Questionnaire-9 (PHQ-9)

The PHQ-9 is a nine-item self-report instrument assessing depression severity. It is included because depressive symptoms are among the most common BPD comorbidities and because severe depression at intake may indicate the need for modified curriculum pacing. Item 9, which assesses suicidal ideation, requires immediate clinical follow-up when endorsed above zero regardless of total score.

Over the last two weeks, how often have you been bothered by any of the following problems?

(0 = Not at all, 1 = Several days, 2 = More than half the days, 3 = Nearly every day)

Item	Score (0 to 3)
1. Little interest or pleasure in doing things	
2. Feeling down, depressed, or hopeless	
3. Trouble falling or staying asleep, or sleeping too much	
4. Feeling tired or having little energy	
5. Poor appetite or overeating	
6. Feeling bad about yourself, or that you are a failure, or have let yourself or your family down	
7. Trouble concentrating on things, such as reading the newspaper or watching television	
8. Moving or speaking so slowly that other people could have noticed; or the opposite, being so fidgety or restless that you have been moving around a lot more than usual	
9. Thoughts that you would be better off dead, or of hurting yourself in some way	

Total Score: ______ (0-4 None/Minimal; 5-9 Mild; 10-14 Moderate; 15-19 Moderately Severe; 20-27 Severe)

Critical note on Item 9: Any score above zero on Item 9 requires immediate individual clinical follow-up before the client's next group session. See Appendix D.

Reference: Kroenke, K., Spitzer, R. L., & Williams, J. B. W. (2001). The PHQ-9: Validity of a brief depression severity measure. Journal of General Internal Medicine, 16(9), 606-613.

B.5 Columbia Suicide Severity Rating Scale (C-SSRS) Screener Version

The Columbia Suicide Severity Rating Scale screener version is a five-item clinician-administered tool that assesses both suicidal ideation and suicidal behavior. It distinguishes non-suicidal self-injury from suicidal behavior, which is the distinction that governs clinical response throughout this curriculum (see Session 14 and Appendix D).

Part I: Ideation (ask in order; stop at first No)

Question	Yes	No
1. Wish to be dead: Have you wished you were dead or wished you could go to sleep and not wake up?		
2. Suicidal thoughts: Have you had any actual thoughts of killing yourself?		
3. Suicidal thoughts with method: Have you been thinking about how you might do this?		
4. Suicidal intent: Have you had these thoughts and had some intention of acting on them?		
5. Suicidal intent with plan: Have you started to work out or have you worked out the details of how to kill yourself? Do you intend to carry out this plan?		

Part II: Behavior (past three months)

Question	Yes	No
1. Has the person done anything, started to do anything, or prepared to do anything to end their life?		

Clinical response guidance: Any Yes on items 3, 4, or 5 of Part I, or any Yes on Part II, requires immediate individual crisis assessment outside the group setting. See Appendix D Section D.3 for the full clinical response protocol.

Reference: Posner, K., Brown, G. K., Stanley, B., Brent, D. A., Yershova, K. V., Oquendo, M. A., Currier, G. W., Melvin, G. A., Greenhill, L., Shen, S., & Mann, J. J. (2011). The Columbia-Suicide Severity Rating Scale: Initial validity and internal consistency findings from three multisite studies with adolescents and adults. American Journal of Psychiatry, 168(12), 1266-1277.

Appendix C: Reproducible Client Handouts

Sessions 1 through 30

The handouts in Appendix C are camera-ready for photocopying or digital distribution. They are licensed for clinical use with individual clients within a licensed treatment setting. See the copyright page for full reproduction terms.

Handout Index

Handout	Title	Session
1A	Our Group Agreement	Session 1
1B	The Zero-to-Ten Arousal Scale	Session 1
2A	The Biosocial Theory and My History	Session 2
3A	My Window of Tolerance Map	Session 3
4A	Wise Mind: Finding the Balance	Session 4
5A	Understanding ACEs: Your History and Your BPD	Session 5
6A	Radical Acceptance: What It Is and What It Is Not	Session 6
7A	My Stabilization Network	Session 7
8A	My Stabilization Plan	Session 8
9A	My Abandonment Fear Chain	Session 9
10A	My Splitting Pattern Map	Session 10
11A	My Identity Map	Session 11
12A	My Mode Map	Session 12
12B	The Five BPD Modes in Plain Language	Session 12
13A	My Impulsivity Chain	Session 13
14A	My Self-Harm Function Map	Session 14
15A	Mapping My Chronic Emptiness	Session 15
16A	My BPD Pattern Map	Session 16
17A	Core Mindfulness: The What Skills	Session 17
18A	Core Mindfulness: The How Skills and Wise Mind	Session 18
19A	Crisis Survival Skills: TIPP, ACCEPTS, and Self-Soothe	Session 19
20A	Radical Acceptance and IMPROVE	Session 20
21A	Emotion Regulation: Understanding My Emotional System	Session 21
22A	Emotion Regulation: Opposite Action, PLEASE, and Building Positive Experience	Session 22
23A	Interpersonal Effectiveness: DEAR MAN and GIVE	Session 23
24A	FAST Skills and Limits	Session 24
25A	My Values and Identity Statement	Session 25
26A	My Relational Repair Map	Session 26
27A	My Abandonment Trigger Calendar	Session 27
28A	My Life Worth Living Document	Session 28

Handout	Title	Session
29A	Post-Traumatic Growth in BPD Recovery	Session 29
30A	My Continuing Care Plan	Session 30

Handout 1A: Our Group Agreement

Session 1 | Module A

This agreement belongs to all of us. We built it together in our first session.

What we agreed:

Our Agreement	Why It Matters
What is shared here stays here	Safety depends on confidentiality
We share the impact of our history, not specific details of traumatic events	Protects everyone in the room
No graphic descriptions of self-harm in this group	Protects the whole group including the person sharing
Passing is always available	You are always in charge of your participation
We speak from our own experience	No one speaks for someone else
We stay present in the room	Your presence matters to this group

We also agreed:

____

____

____

Signed by our group on: ____

Handout 1B: The Zero-to-Ten Arousal Scale

Session 1 | Module A

This scale measures where your nervous system is right now. Use it at the start and end of every session.

Number	What It Feels Like
0 to 2	Completely flat: numb, checked out, not fully here, no energy
3 to 4	Below the window: tired, foggy, disconnected, going through the motions
5 to 6	In the window: present, thinking clearly, able to use skills
7 to 8	Above the window: anxious, activated, restless, hard to focus
9 to 10	Flooded: overwhelmed, unable to think clearly, everything feels urgent

My number right now: _______

What I notice in my body at this number:

____

____

I know I am in the window (5 to 6) when:

____

____

Between sessions practice: Check your zero-to-ten number once daily. Just notice. You do not need to do anything with it.

Handout 2A: The Biosocial Theory and My History

Session 2 | Module A

The biosocial theory says that BPD develops when a person with high emotional sensitivity grows up in an environment that consistently invalidates that sensitivity.

Part 1: The two components

Does emotional sensitivity fit your experience? Describe it in your own words:

____

____

Does an invalidating environment fit your history? What did the invalidation look and sound like for you specifically?

____

____

____

Part 2: What the biosocial theory means for how you understand your BPD

Does the biosocial explanation fit? Does it change anything about how you understand your diagnosis?

____

____

____

Part 3: What it produces in you

When you read the sentence "BPD develops in the overlap between emotional sensitivity and an invalidating environment," what is your reaction?

____

____

Handout 3A: My Window of Tolerance Map

Session 3 | Module A

HYPERAROUSAL (Above my window)

What my body does: ____

What my thinking does: ____

What my behavior looks like from outside:

____

What I feel like from inside: ____

THE WINDOW (Inside my window)

What it feels like to be here: ____

What is available to me here that is not available outside:

____

How often I am here, roughly: ____

HYPOAROUSAL (Below my window)

What my body does: ____

What my thinking does: ____

What I feel like from inside: ____

BPD-Specific Addition: My Relational Cues

One relational event that reliably moves me above my window:

____

What my body does first when this cue arrives:

____

Handout 4A: Wise Mind: Finding the Balance

Session 4 | Module A

State of Mind	What It Feels Like	When It Takes Over
Emotion Mind	Emotion feels like the whole truth. Intensity. Urgency. Certainty.	When the window is exceeded or a mode activates
Reasonable Mind	Cool, analytical, distant. Accurate but disconnected from feeling.	When the Detached Protector mode is active
Wise Mind	Both present. Integrated. Grounded. I can feel it and also assess it.	When I am inside my window

From the breathing space practice:

Was there a moment that felt closer to Wise Mind? Describe it:

____

____

If there was no Wise Mind moment, what did you notice?

____

____

My access practice:

The one thing I can do right now to make Wise Mind more accessible:

____

Between sessions: Practice the breathing space exercise once daily in a neutral moment. Notice which state of mind is most present.

Handout 5A: Understanding ACEs: Your History and Your BPD

Session 5 | Module A

(ACE Questionnaire is in Appendix A. Complete it privately before the group discussion.)

My ACE Score: ________ (Private)

After completing the questionnaire:

Does the number help explain anything about your BPD that has felt confusing or unexplained? Write what comes:

____

____

____

The emotional abuse finding:

Research shows emotional abuse is the strongest ACE predictor of BPD. Does your history include emotional abuse, including being told your emotions were wrong, excessive, or shameful? What does that finding mean for how you understand your BPD?

____

____

____

The accountability question:

Does understanding the developmental origins of your BPD change your responsibility for how you act in current relationships and in treatment? What is your honest answer?

____

____

Handout 6A: Radical Acceptance: What It Is and What It Is Not

Session 6 | Module A

Radical Acceptance IS	Radical Acceptance IS NOT
Full acknowledgment of reality as it is	Approval of what happened
Freeing regulatory resources from fighting what cannot be changed	Giving up on change
An internal shift in your relationship to reality	Forgiving the people who caused harm
The prerequisite for effective change	Passivity or resignation

One thing I have been fighting rather than accepting:

____

____

The estimated cost of that fight (in regulatory energy, relationships, or recovery):

____

____

From the acceptance breathing exercise:

What happened when you said internally: "This is what is"?

____

____

Radical acceptance of my BPD specifically:

What would it mean to fully accept that I have a BPD presentation that is the developmental outcome of specific adversity?

____

____

Handout 7A: My Stabilization Network

Session 7 | Module A

Safe People (people whose presence tends to settle my nervous system)

Safe Places (locations where my nervous system tends to settle)

1. ____

2. ____

Safe Activities (things that produce a regulatory effect for my nervous system)

1. ____

2. ____

3. ____

One relationship or context that reliably activates rather than settles me:

____

What I do before or after contact with that activation:

____

The assessment question for safe people: Does this person's presence, on balance, tend to move my zero-to-ten number lower or higher?

Handout 8A: My Stabilization Plan

Session 8 | Module A

My Window of Tolerance Signs

I am above my window when: ____

I am below my window when: ____

My Most Effective Grounding Techniques

Primary technique: ____

Backup technique: ____

Wise Mind Access

The practice that most reliably gives me brief access to Wise Mind:

____

My Safe People, Places, and Activities

Safe person I will contact first: ____

Safe place I can go: ____

Safe activity that regulates me: ____

Radical Acceptance Practice

One specific thing I am currently practicing accepting:

____

When I notice I am approaching high-risk territory, the first thing I will do:

____

____

Handout 9A: My Abandonment Fear Chain

Session 9 | Module B

Work backward from link five. Leave blank what you cannot yet access.

Link	What to Map	My Entry
Link 5	The behavioral response (what I did)	
Link 4	The emotional activation (what I felt, specifically)	
Link 3	The somatic state (what was happening in my body before the emotion had a name)	
Link 2	The perceptual cue (change in tone, missed message, moment of disconnection, session ending)	
Link 1	The developmental calibration (what my history taught my nervous system to watch for)	

The earliest link I could access:

____

An observation about the calibration (the lesson my nervous system learned):

____

____

Between sessions: When the abandonment fear activates in real time, identify the earliest link you can access. One sentence: "The earliest link I noticed was ___."

Handout 10A: My Splitting Pattern Map

Session 10 | Module B

A relationship where the splitting pattern is most active:

____

The specific cue that most reliably triggers the shift from idealization to devaluation:

____

____

The somatic signature of the shift (what happens in my body when the splitting shift begins):

____

____

What the idealization phase looks like for me:

____

What the devaluation phase looks like for me:

____

The developmental origin (what the original environment required this categorical processing to do):

____

____

Between sessions: Notice once when the somatic signature of a splitting shift begins. Not to stop it. To notice it.

Handout 11A: My Identity Map

Session 11 | Module B

My experience of identity disturbance (which fits most closely: absence, instability, inauthenticity, or real only in extremity):

____

____

Using the mode framework:

Mode	What It Says About Who I Am	How Active in My Presentation (1-3)
Vulnerable Child		
Angry/Impulsive Child		
Detached Protector		
Punitive Parent		
Healthy Adult		

The mode-state self-concept that is most painful:

____

Is there anything that persists across mode states? Any quality, value, or characteristic that appears regardless of which mode is active:

____

____

Handout 12A: My Mode Map

Session 12 | Module B

Use Handout 12B for mode descriptions.

Mode	How Active in My Presentation (1-3)	How It Specifically Expresses in My Behavior or Self-Concept
Vulnerable Child		
Angry/Impulsive Child		
Detached Protector		
Punitive Parent		
Healthy Adult		

For my two highest-rated modes, where do they likely come from in my history?

Mode: _________ | Origin: ____

Mode: _________ | Origin: ____

The mode check-in (used from Session 12 onward):

"Which mode is most present right now?" ____

Handout 12B: The Five BPD Modes in Plain Language

Session 12 | Module B | Reference Card

The Vulnerable Child

The part of you that carries the original pain. Terror of being alone. Grief of what was never there. Longing for care that the adversity made genuinely hard to find. When this part is most active, you are in pain and reaching for care, often in ways that others cannot fully meet.

The Angry/Impulsive Child

The part that holds the rage at what was done. The entitlement to have needs met. The urgency that acts before the thinking brain can catch up. When this part is most active, you escalate, test limits, or do things before you have decided to do them.

The Detached Protector

The part that learned to survive by becoming unreachable. Not indifference. The specific emotional distance that protected you when emotional presence was genuinely dangerous. When this part is most active, you are here but not fully here.

The Punitive Parent

The part that took the harsh or dismissive voice from the adversity environment and turned it on yourself. When this part is most active, you tell yourself you deserve what you are getting, that the pain is your fault, that you should not be struggling.

The Healthy Adult

What treatment is building. The part that can see all the other modes, hold them with some compassion, and choose behavior from your values rather than from the mode's historical logic. This is the goal. Its unfamiliarity right now is not evidence of its impossibility.

Handout 13A: My Impulsivity Chain

Session 13 | Module B

Work backward from link five.

Link	What to Map	My Entry
Link 5	The impulsive action	
Link 4	The urge state (what the urgency felt like, specifically, in my body)	
Link 3	The regulatory collapse (signs I was above my window)	
Link 2	The mode that activated (which mode was running the room?)	
Link 1	The trigger (what relational or perceptual cue initiated the chain?)	

The earliest link I could access:

____

The mode at link two:

____

One intervention I might try at the earliest accessible link:

____

____

Handout 14A: My Self-Harm Function Map

Session 14 | Module B

This handout is about the function of self-harm, not the specific details. No graphic content.

Which functions apply to my self-harm history? (Check all that apply and describe in general terms)

Function	Applies?	In General Terms, What the Behavior Does for My Nervous System
Regulatory: shifts autonomic state from flooding to manageable		
Communicative: conveys pain that verbal expression has not reached		
Dissociation-interrupting: grounds in body when dissociated or numb		
Self-punishing: enacts the Punitive Parent's message that pain is deserved		

For my most active function, what state is my nervous system in before the behavior:

____

One alternative that might address the same function:

____

The barrier to accessing that alternative in the moment:

____

Handout 15A: Mapping My Chronic Emptiness

Session 15 | Module B

The quality of my chronic emptiness (not the emotion words, the phenomenological texture. What does it feel like from inside?):

____

____

____

Where it lives in my body, if it has a location:

____

What I use to fill it or escape it (at least two things, without judgment):

1. ____
2. ____
3. ____

Connecting to history:

When did you first notice this quality? ____

Does the attunement-deprivation explanation fit? (The idea that emotional attunement would have filled what is now absent):

____

____

Handout 16A: My BPD Pattern Map

Session 16 | Module B

Use all seven Module B handouts as reference. Enter the most essential finding from each layer.

Layer	My Key Finding
1. Abandonment chain (the five links)	
2. Splitting pattern (the cue, the somatic signature, the categorical shift)	
3. Identity disturbance (which form, which mode carries the most painful self-concept)	
4. Schema modes (which modes are most active, what each does)	
5. Impulsivity chain (the mode at link two, the regulatory collapse at link three)	
6. Self-harm function (the primary function, the alternative identified)	
7. Chronic emptiness (the phenomenology, the connection to attunement deprivation)	

Cross-layer patterns (things that appear in more than one layer simultaneously):

Pattern 1: ____

Pattern 2: ____

The most precise description of what my BPD has been organized around:

____

____

Handout 17A: Core Mindfulness: The What Skills

Session 17 | Module C

The Three What Skills

Skill	What It Means	The BPD Barrier
Observe	Notice what is present in experience without evaluating or modifying it	Detached Protector blocks internal access; amygdala hypervigilance resists turning inward
Describe	Put words on observations without adding interpretation	Invalidation history makes trusting internal experience feel dangerous
Participate	Engage fully in the present moment without self-monitoring	Abandonment-vigilant nervous system monitors the external environment during inward attention

From the Observe practice:

What I noticed: ____

The resistance that arose (if any): ____

The Pattern Map connection:

Where on my Pattern Map would the Observe skill create an intervention opportunity?

____

Between sessions: Practice Observe for two minutes once daily in a neutral moment. Notice the specific form of resistance.

Handout 18A: Core Mindfulness: The How Skills and Wise Mind

Session 18 | Module C

The Three How Skills

Skill	What It Means	My Primary Mode Barrier
Nonjudgmentally	Observe without adding an evaluation layer	Punitive Parent (turns observation into self-contempt)
One-Mindfully	Full attention to one thing at a time	Hypervigilant amygdala divides attention between internal experience and relational threat monitoring
Effectively	Do what works, not what is right or satisfying in principle	Angry/Impulsive Child demands justice; Punitive Parent prefers self-punishment

From the Wise Mind body scan:

Mode present at the start: ____

What I observed from outside the mode:

____

What Wise Mind offered about the Pattern Map layer I brought in:

____

My Wise Mind access practice:

The mode check I will do before the body scan:

____

Daily practice target: Two minutes of Wise Mind body scan, beginning with the mode check.

Handout 19A: Crisis Survival Skills: TIPP, ACCEPTS, and Self-Soothe

Session 19 | Module C

TIPP Practice Ratings (1 = no effect, 2 = mild shift, 3 = clear shift)

Component	Mechanism	My Rating	What I Noticed
Temperature (cold water on wrists or face)	Activates mammalian diving reflex, parasympathetic shift		
Intense Exercise (60 seconds vigorous movement)	Burns stress hormones, reduces cortisol and adrenaline		
Paced Breathing (exhale slightly longer than inhale)	Shifts autonomic balance toward parasympathetic		
Paired Muscle Relaxation (tense then release)	Addresses somatic tension component of hyperarousal		

My primary TIPP tool: ____

My ACCEPTS personalization (three strategies most accessible for my nervous system):

1. ____

2. ____

3. ____

The mode state from which ACCEPTS is most accessible:

____

Pattern Map location: These skills address link _______ and link _______ of my impulsivity chain.

Handout 20A: Radical Acceptance and IMPROVE

Session 20 | Module C

Turning the Mind Practice

The Pattern Map layer I turned toward acceptance:

____

The resistance that arose: ____

What happened in my body when I turned:

____

Willingness versus Willfulness

Willingness	Willfulness (my expression)
Open to what is	
Participating in life as it actually is	
Responding from Wise Mind	

IMPROVE Personalization (three components most accessible for my nervous system):

Between sessions: Practice Turning the Mind once daily toward one specific Pattern Map layer.

Handout 21A: Emotion Regulation: Understanding My Emotional System

Session 21 | Module C

One recent emotional episode:

The visible (secondary) emotion: ____

Underneath it, the primary emotion: ____

What the primary emotion was detecting:

____

Was the detection calibrated to the current situation, or to a historical one?

____

My three-part BPD emotional profile:

My emotional sensitivity (high, medium, low and describe):

____

My emotional reactivity (what activates it):

____

My return to baseline (how long it typically takes):

____

My PLEASE vulnerability factors:

Factor	Current Status	One Concrete Change
Physical illness		
Eating		
Avoiding substances		
Sleep		
Exercise		

Handout 22A: Emotion Regulation: Opposite Action, PLEASE, and Building Positive Experience

Session 22 | Module C

Opposite Action Practice

One emotional episode: ____

The primary emotion: ____

Its action urge (what the emotion wanted me to do):

____

The opposite action (what would directly contradict the action urge):

____

The mode that would need to be present for opposite action to be possible:

____

Building Positive Experience: My Somatic Start

One two-minute somatic positive experience I will try:

____

What I noticed when I tried it: ____

Pattern Map connection:

Opposite Action addresses which Pattern Map layer?

____

Handout 23A: Interpersonal Effectiveness: DEAR MAN and GIVE

Session 23 | Module C

My DEAR MAN Script

The interaction and my objective: ______________________________________

Component	My Script	Mode Most Likely to Interfere
Describe (the situation behaviorally)		
Express (impact in feeling language)		
Assert (one specific request)		
Reinforce (benefit to the other person)		
Mindful (stay with the request)		
Appear confident (grounded, steady)		
Negotiate (willing to find different ways)		

GIVE Self-Assessment

The relationship where maintaining the connection is the primary goal:

____

Which GIVE component is hardest for my nervous system and why:

____

Handout 24A: FAST Skills and Limits

Session 24 | Module C

FAST Self-Assessment

Component	What It Means	My Punitive Parent's Interference	What the Healthy Adult Would Do
Fair	Treat yourself with the same standards you apply to others		
No Apologies	Do not apologize for your existence or values		
Stick to values	Maintain your values under relational pressure		
Truthful	Do not lie to maintain a relationship		

My Limits Framework

Relational limits (conditions my nervous system needs for recovery):

____

Disclosure limits (what I share, with whom, and when):

____

Self-harm limits (alternative I have prepared for the next urge):

____

Module C Skill Access Map

Module	Most Accessible Skill	Skill Requiring Most Practice	Mode Blocking Practice
Mindfulness			
Distress Tolerance			
Emotion Regulation			
Interpersonal Effectiveness			

Handout 25A: My Values and Identity Statement

Session 25 | Module D

Values that persist across my mode states (3 to 5, from the values inventory):

1. ____ How it expresses when I am in Healthy Adult: ____

2. ____ How it expresses when I am in Healthy Adult: ____

3. ____ How it expresses when I am in Healthy Adult: ____

4. ____

5. ____

My Identity Statement (2 to 3 sentences, values language, beyond the diagnosis):

____

____

____

____

Between sessions: Read your identity statement once daily. Notice which mode receives it.

Handout 26A: My Relational Repair Map

Session 26 | Module D

Section 1: Relationship Categorization

Section 2: DEAR MAN Repair Script (one repair-possible relationship)

What I am offering (not requesting): ____

Describe (the pattern's impact on the relationship):

____

Express (what the impact cost both people):

____

Assert (what I am offering): ____

Section 3: Turning the Mind (one acceptance-needed relationship)

The loss I am accepting: ____

What the resistance says: ____

What happened when I turned: ____

Handout 27A: My Abandonment Trigger Calendar

Session 27 | Module D

Section 1: The Program Ending (most immediate trigger)

My zero-to-ten right now when I think about the program ending: _______

Who I will contact in the seven days following my last session:

____

Regulatory practices I will use in that week:

____

What I need to have in place before the last session rather than after:

____

Section 2: Relational Transitions (first six months)

Section 3: Calendar-Based Trigger Windows (next twelve months)

Section 4: When the Pattern Returns

"When the abandonment fear activates and the pattern returns, I will remember:"

____

____

Handout 28A: My Life Worth Living Document

Session 28 | Module D

Section 1: My Values and Direction (from Session 25's identity statement)

Three to five values organizing the life I am building:

1. ____

2. ____

3. ____

Section 2: Life Domains

Domain	Values-Based Action in This Domain Looks Like
Relationships	
Work or Purpose	
Health	
One more domain that matters to me:	

Section 3: Committed Actions (one specific, observable action per domain in the first thirty days)

Domain _______________: I will ____

Domain _______________: I will ____

Domain _______________: I will ____

Section 4: The Honest Version

The life I am building is not ____ yet.

But it is genuinely moving toward ____.

Handout 29A: Post-Traumatic Growth in BPD Recovery

Session 29 | Module D

The despite-structure: "Despite the cost of ___, I have found ___."

Growth Domain	Growth Visible?	My Despite-Structure Sentence
Personal Strength (changed sense of my own capacity)	Yes / Not yet	
Relating to Others (changed quality of some connections)	Yes / Not yet	
New Possibilities (directions that were not previously available)	Yes / Not yet	
Appreciation of Life (changed relationship to ordinary experience)	Yes / Not yet	
Existential or Meaning Change (changed beliefs about purpose)	Yes / Not yet	

The domain where growth is hardest to find:

____

Radical acceptance of that absence:

"Growth in this domain is not yet visible, and that is the current reality."

What that sentence produces: ____

What this group specifically has given me, in the despite-structure:

Despite ____, I have found ____.

Handout 30A: My Continuing Care Plan

Session 30 | Module D

Regulatory Practices

My top two regulatory practices: ____

My highest-rated TIPP component: ____

Pattern Awareness

The Pattern Map layer most active in my BPD presentation:

____

The earliest chain link at which I can currently intervene:

____

Skills Access

The two most accessible skills from my Module C access map:

____

The one skill requiring the most continued practice:

____

Direction

One sentence from my Life Worth Living Document describing where I am going:

____

____

High-Risk Period

My highest-risk abandonment trigger window in the next twelve months:

____

My proactive plan for that period: ____

Support

My primary safe person: ____ Contact:

____

My individual therapist: ____ Contact:

____

Appendix D: Self-Harm and Suicide Safety Planning Protocol

D.1 Purpose and Scope

This protocol governs clinical response to self-harm and suicidal behavior across all thirty sessions of the curriculum. Every facilitator must read this appendix in its entirety before facilitating Session 1 and must review it with their clinical supervisor before the first session and again before Session 14.

The protocol distinguishes two clinically distinct phenomena that require different clinical responses: non-suicidal self-injury (NSSI) and suicidal behavior. Conflating these phenomena produces both clinical underresponse and overresponse. This protocol provides the clinical decision framework for each.

D.2 NSSI and Suicidal Behavior: The Clinical Distinction

Non-suicidal self-injury is deliberate physical self-harm without suicidal intent. In BPD populations it most commonly functions as a regulatory strategy, a form of communication, a dissociation-interrupting tool, or a self-punishment expression of the Punitive Parent mode. NSSI is clinically serious and requires clinical attention. It does not require the same immediate crisis response as suicidal behavior.

Suicidal behavior includes suicidal ideation with intent, plan, or means; suicide attempts; and completed suicide. Suicidal behavior in BPD presentations requires immediate individual clinical assessment outside the group setting. The group does not continue until the suicidal client has been individually assessed and a safety plan is in place.

How to distinguish them in session: When a group member discloses self-harm, the facilitator asks directly and calmly: "When you hurt yourself, are you trying to die, or are you trying to manage something that is unbearable?" This question is not alarming. It is the clinical act of obtaining accurate information on which the response depends. A clear "no intent to die" answer is clinically meaningful. Any ambiguity or "yes" requires the suicidal behavior protocol.

D.3 In-Session Disclosure Protocol

If a group member discloses recent NSSI with no suicidal intent:

Step 1: Acknowledge directly and without excessive alarm. "I hear that you have been hurting yourself. I am glad you told us, and I want to make sure you have individual support this week."

Step 2: Assess the current state. "What is your zero-to-ten right now? Are you safe right now?"

Step 3: Maintain the group's regulatory state. Offer a brief grounding practice before continuing session content if the disclosure has significantly elevated the collective window.

Step 4: Schedule individual follow-up. The facilitator or program staff contacts the client's individual therapist the same day.

Step 5: Document. See Appendix D Section D.5.

If a group member discloses suicidal ideation with intent, plan, or means:

Step 1: Pause the group calmly and clearly. "I need to step out for a moment with [name]. [Co-facilitator name] will continue holding the space."

Step 2: Move to individual assessment outside the group room. Use the C-SSRS from Appendix B to assess severity.

Step 3: Activate the program's crisis pathway. This includes contacting the on-call clinician, the individual therapist, and, when clinically indicated, emergency services. The client should not be left alone during this process.

Step 4: Return to the group only after the suicidal client has been individually held. The group will have been held by the co-facilitator during this time.

Step 5: Acknowledge the disruption to the group briefly and directly. "Something came up that required individual attention. Everyone in this group matters to us, and so does the group itself. Let's check our windows and return to where we were."

D.4 Between-Session Crisis Protocol

Clients in this program must have access to a crisis contact outside of group session hours. Every client should have the following confirmed at intake and reviewed in Session 1:

Individual therapist contact information and after-hours coverage procedure.

Program crisis line or on-call clinician number.

National Suicide Prevention Lifeline: 988 (call or text, available 24 hours, United States).

Crisis Text Line: Text HOME to 741741 (United States).

Local emergency services: 911 or local equivalent.

The program's specific crisis response procedure, including whether group members are given the facilitator's direct contact or a program number, should be determined by the program before the curriculum begins and communicated clearly to all group members in Session 1.

D.5 Documentation Requirements

Every clinical event involving self-harm disclosure, suicidal ideation, or crisis response requires documentation on the same day it occurs. Documentation should include: the specific disclosure or behavior; the clinical assessment performed; the clinical response and rationale; the individual therapist contact and their response; and the plan for the next group session.

Facilitators should review their program's specific documentation requirements before the curriculum begins. For programs using electronic health records, the documentation should flag the event for supervisor review.

D.6 Facilitator Self-Care After Crisis Events

Session 14 and any session involving self-harm disclosure or suicidal behavior requires post-session facilitator debrief. The debriefing should address: the facilitator's regulatory state during and after the event; any countertransference activated by the disclosure; the clinical accuracy of the response; and what the facilitator needs before the next session.

This debrief belongs in the supervision session identified in the Facilitator Competencies and Training Recommendations. It should not be deferred.

Appendix E: 12-Week IOP and 8-Week PHP Implementation Guides

E.1 12-Week IOP Implementation Guide (Three Sessions Per Week)

This guide assumes three sessions per week, ninety minutes each, totaling thirty-six available sessions. The thirty sessions of the curriculum leave six sessions for review, skills practice reinforcement, and clinical contingency.

Week	Sessions	Module	Clinical Notes
1	1-3	A	Sessions 1, 2, 3. Do not schedule Sessions 2 and 3 on consecutive days. Allow one session between biosocial theory and window of tolerance.
2	4-6	A	Sessions 4, 5, 6. Session 5 (ACE framework) is the highest-activation Module A session. Schedule individual therapist availability the same day.
3	7-8 + Review	A to B	Session 7, Session 8, Module A Review session. Use the review session to complete Stabilization Plans for any client who did not complete in session.
4	9-11	B	Sessions 9, 10, 11. Do not schedule Sessions 9, 10, and 11 on consecutive days without at least one grounding or review session between them.
5	12-14	B	Sessions 12, 13, 14. Session 14 (self-harm) is the highest-activation session of the curriculum. Schedule individual therapist availability the same day and the following day. Supervisor review of Session 14 facilitation required before independent delivery.
6	15-16 + Review	B	Sessions 15, 16, Module B Review. Ensure BPD Pattern Maps are complete before any client enters Module C.
7	17-19	C	Sessions 17, 18, 19. Module C regulatory prerequisite check: confirm all clients have a working grounding toolkit and zero-to-ten monitoring practice before beginning.
8	20-22	C	Sessions 20, 21, 22.
9	23-24 + Review	C	Sessions 23, 24, Module C review. Skill access maps completed.
10	25-27	D	Sessions 25, 26, 27. Session 27 addresses the program ending three sessions ahead. Begin naming it here.
11	28-29 + Review	D	Sessions 28, 29, and a clinical review session for Life Worth Living Documents and growth domain work.
12	30 + Transition	D	Session 30 Graduation. Final individual clinical meetings with all clients recommended in the week before graduation.

Extension guidance: If clinical assessment before Module B indicates insufficient regulatory foundation, extend Module A by one to two additional review sessions using any combination of Sessions 1 through 8 content. This extends the program to fourteen weeks. This extension is always preferable to proceeding to Module B with a group whose window stability is inadequate for the pattern recognition content.

E.2 8-Week PHP Implementation Guide (Five Sessions Per Week)

This guide assumes five sessions per week, ninety minutes each, totaling forty available sessions. The thirty sessions leave ten available for review, diary card work, skills reinforcement, and clinical contingency.

Week	Sessions	Module	Clinical Notes
1	1-5	A	Full Module A delivered Monday through Friday. Session 5 (ACE framework) on Wednesday or Thursday, with individual follow-up available that day.
2	6-8 + Reviews	A	Sessions 6, 7, 8, and two review sessions. Use review sessions for Stabilization Plan completion and somatic practice reinforcement. All clients must have working regulatory practices before Week 3.
3	9-12 + Review	B	Sessions 9, 10, 11, 12. Schedule a review session after Session 12 for mode map completion. Do not schedule Sessions 9, 10, and 11 on consecutive days in the same week without a review session between.
4	13-16 + Review	B	Sessions 13, 14, 15, 16 plus one review session. Session 14 on Tuesday or Wednesday with individual support available for the full week. Pattern Maps must be complete before Week 5.
5	17-20 + Review	C	Sessions 17, 18, 19, 20, plus one review session for TIPP and skills reinforcement.
6	21-24 + Review	C	Sessions 21, 22, 23, 24, plus one review. Module C skill access maps completed by end of week.
7	25-28 + Review	D	Sessions 25, 26, 27, 28, plus one review session for Life Worth Living Document completion.
8	29-30 + Transitions	D	Session 29 Monday, Session 30 Graduation Wednesday or Thursday. Tuesday, Friday, and the final day available for individual clinical meetings and transition planning.

Diary card integration: PHP programs that use DBT diary cards alongside group skills training should integrate them beginning in Module C, Week 5. Diary cards address the between-session generalization of skills and should be reviewed briefly at the opening of each Module C session rather than in a separate diary card review session. The diary card review takes five minutes and replaces the take-home reflection check-in in the opening ritual.

E.3 Rolling Admissions Adaptation

As established in the Front Matter, rolling admissions in BPD group programs requires stronger closed-cohort protocols than in addiction programs. The recommended rolling admissions structure:

Module A as an open, rolling-entry group: New members may join Module A on any session, with orientation provided by the facilitator at the start of each new member's first session. Module A's content is cyclical enough that clients can enter at any point and receive adequate orientation within two sessions.

Modules B through D as closed cohorts: Each closed cohort opens when a minimum of four and a maximum of eight Module A completers are ready to proceed. The cohort is closed at Session 9 and remains closed through Session 30. Under no circumstances should new members enter an existing Module B, C, or D cohort.

Minimum cohort interval: No new Module B cohort should begin until at least eight weeks have elapsed since the previous cohort's Session 9. This interval allows adequate individual clinical preparation and prevents program-level resource depletion.

Appendix F: Facilitator Self-Care: Managing Splitting, Idealization, and Secondary Traumatization

F.1 Why This Appendix Is Not Optional

Chapter 5 established that the facilitator's regulatory state is the primary clinical instrument in BPD treatment. Appendix F exists because that instrument requires maintenance, and the specific maintenance required in BPD group facilitation is different from what most clinical training prepares facilitators for.

The material in this appendix is not generic self-care guidance. It is specific to the countertransference dynamics that BPD presentations produce and to the secondary traumatization that sustained exposure to high-ACE clinical content generates. Every facilitator delivering this curriculum should read this appendix before Session 1 and return to it after any session that produces significant countertransferential activation.

F.2 Managing Splitting and Idealization

When you are being idealized: The idealization of the BPD facilitator is not a clinical complication to be managed. It is a clinical process to be understood. A group member in the idealization phase is experiencing the Vulnerable Child mode's hope that this relationship will provide what prior relationships have not. The clinical task is not to disabuse the idealization abruptly, which replicates abandonment, nor to accept it and act from it, which sets the stage for the devaluation that follows. The task is to be consistently warm, consistent, and genuinely present without accepting the omnipotence that idealization assigns.

Signs that idealization is affecting facilitation: excessive preparation anxiety about not meeting the group member's expectations; reluctance to give clinical feedback that might disrupt the positive regard; a quality of performance in the facilitation that is aimed at maintaining the idealized image rather than at delivering the clinical content.

When you are being devalued: Devaluation is the most clinically destabilizing experience in BPD facilitation for most practitioners. The specific quality of the devaluation, its directness, its certainty, and its occasional accuracy (BPD clients are perceptive observers of relational dynamics), makes the non-defensive response genuinely difficult.

Signs that devaluation is affecting facilitation: withdrawal from the group member producing the devaluation; over-explanation or over-justification of clinical decisions; a quality of clinical coldness that is organized by self-protection rather than by clinical judgment; or the opposite: excessive accommodation to the devaluing group member that abandons the clinical frame.

The supervised response to devaluation: name it, non-defensively, and bring it to supervision. "I am experiencing devaluation from this group member, and it is activating something in me that I need to examine before the next session."

F.3 Secondary Traumatization Prevention

Sustained exposure to high-ACE clinical content, particularly the childhood emotional abuse, emotional neglect, and developmental adversity described across Modules A and B, produces secondary traumatization in clinicians who work with it without adequate protective structures. Secondary traumatization is not a sign of insufficient professional resilience. It is the predictable outcome of empathic engagement with traumatic material over time without the regulatory support structures that make sustained exposure clinically sustainable.

The three protective structures for BPD group facilitators:

Regular clinical supervision with access to all three supervision domains described in the Front Matter: clinical decision-making, facilitator state, and countertransference to BPD specifically.

Peer consultation with at least one colleague who understands the clinical demands of BPD group facilitation. Peer consultation supplements supervision rather than replacing it. Its specific function is normalization: the experience of "this is what this work produces" from someone who has encountered the same clinical terrain.

Personal regulatory practice maintained independently of clinical performance: the same zero-to-ten monitoring, grounding practice, and Wise Mind access that the curriculum teaches clients to build. A facilitator whose own regulatory practice exists only in theory cannot credibly hold the group's regulatory field.

F.4 The Pre-Session Regulatory Check

Before every session, the facilitator completes a self-assessment that takes two minutes and is non-negotiable.

Zero-to-ten: Where am I right now? If above five, take one regulatory action before entering the room.

Mode check: Which mode is most present right now? The Detached Protector that protects against the session's emotional intensity will produce flat facilitation. The Vulnerable Child activated by the group member who is struggling will produce over-identification. The Punitive Parent activated by group dynamics will produce clinical coldness. Name the mode. Take one Healthy Adult action: one breath, one orienting scan, one Wise Mind moment.

Residual activation from prior sessions: Am I carrying anything from the previous session into this one? If yes, it belongs in supervision, not in the next session.

F.5 Burnout Recognition

Burnout in BPD group facilitation has a specific signature that differs from general clinical burnout: it tends to appear as emotional flatness in the group room rather than as exhaustion outside it; as a quality of going through the clinical motions while the genuine relational engagement has withdrawn;

or as a gradual erosion of the non-retaliatory response to testing behavior, producing either subtle aversion or subtle collusion.

The clinical cost of unrecognized burnout in BPD group facilitation is significant. The Relational Update that Chapter 5 identified as the primary treatment mechanism depends on the facilitator's genuine regulated presence. A facilitator operating from burnout cannot provide that presence, and the group's clinical progress depends on it.

If a facilitator recognizes the burnout signature in themselves, the clinical response is not to push through the next session. It is to bring it to supervision immediately, to discuss the need for a session pause, a co-facilitation adjustment, or a clinical consultation before proceeding.

Appendix G: Evidence Base Summary

G.1 Purpose

Appendix G provides a summary of the five foundational evidence bases that this curriculum integrates, with references to the primary literature that facilitators and clinical directors can use to deepen their understanding of the clinical framework. The summary is organized to parallel the curriculum's clinical architecture: ACE research and biosocial theory inform Modules A and B; schema therapy and DBT inform Module C; and mentalization-based treatment informs the relational dimensions of Module D.

G.2 Dialectical Behavior Therapy (DBT)

Dialectical Behavior Therapy is the gold-standard treatment for borderline personality disorder, with the largest and most rigorous evidence base of any BPD treatment currently available. The foundational texts are Linehan's (1993) original treatment manual and her (2015) skills training manual, second edition. The core DBT evidence base demonstrates significant reductions in self-harm behavior, hospitalization rates, and treatment dropout in BPD populations relative to treatment as usual.

The Module C skills training in this curriculum delivers the four DBT skill modules exactly as Linehan describes them. Facilitators who have not completed formal DBT skills training should read the 2015 Skills Training Manual before facilitating Module C.

For the emerging evidence on trauma-focused DBT adaptations, see Bohus and colleagues' (2020) DBT-PTSD randomized controlled trial and Prillinger and colleagues' (2024) systematic review of DBT variants for PTSD. Both support the argument this curriculum makes for addressing developmental trauma alongside standard DBT skills training.

Key references: Linehan (1993); Linehan (2015); Bohus et al. (2020); Prillinger et al. (2024).

G.3 Schema Therapy

Schema therapy, developed by Jeffrey Young and colleagues, provides the clinical vocabulary for the early maladaptive schemas and schema modes that this curriculum applies across Module B and throughout Module D. The schema mode framework, specifically the five BPD-relevant modes of Vulnerable Child, Angry/Impulsive Child, Detached Protector, Punitive Parent, and Healthy Adult, provides the internal map that makes DBT skills training more targeted and more accessible.

Randomized controlled trials support schema therapy's efficacy for BPD, with Nadort and colleagues (2009) demonstrating effective implementation of outpatient schema therapy in regular mental healthcare settings. The combination of schema therapy concepts with DBT skills delivery is the specific integration that this curriculum advances.

Key references: Young, Klosko, and Weishaar (2003); Nadort et al. (2009); Fassbinder, Schweiger, Martius, Brand-de Wilde, and Arntz (2016).

G.4 Biosocial Theory

Linehan's (1993) biosocial theory of BPD, describing the interaction between emotional sensitivity and an invalidating environment as the developmental mechanism producing BPD, is the foundational theoretical model of Chapters 1 and 2 and the organizing framework of Module A's psychoeducation. Session 2 delivers the biosocial theory in group settings as the primary de-shaming clinical intervention of Module A.

The biosocial theory's empirical foundation has strengthened substantially since Linehan's original articulation, particularly through the ACE research that established the specific adversity types most strongly associated with BPD: emotional abuse as the strongest predictor, and emotional neglect as the second. This curriculum treats the ACE research as the empirical validation and elaboration of the biosocial theory's invalidating environment construct.

Key references: Linehan (1993); Porter et al. (2020); Fall (2020); Carpenter and Trull (2013).

G.5 ACE Research

The Adverse Childhood Experiences research program, initiated by Felitti and colleagues (1998) at Kaiser Permanente in collaboration with the Centers for Disease Control, established the dose-response relationship between adverse childhood experiences and a broad range of adult health and behavioral health outcomes. The BPD-specific findings from this program are among the most clinically significant findings in personality disorder research.

The 2020 meta-analysis by Porter and colleagues, covering 97 studies and more than 11,000 individuals with BPD, documented the 13.91 adjusted odds ratio for childhood adversity in BPD relative to non-clinical controls. The NESARC-III analysis by Fall (2020) established the specific ACE category odds ratios, with emotional abuse at 3.00 and emotional neglect at 2.30 as the strongest independent BPD predictors.

This curriculum applies the ACE research in two specific clinical ways: as the empirical foundation for the de-shaming reframe that Session 5 delivers, and as the targeting framework that connects Module B's Pattern Map layers to the specific adversity types that produced them.

Key references: Felitti et al. (1998); Porter et al. (2020); Fall (2020); Teicher and Samson (2016).

G.6 Mentalization-Based Treatment

Mentalization-based treatment (MBT), developed by Bateman and Fonagy, addresses the specific impairment in mentalizing, the capacity to understand oneself and others in terms of mental states, that characterizes BPD presentations. MBT's evidence base is comparable to DBT's for BPD outcomes, and its theoretical framework provides the relational attunement concepts that inform the Healthy Adult mode's development in this curriculum.

The curriculum applies MBT concepts most directly in Chapter 5's discussion of the facilitator's relational presence as the primary treatment mechanism, in the Relational Update named concept, and in Module D's relational repair and identity work. The MBT framework's insistence on the centrality of the therapeutic relationship in BPD treatment is fully consistent with the clinical stance this curriculum advances.

Key references: Bateman and Fonagy (2004); Barnicot et al. (2012); Bateman and Fonagy (2016).

Note: Full bibliographic entries for all sources cited in Appendix G are consolidated in the main References section at the end of this volume.

References

Barnicot, K., Katsakou, C., Bhatti, N., Savill, M., Fearns, N., & Priebe, S. (2012). Factors predicting the outcome of psychotherapy for borderline personality disorder: A systematic review. Clinical Psychology Review, 32(5), 400-412. https://doi.org/10.1016/j.cpr.2012.04.004

Bateman, A., & Fonagy, P. (2004). Psychotherapy for borderline personality disorder: Mentalization-based treatment. Oxford University Press.

Bateman, A., & Fonagy, P. (2016). Mentalization-based treatment for personality disorders: A practical guide. Oxford University Press.

Bohus, M., Kleindienst, N., Hahn, C., Müller-Engelmann, M., Ludäscher, P., Steil, R., Fydrich, T., Kuehner, C., Resick, P. A., Stiglmayr, C., Schmahl, C., & Priebe, K. (2020). Dialectical behavior therapy for posttraumatic stress disorder (DBT-PTSD) compared with cognitive processing therapy (CPT) in complex presentations of PTSD in women survivors of childhood abuse. JAMA Psychiatry, 77(12), 1235-1245. https://doi.org/10.1001/jamapsychiatry.2020.2148

Carpenter, R. W., & Trull, T. J. (2013). Components of emotion dysregulation in borderline personality disorder: A review. Current Psychiatry Reports, 15(1), 335. https://doi.org/10.1007/s11920-012-0335-2

Domes, G., Schulze, L., & Herpertz, S. C. (2009). Emotion recognition in borderline personality disorder: A review of the literature. Journal of Personality Disorders, 23(1), 6-19. https://doi.org/10.1521/pedi.2009.23.1.6

Fall, E. A. (2020). Association between adverse childhood experiences and borderline personality disorder: Findings from the National Epidemiologic Survey on Alcohol and Related Conditions (NESARC)-III [Master's thesis, Georgia State University]. ScholarWorks @ Georgia State University. https://scholarworks.gsu.edu/iph_theses/721/

Fassbinder, E., Schweiger, U., Martius, D., Brand-de Wilde, O., & Arntz, A. (2016). Emotion regulation in schema therapy and dialectical behavior therapy. Frontiers in Psychology, 7, 1373. https://doi.org/10.3389/fpsyg.2016.01373

Felitti, V. J., Anda, R. F., Nordenberg, D., Williamson, D. F., Spitz, A. M., Edwards, V., Koss, M. P., & Marks, J. S. (1998). Relationship of childhood abuse and household dysfunction to many of the leading causes of death in adults: The Adverse Childhood Experiences (ACE) Study. American Journal of Preventive Medicine, 14(4), 245-258. https://doi.org/10.1016/S0749-3797(98)00017-8

Harned, M. S., Korslund, K. E., & Linehan, M. M. (2014). A pilot randomized controlled trial of Dialectical Behavior Therapy with and without the Dialectical Behavior Therapy Prolonged Exposure protocol for suicidal and self-injuring women with borderline personality disorder and PTSD. Behaviour Research and Therapy, 55, 7-17. https://doi.org/10.1016/j.brat.2014.01.008

Kroenke, K., Spitzer, R. L., & Williams, J. B. W. (2001). The PHQ-9: Validity of a brief depression severity measure. Journal of General Internal Medicine, 16(9), 606-613. https://doi.org/10.1046/j.1525-1497.2001.016009606.x

Linehan, M. M. (1993). Cognitive-behavioral treatment of borderline personality disorder. Guilford Press.

Linehan, M. M. (2015). DBT skills training manual (2nd ed.). Guilford Press.

Linehan, M. M., Korslund, K. E., Harned, M. S., Gallop, R. J., Lungu, A., Neacsiu, A. D., McDavid, J., Comtois, K. A., & Murray-Gregory, A. M. (2015). Dialectical behavior therapy for high suicide risk in individuals with borderline personality disorder: A randomized clinical trial and component analysis. JAMA Psychiatry, 72(5), 475-482. https://doi.org/10.1001/jamapsychiatry.2014.3039

Nadort, M., Arntz, A., Smit, J. H., Giesen-Bloo, J., Eikelenboom, M., Spinhoven, P., van Asselt, T., Wensing, M., & van Dyck, R. (2009). Implementation of outpatient schema therapy for borderline personality disorder with versus without crisis support by the therapist outside office hours: A randomized trial. Behaviour Research and Therapy, 47(11), 961-973. https://doi.org/10.1016/j.brat.2009.07.013

Porter, C., Palmier-Claus, J., Branitsky, A., Mansell, W., Warwick, H., & Varese, F. (2020). Childhood adversity and borderline personality disorder: A meta-analysis. Acta Psychiatrica Scandinavica, 141(1), 6-20. https://doi.org/10.1111/acps.13118

Posner, K., Brown, G. K., Stanley, B., Brent, D. A., Yershova, K. V., Oquendo, M. A., Currier, G. W., Melvin, G. A., Greenhill, L., Shen, S., & Mann, J. J. (2011). The Columbia-Suicide Severity Rating Scale: Initial validity and internal consistency findings from three multisite studies with adolescents and adults. American Journal of Psychiatry, 168(12), 1266-1277. https://doi.org/10.1176/appi.ajp.2011.10111704

Prillinger, K., Goreis, A., Macura, S., Hajek Gross, C., Lozar, A., Fanninger, S., Mayer, A., Oppenauer, C., Plener, P. L., & Kothgassner, O. D. (2024). A systematic review and meta-analysis on the efficacy of dialectical behavior therapy variants for the treatment of post-traumatic stress disorder. European Journal of Psychotraumatology, 15(1), 2406662. https://doi.org/10.1080/20008066.2024.2406662

Prins, A., Bovin, M. J., Smolenski, D. J., Marx, B. P., Kimerling, R., Jenkins-Guarnieri, M. A., Kaloupek, D. G., Schnurr, P. P., Kaiser, A. P., Leyva, Y. E., & Tiet, Q. Q. (2016). The Primary Care PTSD Screen for DSM-5 (PC-PTSD-5): Development and evaluation within a veteran primary care sample. Journal of General Internal Medicine, 31(10), 1206-1211. https://doi.org/10.1007/s11606-016-3703-5

Tedeschi, R. G., & Calhoun, L. G. (2004). Posttraumatic growth: Conceptual foundations and empirical evidence. Psychological Inquiry, 15(1), 1-18. https://doi.org/10.1207/s15327965pli1501_01

Teicher, M. H., & Samson, J. A. (2016). Annual research review: Enduring neurobiological effects of childhood abuse and neglect. Journal of Child Psychology and Psychiatry, 57(3), 241-266. https://doi.org/10.1111/jcpp.12507

Torgersen, S., Myers, J., Reichborn-Kjennerud, T., Røysamb, E., Kubarych, T. S., & Kendler, K. S. (2012). The heritability of Cluster B personality disorders assessed both by personal interview and questionnaire. Journal of Personality Disorders, 26(6), 848-866. https://doi.org/10.1521/pedi.2012.26.6.848

Young, J. E., Klosko, J. S., & Weishaar, M. E. (2003). Schema therapy: A practitioner's guide. Guilford Press.

Zanarini, M. C., Vujanovic, A. A., Parachini, E. A., Boulanger, J. L., Frankenburg, F. R., & Hennen, J. (2003). Zanarini Rating Scale for Borderline Personality Disorder (ZAN-BPD): A continuous measure of DSM-IV borderline psychopathology. Journal of Personality Disorders, 17(3), 233-242. https://doi.org/10.1521/pedi.17.3.233.22147

Made in the USA
Monee, IL
05 November 2026

67979972R00142